SUDDEN DEATH

The Green Bay Packers, the Baltimore Colts, and the NFL, 1965

By Richard Petre

Sudden Death
Copyright © 2025 by Richard J. Petre Jr.
SC ISBN: 9781645386162
Sudden Death
By Richard J. Petre, Jr.

Cover design by Dana Breunig
Cover image © Milwaukee Journal Sentinel via Imagn Images
All tables prepared by, and printed with the permission of, Sports Reference LLC.

Published by Ten16 Press, an imprint of Orange Hat Publishing

www.orangehatpublishing.com
Wauwatosa, WI

To foremost my parents, Doris and Richard,
and my uncle, John Petre,
for what they did.

AUTHOR'S NOTE

Many have helped with the writing of this book. My acknowledgments appear at the end. But at the outset, a few comments about how this book was written seem helpful.

Unless otherwise noted, any mention or listing of All-Pro and other postseason honors refers to selections made by the Associated Press.

Based on responsibility rather than the coaching title then employed, I have used at times the term "coordinator" to describe an assistant coach who was principally in charge of his team's offense or defense.

In 1965, the terms "conference" and "division" were used nearly interchangeably. I use exclusively the term "conference" when referring to the NFL's Western Conference and Eastern Conference.

This book tells the story of the 1965 NFL season by recounting the historic Western Conference race between the Green Bay Packers and the Baltimore Colts. My goal was to tell that story as though it were taking place, with decisions in September and games in October described without knowledge of what happened in later months and certainly later years. With few, if any, exceptions, I trust for the sake of readers that I succeeded.

Table of Contents

INTRODUCTION

For the nation, the year 1965 was the midpoint in a decade of social and cultural change that began with hope and ended with rancor. Lyndon Johnson, just elected in a landslide, began a full term as president and championed his domestic goals as "the Great Society." In music, the Rolling Stones rocked with "(I Can't Get No) Satisfaction," the Supremes ruled the pop charts, and the Beatles still received hysterical acclaim. The Gemini space program, sandwiched between Mercury and Apollo, successfully completed several missions, each one more daring than the one before. Violence defiled civil rights marches in Selma, Alabama. Congress passed the Voting Rights Act and Medicare. Riots erupted in American inner cities. President Johnson increased the number of Americans fighting in Vietnam to nearly 185,000 and doubled the number who would be drafted each month. Television network anchormen like Walter Cronkite and David Brinkley were revered and led their news broadcasts with war in Asia and civil unrest at home.

Sports provided the country with joy and some solace. In baseball, long the national pastime, the Los Angeles Dodgers with pitching by Sandy Koufax and Don Drysdale won the World Series; Koufax pitched a perfect game captured by Vin Scully's indelible radio call; and Willie Mays, Hank Aaron, Roberto Clemente, and Brooks Robinson drew cheers. In professional basketball, there were only nine teams; the Boston Celtics, led by Bill Russell and John Havlicek, began their pursuit of an eighth consecutive NBA Championship; and Wilt Chamberlain, Oscar Robertson, and Jerry West dazzled those at courtside. In boxing, Muhammad Ali was the sport's greatest heavyweight champion who courted controversy with his recent conversion to the Islam faith and political views.

And then there was professional football. An estimated 45,000,000—nearly three out of every 10 Americans living outside the blacked-out New York City metropolitan area—watched on television the 1958 NFL Championship Game between the Baltimore Colts and the New York Giants. The last-minute and overtime heroics of Johnny Unitas and Raymond Berry captivated sports fans. *Sports Illustrated* called the sudden-death thriller "The Best Football Game Ever Played." Catapulted by the game's drama, the popularity of pro football soared. Booming cities clamored for an NFL team. Rich men with vision like Lamar Hunt wanted to own one. In 1960, NFL owners selected 33-year-old Pete Rozelle as their new commissioner and voted to expand to Dallas and Minnesota, and a second pro football league, the American Football League, began play with eight teams.

For those heading sports programming at all three of the country's television networks, NFL football became the most coveted jewel in Tiffany's window—the sport that for prestige and revenue every network believed it needed. By 1964, pro football had overtaken major league baseball as the country's most popular spectator sport, and the NFL and AFL captured Sunday afternoons in the fall and early winter on both CBS and NBC. Before the 1965 season, teams in the two leagues competed to sign newly drafted college seniors. But recent signings—especially quarterback Joe Namath's $427,000, three-year contract with the AFL's New York Jets—had raised the costs and the stakes in the leagues' ongoing strife, and team owners in the rival leagues furtively visited to probe whether a merger between their leagues might be possible and what the structure of such a merger might look like.

The 1965 NFL season was a bridge year between old and new that showed how a violent game in earlier years was played but also how the sport, like the country, was changing—it was the last year before a merger agreement, a common draft, and the Super Bowl; the last year that the NFL and

AFL, often with creative ruses, battled to sign college players; the last year that a Green Bay backfield would feature Jimmy Taylor and Paul Hornung; the last year before the true emergence of the Dallas Cowboys; the last year that Jim Brown would play; and the first year that Dick Butkus and Gale Sayers did play.

Nearly all 14 NFL teams had star players. In the Eastern Conference, the Cleveland Browns with the great Jim Brown were prohibitive favorites. But in the Western Conference, there were too many good teams with so much talent, and the seven teams in the West and their fans braced for close games and a tight conference race. The favorites to win the Western Conference were the Green Bay Packers and the Baltimore Colts, the defending conference champions. When those two teams met, standing on the sidelines were head coaches Vince Lombardi and Don Shula, and playing on the field were 16 future members of the Pro Football Hall of Fame such as Johnny Unitas, Bart Starr, Raymond Berry, Jim Taylor, Lenny Moore, Ray Nitschke, Forrest Gregg, and John Mackey. But each of the other five teams in their conference showcased All-Pro players and believed it could win, especially the Chicago Bears who, with rookie sensations Butkus and Sayers, were the league's best team in the season's final weeks and were surging in December's stretch run.

In both Green Bay and Baltimore, the coaches and players felt urgency and faced questions. Both teams had aging players. The Packers had not won a league championship or even the conference since 1962. And even in the unforgiving profession of NFL coaching that counted only wins and losses, Vince Lombardi's need to win was obsessive—the Packers could not finish second again.

With the Colts, defensive end Gino Marchetti and middle linebacker Bill Pellington had just retired. There was uncertainty over who would replace them and how badly they would be missed. And Don Shula, Baltimore's 35-year-old head coach, had a demanding owner, Carroll Rosenbloom, whose team had won two championships and who was seething that his team had not just won a third.

The NFL's 1965 Western Conference race proved thrilling, and the sudden-death overtime playoff game that decided the conference and still angers Baltimore fans proved historic. Opening day in 1965 was September 19. But the story of that NFL season did not begin with week-one games or training-camp openings at remote colleges. It began earlier on a harsh late December afternoon in Cleveland when the underdog Cleveland Browns and the Baltimore Colts played for the 1964 NFL Championship.

1

Cleveland, December 27, 1964: The NFL Championship

The 1964 NFL Championship Game was played two days after Christmas in Cleveland. The temperatures were near freezing. Furious winds off Lake Erie whipped flags and blew debris. Few outside Cleveland thought the Browns could win. With sandwiches made at home, thermos jugs of hot chocolate, and pocketed whiskey bottles and flasks, Browns fans advanced up West Third, Ontario, and East Ninth to Municipal Stadium, a cavernous, double-decked stadium perched on Lake Erie and known for its size and utility rather than any architectural distinction. Red, white, and blue bunting, emblematic of a title game, draped the stadium. The east end zone had bleacher seats and lacked an upper deck. Winds howling from the lake entered the stadium and swirled inside. Of course, the game was a sellout. Though on game day standing-room tickets could still be bought, over 78,000 tickets had been sold. Baltimore fans bought 9,000. The Colts Marching Band traveled in older coach buses to Cleveland. In the west end zone, one audacious Colt fan, wearing a raccoon coat and a derby hat, paraded a sign that read "Colts 49 Browns 0." To watch on television a blacked-out game, thousands of Browns fans drove to motels in cities at least 75 miles from Cleveland like Toledo and Erie.

To the delight of CBS, which was broadcasting its first NFL title game, and the NFL, whose sport was now challenging baseball as the nation's most popular, this Championship Game offered the league's two best offenses and the sport's two biggest stars—Baltimore quarterback Johnny Unitas and Cleveland fullback Jim Brown. In the 1958 NFL Championship, Unitas became a football legend. He coupled daring play selection and physical toughness with a sense of theater that defined his position—the unflinching field general who willed improbable comeback wins in the cold and the rain, as later dramatized by NFL Films with its stirring words and swelling music. In 1964, Unitas passed for 2,824 yards with 19 touchdowns and only six interceptions, leading Baltimore to its best record ever and its third Western Conference championship. For the second time, Unitas won the NFL's highest individual honor—Most Valuable Player.

Controversial off the field with Hollywood hopes, Cleveland's Jim Brown was a generational talent. In high school and at Syracuse, he was a star in every sport he played and perhaps the greatest college lacrosse player ever. But it was football where Jim Brown, setting records with prodigious numbers, achieved true stardom. He was often bigger than the linebackers and faster than the defensive halfbacks he faced. He could run with violence, using shoulders and forearms to batter defenders he needed to run over. He ran holding the football with his left hand to use his right hand and arm as a club. Jim Brown never backed down. He rarely complained. And he never missed a game. In his eight years from his 1957 rookie season through 1964, Brown seven times led the league in rushing and was named first-team All-Pro, and twice was voted the NFL's Most Valuable Player. The 1963 season was his greatest year. Playing with a broken big toe, Jim Brown ran for 1,863 yards—he averaged 6.4 yards per carry and 133 rushing yards per game. In 1964, Brown rushed and caught passes for 1,786 yards; in the voting for the league's Most Valuable Player, he finished second to Unitas.

Driven by football's two greatest players, the two offenses with overlooked but skilled offensive lines were prolific. In scoring offense, Baltimore led the league, averaging almost 31 points per game, but Cleveland's offense was second with nearly 30 points each game. On offense, Baltimore had star players other than Unitas. Through relentless repetition and study, receiver Raymond Berry at his position was the game's top student and finest artisan, running his pass routes with unmatched precision. Flanker Jimmy Orr used quickness in his routes to constantly get open, especially on deep patterns. Both receivers almost never dropped a pass. Though in his second year still learning how to play tight end, John Mackey, with a football in the open field, was a bowling ball looking for defenders to run over. And recapturing the magic of his early years and scoring 19 touchdowns, halfback Lenny Moore was the 1964 Comeback Player of the Year.

Cleveland's offense was also more than one great player. The Browns' quarterback was Frank Ryan, who was better known for classroom achievement than for football excellence. Ryan was months away from receiving his doctorate in mathematics from Rice, where, as an undergraduate, he studied physics but did not start at quarterback. Though blessed with a strong arm and stature, Ryan did not become a starter until the middle of the 1962 season, his fifth year in the league, after he was traded to Cleveland. For Ryan, 1964 was a triumphant season: the Browns won their conference, and he threw for 2,404 yards and 25 touchdowns.

Ryan had two top receivers. One was Gary Collins, who two years earlier was the fourth pick in the NFL draft after Ernie Davis, Roman Gabriel, and Merlin Olsen. Hardened by an upbringing in Pennsylvania's coal country, Collins, at six-foot-four and 215 pounds, towered over defensive backs. Outjumping defenders and surprising them with deceptive speed, Collins ranked high among receivers in catching touchdowns.

But even in a league with men who, before professional football, had always been their team's best player, Paul Warfield in his first year stood out. Watching game film for instruction, coaches marveled at how Warfield, using speed and quickness in his pass patterns, effortlessly created separation from defensive halfbacks. Watching games for enjoyment, fans took delight in his grace and artistry. At Ohio State, Warfield was a football and track and field standout at Ohio State who set records in the broad jump and low hurdles. In

1964, he caught 52 passes for nine touchdowns. Cleveland head coach Blanton Collier, an astute judge of talent, believed Warfield could become one of the game's greatest receivers ever. Baltimore's top defensive coach, Charlie Winner, called him the best rookie receiver he had ever seen.

With one exception, the two defenses lacked the special players routinely named All-Pro. Capable players largely made up the Cleveland defense, but linebacker Galen Fiss, defensive end Bill Glass, and defensive halfback Bernie Parrish had played in Pro Bowl games. The 1964 season brought Pro Bowl honors to linebacker Jim Houston and finally to Dick Modzelewski, a defensive tackle in his 12th season. After the 1963 season, Cleveland seeking leadership traded with the New York Giants for Modzelewski. He challenged his new teammates: "You have all the talent to win a championship but don't really believe that you can." You just need to believe, Modzelewski said, that you can do it.

Playing defense for Baltimore were defensive halfback Bobby Boyd and other players on the cusp of postseason honors. In 1964, Boyd, a former Oklahoma quarterback, had nine interceptions and earned first-team All-Pro honors. But the Colts defense featured two player-coaches who had announced that 1964 would be their final year: defensive end Gino Marchetti and middle linebacker Bill Pellington. Baltimore coach Don Shula, when a Colts player, had roomed with both. At the time, all three had a reputation for rowdiness, especially Pellington. Cut by Cleveland's Paul Brown in 1952 after one week of training camp for being too violent, Pellington was playing his 12th year in Baltimore. Even for his time, he was known for vicious play. His nickname was "the Hangman." His signature takedown was the clothesline tackle where he used his forearm to hook opponents across their neck, knocking them backwards.

The game's one defensive player whose accomplishments and talent could match those of Johnny Unitas and Jim Brown was Baltimore's Gino Marchetti. Quitting high school to fight in a world war, Marchetti, an Army infantryman, turned 19 in

Belgium during the Battle of the Bulge. Graduating from the University of San Francisco, he was drafted by the New York Yanks in 1952. In his early years, Marchetti was known as a dirty player, an enforcer, in an era known for lawless play. He once tackled Detroit's standout halfback Doak Walker and then ground the heel of his hand into Walker's nose. Walker, a Heisman Trophy winner who was five inches and 70 pounds smaller, stood up and silently glared at Marchetti. Ashamed, Gino Marchetti largely changed how he played after tackles were made and whistles were blown. But he remained a feared opponent and was routinely named All-Pro.

Standing six-foot-four, Marchetti paired strength with exceptional quickness. He relentlessly hunted quarterbacks and ballcarriers. Once after a game with San Francisco, 49er All-Pro tackle Bob St. Clair on the field chased after Marchetti, his former college teammate, to offer congratulations: "I just want to say I touched you once today." For much of his career, Gino Marchetti was football's top pass-rusher and most dominant defensive player. At 38 years old, he was still a disruptive defensive end.

And football fans wondered whether an Eastern Conference team like Cleveland could win an NFL championship. Playing in the clearly stronger Western Conference, Baltimore had the better regular-season record, 12-2, to Cleveland's 10-3-1 finish. A month before the title game, *Sports Illustrated* featured an article titled "How the West Has Won." The writer, Edwin Shrake, noted that Western Conference teams had won six of the last seven NFL championships—the exception was Philadelphia's 17-13 win in 1960 over a young but emerging Green Bay Packers team, which should have won. "This year it is yawningly conceded that the Eastern champion—probably Cleveland—will be playing for the dubious pleasure of being thrashed by Baltimore on December 27," Shrake wrote. "There are at least three teams in the West that are superior to any in the East." And he added that the true 1964 Championship Game had already been played. "Baltimore won it in October by beating Green Bay for the second time."

For those who gambled, Baltimore was a touchdown favorite. Previewing the title game for *Sports Illustrated*, Tex Maule, the magazine's chief pro football writer, predicted a "decisive" Baltimore win. In many statistical categories, Baltimore's defense ranked as one of the league's best and Cleveland's as one of the worst. The Browns were last in total defense or yards given up, and in quarterback sacks. But in scoring defense or points given up, Cleveland's defense finished fifth in the league. Conservative on defense, the Browns favored zone coverage on passing downs and rarely blitzed quarterbacks. Maule quoted an unnamed New York Giant that Baltimore quarterback Unitas, especially adept against zone defenses, "would cut the Browns to pieces." And Maule's analysis highlighted the obvious mismatch between Jim Kanicki, Cleveland's second-year defensive tackle, and Baltimore guard Jim Parker, a first-team All-Pro at offensive tackle or guard every year since 1957. "Although the Browns are a sound, intelligent, and even explosive football team," Maule concluded, "they stand little chance of upsetting the Baltimore Colts." But the game preview hardly mentioned the teams' contrasting head coaches, Baltimore's 34-year-old Don Shula and Cleveland's 58-year-old Blanton Collier, whose lives had crossed and whose coaching had been shaped by Paul Brown.

* * * * *

At game time, Paul Brown, with his stern visage and judgmental gaze, in a dark suit and tie and fedora hat, would not be standing on the Cleveland sideline. He was no longer the head coach of the Browns, the team that he had coached and run with an iron hand for 17 years and that bore his name. But the 1964 Cleveland Browns were still very much Paul Brown's team. The long-time coach had picked and trained their coaching staff and much of their roster. For nine years, Collier was Paul Brown's most valued assistant. And Brown's stamp on the Baltimore Colts was unmistakable. His coaching methods and approach to football had instructed not only Shula, a former player in 1951 and 1952, but also the coach who built the team that Shula inherited, Weeb Ewbank.

Paul Brown was a giant in his sport. Everywhere Paul Brown went, he won. And over his three decades of coaching football, he changed how the game was played. In the 1930s, he made Massillon Washington High School in Ohio a dominant program—in nine years, he achieved an 80-8-2 record and won six consecutive state championships in a big state that took football seriously. In 1941, he moved to Ohio State, claiming a national championship in his second year. Called to military service, Brown continued to excel as the football coach of the Great Lakes Naval Training Station teams. In 1946, he became the head coach and general manager of the Cleveland franchise in the new All-America Football Conference. His team was called the Browns, and Paul Brown so completely dominated the new league, winning four straight championships, that he destroyed it.

In December 1949, the NFL merged with the crippled AAFC, accepting the Browns and two other teams. Though now facing tougher competition, the Browns remained a superior team. From 1950 through 1957, they played in the NFL Championship Game every year but 1956 and won three titles. With a true talent for organization and an obsession with professional success, Brown proved a remarkable innovator—extensive classroom instruction and testing, an expanded year-round coaching staff with position coaches, regimented practice routines, intelligence and personality tests, 40-yard speed testing of players, the early signing of Black players like Marion Motley and Bill Willis, emphasis on film study, and the development of the passing game. Brown even invented the single-bar facemask, a creation prompted by a defender out of bounds intentionally pounding his elbow in the face of Cleveland's star quarterback, Otto Graham, who at halftime received 15 stitches inside his mouth.

But there was a dark side to Paul Brown. With his players, he was cold and often cutting and unforgiving. "You always choke," he taunted Cleveland receiver Ray Renfro, returning to the sideline after dropping a pass. Angry that a former Browns assistant coach, Creighton Miller, led as a lawyer in 1956 a drive for NFL players to start a union, Brown had

Miller's image removed from the 1946 team photograph in his office, a tainted practice associated with Joseph Stalin erasing purged deputies from Kremlin photographs.

In the new decade of the 1960s, Paul Brown would finally face an owner he could not intimidate and a player he could not silence. In 1961, Art Modell, a brash, self-made 35-year-old advertising executive from New York, bought the Cleveland Browns for $4,000,000, largely with money that he had borrowed. Modell loved the limelight and welcomed nightclub dinners with his players. He saw himself as an active and key member of the Browns hierarchy. Expecting owners like players to be silent and subservient, Paul Brown saw Modell as a meddlesome intruder.

With the first pick in the 1962 draft, the Washington Redskins selected Ernie Davis, the 1961 Heisman Trophy winner from Syracuse where he wore Jim Brown's number and as a junior averaged nearly eight yards every carry. Paul Brown coveted Davis, seeing him as the big halfback he wanted to pair with Jim Brown. For Washington's rights to sign Davis, Paul Brown traded to the Redskins Bobby Mitchell, a superb halfback and receiver who was Jim Brown's roommate. Ernie Davis would tragically die of leukemia in 1963 and never play a regular-season game for Cleveland. In making the deal, Paul Brown never spoke with Art Modell. The Cleveland owner learned of the swap when he was called by Redskins' owner George Preston Marshall. Astonished that Modell knew nothing about the trade, Marshall lectured Modell that he, not Paul Brown, owned the team. "Don't ever let that happen again. You're the owner. You own the franchise. It's yours." His fortune and identity tied to the Cleveland Browns, Modell would not forget Marshall's admonishment.

Though Paul Brown in the 1950s had been among the first in the NFL to sign Black players, his relationship with the game's greatest running back, Jim Brown, had turned increasingly sour. Used to total control as the team's head coach and general manager, Paul Brown demanded obedience from his players and banished those hesitant to show it. For the first time, even Paul Brown recognized that he coached someone whose talent was so great and whose personality was so strong that the player could challenge his autocratic authority. The 1960s were a time of social change, but Paul Brown increasingly welcomed only game changes which he authored and for which he could claim credit.

In its four seasons after 1958, Cleveland flirted with mediocrity, the industry leader that, successful and innovative for so long, had resisted change and become stagnant. From 1959 through 1961, the Browns finished each year second or third in the Eastern Conference. In 1962, Cleveland's offensive players, seeing too often defenders shouting out their plays before the center snap, had grown tired of Paul Brown's insistence that he call every offensive play and that his quarterback without exception run the play called.

Before Cleveland's December 1962 game in New York, Paul Brown bizarrely ordered his team to practice in a blizzard and watched the workouts from his car. For instruction, his quarterbacks ran back and forth from the field to their coach's sedan. On Sunday, December 9, the Giants beat Cleveland 17-13, and the Browns fell to 6-6-1 and third place in the Eastern Conference, more than four games behind New York and even behind the Pittsburgh Steelers. Flying back to Cleveland from New York, Jim Brown, John Wooten, Bernie Parrish, and Mike McCormack agreed they would confront their head coach and insist on changes. If Paul Brown refused, Jim Brown was ready to demand a trade or quit football. Learning of the mutinous sentiment, Modell counseled the players to back off, ensuring them that he would intervene. On January 9, 1963, after a disappointing 7-6-1 season, Art Modell summoned Paul Brown, announcing that he would no longer coach the Browns. Without a word, Brown immediately walked out of Modell's office. "He's taken my team from me," he bemoaned to his son Mike.

Modell offered the Browns' head coach job to Blanton Collier, the team's chief assistant coach. In a display of loyalty, Collier told Modell that before accepting, he first wanted to speak with Paul Brown. In their conversation, Brown advised

Collier to take the job: "You owe it to your family." But shortly later, Mike Brown called Collier, urging him to reject the offer. Collier accepted the job. Paul Brown never forgave him for doing so.

* * * * *

For 16 years, Blanton Collier coached football and taught math at Paris High School in his native Kentucky. In 1944, at the Great Lakes Naval Training Station, he caught the attention of Paul Brown, head coach of the Great Lakes team. In 1946, Collier joined Brown to coach in Cleveland in the new AAFC. In his first stint with the Browns, Collier coached for eight years. Under Brown's tutelage, he excelled in studying game film, grading during off-seasons every Cleveland play and player.

In 1954, Baltimore wanted to hire Collier as its head coach. Paul Brown, fearful of losing his star assistant to an NFL competitor, told the Colts that Collier had no interest. He never told Blanton of Baltimore's overture. Collier later learned of the Colts' inquiry and decided that year to leave Cleveland, though not for Baltimore. He returned to his home state to become head coach at the University of Kentucky, replacing the successful Bear Bryant, who objected to the school's new recruiting restrictions and had grown tired of competing in Lexington for attention against Kentucky basketball and its haughty coach Adolph Rupp. At Kentucky, Collier built a superb coaching staff with assistants like Howard Schnellenberger, Chuck Knox, Bill Arnsparger, and in 1959 a young Don Shula. Though Collier's technical knowledge of the game was superior to Bryant's, success at the college level required good recruiting. At Kentucky, Collier struggled to recruit. Finding Collier's eight-year record of 41-36-3 wanting, Kentucky after the 1961 season fired its head coach. Collier was quickly rehired by Paul Brown.

In 1963, Blanton Collier was the right choice to be Cleveland's head coach. With his thick glasses, thinning hair, and courteous manners, he looked like a high school principal in a small town. But behind his modest façade, Collier was a remarkable student and teacher of football. Otto Graham thought him the game's finest offensive coach. And along with technical mastery and sound organization, he offered his players not familiarity but decency and an openness to their views. Tellingly, he shook hands with his left hand, saying it was closer to his heart. In Collier's first year as head coach, the Browns showed improvement, finishing with a 10-4 record, one game behind the New York Giants in the Eastern Conference. During the season, racial issues surfaced, threatening to divide the team. Collier quickly restored peace. And he worked assiduously to improve the mechanics and bolster the confidence of his quarterback, Frank Ryan.

* * * * *

The title game was played two weeks after the regular season ended, giving the coaches an extra week to prepare. The two head coaches agreed to exchange game film for six games rather than the customary five. The more time Collier and his coaches watched Baltimore's game film, the more they believed the Browns would win. Cleveland's challenge was how to stop Unitas and the Colts' passing attack. The Browns' defensive coaches and players heard the criticism that their defense was mediocre and that their defensive backs were too small and could not play man coverage. Studying Baltimore's game film, Cleveland's coaches saw that Baltimore's passing game was built on timing--Unitas throwing quick passes to receivers Raymond Berry and Jimmy Orr running exact routes against defensive backs who often lined up yards from the line of scrimmage in soft coverage. During the regular season, Cleveland played a conservative defense intended to prevent touchdowns rather than yards gained away from its goal line. To disrupt the precision of Baltimore's passing offense, Cleveland devised a different defensive plan that was simple but daring--the Browns would challenge the Baltimore receivers with tight coverage and even blitz or rush extra defenders. But could they do it?

Fearful that a windstorm might delay air travel, the Colts flew into Cleveland on Christmas night. On Saturday, they conducted a walk-through at Municipal Stadium. The Colts expected to win. On Christmas Eve, the *Baltimore Sun* carried a game article with the headline "Colt Team Denies Complacency" and the subhead "Colts Deny Smugness." "I hope you don't embarrass us," Art Modell graciously told Colts owner Carroll Rosenbloom the day before the game. "We'll try not to," responded Rosenbloom without a hint of levity. Charles Heaton, one of the few sportswriters predicting a Browns win, reported in his *Cleveland Plain Dealer* column that Baltimore newspaper writers feared the Colts were overconfident. In their game preparation, Baltimore's defensive players could see Cleveland's talent on offense with fullback Jim Brown, receivers Paul Warfield and Gary Collins, and a sturdy offensive line. But on game film, the Browns defense, lacking the great players who change offensive game plans, looked less formidable than the Western Conference defenses the Colts had repeatedly played against and beaten.

On the Saturday night before the game, both teams went to the same downtown movie theater to watch the newly released James Bond movie, *Goldfinger*. The Browns were seated in front of the Colts. Some Colt players behaved like wayward adolescents. Their antics prompted Frank Ryan, despite the allure of Honor Blackman's Pussy Galore and the menace of Harold Sakata's Oddjob, to leave the theater before the movie ended. The next morning, members of a Colts fan corral, booked at Cleveland's Pick-Carter Hotel where the Browns were staying, began playing taps when Brown players were spotted. Hearing the bugle call shortly before he left the hotel on game day, Jim Brown told his teammates, "We're going to kick the hell out of these guys."

* * * * *

On the morning of the game, Colt receivers Jimmy Orr and Alex Hawkins met defensive halfback Bobby Boyd in his hotel room. Orr pushed back window curtains to see what the weather was like. He immediately commented on the wind—an American flag outside the hotel was fully extended out. Though the skies were a wintry grey and the temperature hovered at freezing at opening kickoff, there was no rain degrading further a barren field that was already muddy and no snow delighting television viewers after Christmas. With wind gusts off Lake Erie up to 30 miles per hour, the wind would be a factor. But at Municipal Stadium, Cleveland team officials were determined that the Colts Marching Band would not be. After a pregame march around the field, the band's members, cheerleaders, and majorettes had to surrender their instruments, pom-poms, and batons. Like contraband, they were placed under police guard for the game.

* * * * *

Cleveland won the coin toss and elected to receive with Baltimore choosing the wind. On the Browns' first series, Jim Brown made a one-handed catch between defenders, and Cleveland pushed the ball to midfield before punting only 27 yards into the wind. After Lenny Moore ran for 15 yards, fullback Jerry Hill fumbled Unitas's handoff, and the ball squirted to Cleveland's tackle Dick Modzelewski. The Browns moved the ball to the Baltimore 34. Frank Ryan, throwing into the wind, attempted to hit Paul Warfield sandwiched between two defenders. The ball fluttered. Trying to reach back for the ball, Warfield slipped, and Don Shinnick intercepted the pass. Baltimore drove to the Cleveland 21-yard line as the first quarter ended. But with the wind at their backs, the Colts had failed to score. Retreating to pass, Unitas saw receivers tightly covered. Harried by Cleveland's defensive linemen, he too often had to run.

Baltimore's drive stalled at the Cleveland 19. The Colts' field-goal unit entered the field. On the center's snap to holder Bobby Boyd, a gust of wind pushed the ball to the right. Boyd dropped the ball and tried running for a first down. He was tackled for a loss. In the second period, the teams traded punts. With Cleveland blitzing a linebacker, Unitas looked to his left and threw a screen pass to Lenny Moore. Four Colts, running ahead of Moore, began setting up blocks. The screen pass seemed a perfect call. But Galen Fiss, the lone Brown defender near the play, ran past the blockers and barreled into Moore's legs. The Colts still drove into Cleveland territory when Unitas threw a waist-high pass to John Mackey at the

Cleveland 30. Thrown slightly behind the tight end, the ball bounced off Mackey upwards into the hands of linebacker Vince Costello. His interception ended the Baltimore threat and ensured a scoreless first half. During the intermission, the high-stepping Florida A&M marching band, personally selected by Art Modell, performed.

The third quarter would not be scoreless. Beginning the second half, Baltimore wanted the ball, and Cleveland wanted the wind, fearful that otherwise the Colts might end the third quarter with a substantial lead and even that the violent gusts could later shift. On Baltimore's first drive, Jerry Hill on third down dropped a screen pass with three blockers in front of him. Tom Gilburg's punt went only 25 yards to the Baltimore 48. Six plays later, Cleveland's Lou Groza kicked a 43-yard field goal. At 11:39 in the third quarter, Cleveland led 3-0.

On the Colts' next series, Jim Kanicki sacked Unitas, causing Baltimore deep in its own territory to punt again. The Browns had the ball at their own 36-yard line on the left hashmark. The Browns shifted into their double-wing formation with fullback Ernie Green lined up as a flanker to the short side of the field. Believing that Bill Pellington had changed the defensive formation, safety Jim Welch retreated from the line of scrimmage. He was mistaken and out of position. On the center's snap, right linebacker Don Shinnick stepped to his left, expecting an inside run. But Ryan pitched the ball to Jim Brown. Running to his left, he ran down the sideline and cut into the middle of the field before he was finally tackled from behind by Jerry Logan after a 46-yard gain. On the next play, Frank Ryan dropped back to pass. He stutter-stepped forward in the pocket for more time to throw and saw Gary Collins running across the end zone to his left. Feeling defensive tackle Fred Miller tugging on the back of his jersey, Ryan threw to the Cleveland receiver. The pass nearly hit the goalposts' crossbar. Collins momentarily juggled the ball before securing it for an 18-yard touchdown. With 8:34 remaining in the third quarter, Cleveland led 10-0.

Once more, Baltimore's offense could do little, and Gilburg's punt into the wind traveled 27 yards. With the ball at the Baltimore 42, Gary Collins faked an inside move, Ryan pumped the ball as though passing, and Collins ran towards the end zone. Jerry Logan, trying to bump Collins, fell. Open by 10 yards, Collins caught Ryan's pass at the 15 and scored an easy touchdown. A Colt safety had misread Cleveland's formation and failed to line up deep in the middle of the field. The score was now 17-0. "And all of a sudden," bewailed WBAL play-by-play announcer Frank Messer on the Colts' radio broadcast, "this football game has taken on a completely different complexion."

The Browns still had six minutes in the third quarter to take advantage of the wind. On Baltimore's next series, Lenny Moore fumbled away a handoff. When the third period ended, Cleveland was deep in Baltimore territory at the 14-yard line. As the final quarter began, Paul Warfield made a diving catch a yard shy of the Baltimore goal line. The Colts' defense stiffened, but Lou Groza kicked his second field goal to put Cleveland ahead 20-0. With six minutes left to play, the Browns had the ball at midfield. Ryan dropped back to pass. Baltimore blitzed two linebackers. Evading Colt defenders, Ryan threw once more to Collins running downfield. With Bobby Boyd on his back, Collins at the Baltimore 10-yard line stretched out for Ryan's pass and caught his third touchdown of the game before running into a gaggle of Cleveland fans behind the end zone. The scoreboard incredibly read 27-0.

With the game clock showing less than a minute, Frank Ryan ignored convention and added final drama to Cleveland's upset win. With the ball at Baltimore's 38-yard line, Ryan threw downfield to tight end Johnny Brewer, who had not scored a touchdown. The pass attempt enraged Baltimore's defense, particularly Gino Marchetti. With less than 30 seconds left, 1,500 Cleveland fans stormed the field, intent on tearing down goalposts or desperate to claim a field flag or a handful of turf as a game memento. The game officials wisely called the game over, and Cleveland police officers surrounded players like Jim Brown struggling to leave the field.

* * * * *

Amidst their locker room jubilation, Cleveland's defensive players gloated, especially its defensive backs whose size and ability in man coverage had been questioned. "Were we tall enough out there, baby!" safety Bernie Parrish crowed. "We grew a few inches this afternoon." Transforming their defense, the Browns did what few believed was possible. "We crowded them, especially when they were throwing into the wind, and we knew they could not throw long," Browns defensive coach Nick Skorich explained. "If you cover Jimmy Orr and Raymond Berry tight up close, you force them to change their cuts and patterns, and you take away the timing and the precision."

The Baltimore locker room remained closed for 15 minutes after the game. When Shula emerged to take questions, he looked dazed. Gordon White, covering Shula's post-game appearance for the *New York Times*, wrote that Shula appeared as shocked by the outcome as his players. "Of course, you can't talk about our defense without talking about our lack of offense," said Shula. "The offense didn't give the defense any kind of break at all. We couldn't move the ball, and when we did move it, we gave it up on fumbles and interceptions." White reported, "Without mentioning names, Shula expressed disappointment at the performance of his offense, led by Unitas." Offering a stronger account of Shula's postmortem analysis, the *Cleveland Plain Dealer* ran the headline "Colts' Shula Is Disgusted With Offense."

Baltimore's offense certainly played poorly. The Colts turned the ball over four times and managed just 11 first downs and 181 yards, and Unitas completed only 12 passes on 20 attempts for 95 yards. The high winds favored Cleveland with the better running game. With tight coverage and frequent blitzes, Cleveland's defense surprised the Colts, who failed to adjust to what the Browns' defense was doing. And Cleveland's defensive line proved surprisingly dominant with young Jim Kanicki outplaying All-Pro guard Jim Parker. But in the second half, the Colts' defense missed assignments, allowed big plays, and gave up 27 points. Its surrender of 17 points in a six-minute span in the third quarter decided the game. Baltimore, seemingly overconfident and certainly outcoached, played its worst game of the year, and Cleveland played its best.

With a 12-2 regular-season record, 34-year-old Don Shula would win Coach of the Year honors. But Shula's postgame comments, though given in an emotionally charged moment, would rankle. When we win, we win as a team, thought receiver and special-teams standout Alex Hawkins, but when we lose, Unitas and the offense lost the game. On the Colts' flight home to Baltimore on that late December evening, the mood on board was funereal. Shula, sitting in front of the plane, was still stunned, and Johnny Unitas, seated in the rear, was smoldering with resentment. Unitas, accomplished and proud, already had a contentious relationship with Shula. He could not have missed that Shula, though not using his name, had blamed the quarterback and the offense he led for the upset loss. For the Baltimore Colts, as the 1964 season ended and with the start of a new season seven months away, the pain of a Championship Game debacle would linger.

2

Green Bay: "The Packers Will Win It All"

Vince Lombardi, head coach and general manager of the Green Bay Packers, was a man of intense emotions and, with operatic mannerisms, was a master at conveying them. New York Giants owner Wellington Mara, for whom Lombardi worked as an assistant coach, joked that he could hear Lombardi laughing five blocks away. Dallas Cowboys head coach Tom Landry, a coaching colleague in New York, noted Lombardi's manic swings between elation and depression and caustically called him "Mr. High-Low." Lombardi smiled often, flashing the big gap in his front teeth, and laughed boisterously. His players knew his desperate need to win and quick rage—the face distorted, the body shaking in anger, the voice loud and uniquely piercing, and the message biting. But with sudden praise and tight embraces, he inspired those needing encouragement. And he easily became tearful—he openly wept at the ordination to the priesthood of a young man he had coached in high school. During his coaching career, Lombardi had known uncertainty and difficult moments. By his high standards, the Packers' 1964 season was not a good one. As the new year of 1965 began, the disappointment of 1964 turned darker.

On a frigid February 1959 day at Green Bay's Hotel Northland, Lombardi, a stocky man of average height with glasses and wavy hair, was formally introduced as the Packers' head coach. "I want it understood that I'm in complete control," Lombardi announced with the team's unwieldy board of directors in attendance. "I expect full cooperation from you people, and you will get full cooperation from me in return." Exercising total control would mark Lombardi's years as head coach. "I have never been associated with a loser before," he added, "and I don't expect to be now." Great success followed. In his first year in 1959, the Packers won their season opener at home against their most detested rivals, the Chicago Bears, with players hoisting Lombardi on their shoulders, and Green Bay had its first winning season since 1947. In 1960, Green Bay won the Western Conference but lost the title game to Philadelphia 17-13. It was a game Green Bay should have won. The Packers had nine more first downs, 105 more yards, and two fewer turnovers than the Eagles, but were stopped three times inside Philadelphia's 10-yard line without scoring points. Lombardi blamed himself for not kicking field goals. After the game, he told his players they would never again lose a championship game.

In 1961 and 1962, with so many star players at the peak of their careers, the Packers became the league's dominant team and won the championship both years. The 1962 season was historic. The Packers finished the regular season 13-1. They scored 415 points and gave up only 148--Green Bay's average margin of victory was 19.1 points, the league's best since Philadelphia's 19.2-point margin in 1949.

But the 1963 season began with disappointment. In April, the league suspended indefinitely Packer halfback Paul Hornung, Lombardi's favorite player, for betting on NFL games. The Packers ended that season with an 11-2-1 record, finishing second in the conference behind Chicago, which went 11-1-2 and beat Green Bay twice. After the season, the Packers traded veteran center Jim Ringo to Philadelphia, and linebacker Bill Forester, the team's defensive captain, retired; both were All-Pro players.

In 1964, Hornung was reinstated, but the Packers with championship expectations struggled, finishing 8-5-1. Guard Jerry Kramer missed the entire season, nearly dying from an intestinal illness caused by a childhood accident and undergoing eight abdominal surgeries. The team's other guard,

Fuzzy Thurston, sat out games because of injury. Returning from his suspension, Hornung faltered as a placekicker, making only 12 of his 38 field-goal attempts. Green Bay lost three of its first six games by a total of five points—one-point defeats against Baltimore and Minnesota and then a wrenching three-point loss to Baltimore in which Hornung missed five field goals. Finishing three and a half games behind Baltimore in the Western Conference, Green Bay tied with Minnesota for second place in the West. The Packers played for the second consecutive year in the Playoff Bowl, a postseason exhibition in Miami that pitted the two conference runners-up a week after the NFL Championship was played. The match's true purpose was admirable—to raise money for the players' pension fund. But it was a contest that Lombardi derided as a game for losers. Green Bay played badly, losing to the St. Louis Cardinals 24-17, a fitting coda to a forgettable season. The Packers managed only 131 net yards on offense. Unhappy about playing in the Playoff Bowl for the second consecutive year, Lombardi was incensed over his team's performance, telling reporters after the game, "We played the game like we were still in our sleep."

In February 1965, domestic crisis struck. Lombardi routinely told his players each year that their priorities were God, family, and the Packers. But in a time when a husband's role was largely breadwinner and in a profession that demanded long hours and, regardless of effort, successful results, family for Lombardi was at times a distant third. Like other marriages, the 24-year marriage of Vince Lombardi and Marie Planitz concealed private struggles. Though Vince and Marie would have two children, an early pregnancy ended with the baby dying in the womb at seven months. Another pregnancy ended with a baby girl dying two days after birth. With an absent yet demanding husband, Marie had long earlier turned to alcohol. In February 1965, her daughter, Susan, found her unconscious in bed with a container of pills nearby, and Marie was rushed to a local hospital.

* * * * *

A child of Brooklyn, Vincent Lombardi was the eldest of five children in an Italian family. His father was a butcher, and his mother was one of 13 children in the Izzo family. Deeply religious even as a youngster, he attended a Brooklyn diocesan preparatory school, Cathedral College of the Immaculate Conception, which offered a six-year program for boys interested in becoming a priest. The school, considered a minor seminary, required Latin, Greek, and Mass each morning. It did not offer football. Recognizing Lombardi's maturity and leadership, classmates elected Vincent class president four times. Though he was devoutly Catholic and would make daily Mass a lifelong practice, Lombardi left Cathedral College after four years. His wanting to play football was one reason.

Failing to complete Cathedral College's six-year program, Lombardi enrolled in Brooklyn's St. Francis Preparatory School to obtain his high school diploma. At St. Francis Prep, Vince played football for Harry Kane, who had coached in high school New York Yankee star Lou Gehrig, and he played against future Chicago Bear great Sid Luckman at Brooklyn's Erasmus High School, which Al Davis and Barbra Streisand would later attend. In 1933, as the Great Depression deepened, Lombardi graduated from St. Francis Prep days before his 20th birthday.

Lombardi's high-school play earned Vince a scholarship at Jesuit Fordham University in the Bronx. At Fordham, Lombardi's head coach was Jim Crowley, and an assistant coach was Frank Leahy. Crowley, nicknamed "Sleepy Jim" because of drooping eyelids, won a Wisconsin State Championship in 1920 at Green Bay East High School where his coach was Curly Lambeau; he played later for Knute Rockne at Notre Dame in the early 1920s, becoming one of the fabled "Four Horsemen." Leahy played for Rockne at Notre Dame on two national championship teams; in 1941, he returned to South Bend as Notre Dame's new head coach.

Before his senior year at Fordham, Lombardi struggled, beset by injuries and other health problems. But as a senior, Lombardi started at guard, one of the "Seven Blocks of Granite" on Fordham's 1936 team. That Fordham squad finished

5-1-2, shutting out three opponents and never allowing more than seven points in any game. In college, Lombardi was known for his passion for playing football, not for his talent. "There never was a more aggressive man who played for me than Vincent," his coach Frank Leahy noted. "There were times I genuinely worried that he might be too aggressive."

Lombardi graduated from Fordham in 1937 when the country's unemployment rate was once again climbing and would soon reach 19 percent. After college, Lombardi, like so many others searching for a livelihood and a future, drifted—he held several jobs, played minor league football for the Brooklyn Eagles, and attended law school at Fordham for one semester at night before dropping out.

In 1939, in Englewood, New Jersey, across the Hudson from New York, Lombardi found his calling. St. Cecilia High School hired as its new football coach Andy Palau, Lombardi's former quarterback at Fordham. The new head coach recruited Lombardi to coach as an assistant and teach at the Englewood school. Lombardi accepted Palau's offer and spent eight years at St. Ceciia.

Taking classes at Seton Hall to prepare for his classroom duties, Lombardi, just a solid student in his schoolboy days, taught demanding subjects—Latin, physics, and chemistry. Lively and repetitive in presentation, Lombardi had a gift for making difficult lessons simpler. Aware and understanding when slower students struggled, he excelled as a teacher. But the Lombardi legend began not in a classroom but on the football field. As a football assistant and head basketball coach, Lombardi quickly learned the effectiveness of lessons distilled and repeatedly drilled, the importance of emotion on playing fields, and the need to motivate differently those too comfortable and those unsure. Head coach Palau once asked assistant Lombardi to give their team a pregame pep talk. "I was shaking in my boots when it was over," said Palau. "And I know the team was too."

In 1942, after Fordham hired Palau as a football assistant coach, St. Cecilia named Lombardi its new head coach. He lost his first game as head coach but then went undefeated for 32 consecutive games. During Lombardi's time at St. Cecilia, the school won six straight state championships. His undefeated 1943 team, scoring 267 points and giving up only 19, was named national champions. In 1947, Fordham finally called with a job offer. Lombardi coached at Fordham for two years, the second year as the school's chief offensive coach.

* * * * *

In the 1940s, Army football was nationally celebrated, as was its head coach, Earl Blaik, known by his nickname "Red" but often called "Colonel." After seven years coaching at Dartmouth, Blaik, a graduate of both Miami University in Ohio and the Military Academy, returned to West Point. Aided by World War II's disruption of college football, Army with Blaik's coaching was nationally ranked first or second each year from 1944 through 1946 and won five times from 1944 through 1949 the Lambert Trophy, given by New York football writers to the best college football team in the East. After the 1948 season, Army's offensive line coach, Sid Gillman, left West Point to be head coach at the University of Cincinnati. At an Eastern College Athletic Association meeting, Blaik asked Tim Cohane, a sportswriter and a former sports-information director at Fordham, whether he knew of anyone for a coaching vacancy. Following closely Lombardi's coaching career, Cohane recommended the Fordham assistant. Blaik gave Lombardi an interview. It lasted two hours, with the two coaches, both obsessed by the game's detail, dissecting pulling and blocking techniques. After the interview, Cohane called Blaik to see how the meeting had gone. Impressed by Lombardi's football knowledge, Blaik responded with typical sparseness, "He's all right. He's a rough soul."

In both appearance and temperament, Red Blaik, a tall, trim Scotsman with a shock of dark hair, high forehead, and military bearing, was Lombardi's opposite. Reserved and single-minded, Blaik was known not for stirring pep talks but for his unsparing emphasis on detail and quest for flawless execution. On the pastoral fields of West Point, bordered by a twisting Hudson River and dotted with red and yellow when mid-October beckoned, Blaik's coaching methods, compared to the Academy's stirring surroundings, seemed prosaic. But at West Point, Red Blaik became Lombardi's true instructor and mentor, the man Lombardi would always insist was the greatest coach he had ever known. Shortly after retiring from West Point in 1959, Blaik, with Tim Cohane, wrote a book fittingly titled *You Have to Pay the Price*. For Army coaches, workdays ended at midnight during spring football and the fall season. From Blaik, Lombardi learned the need for organization—at Army, practices were scripted by the minute. Another lesson was the importance of film study, however laborious, with a study of each play and each player in a search for weakness and a pursuit for excellence. Appropriately, Blaik's model was that of the United States Army since the Army of the Potomac—victory required only the proper application of superior force. With greater talent and high execution, Blaik sought to demoralize opponents by attacking and overwhelming their strengths.

Though strong-willed, Lombardi was impressionable. He was moved by West Point's majestic setting and especially its mission of defending the nation. West Point's leaders and instructors had been tested in France, in the skies over Germany, and on strange Pacific islands. Colonel Russell "Red" Reeder, an Army instructor who cared for the Academy's athletic fields and became Lombardi's close friend, had commanded a regiment at Utah Beach and days after the Normandy invasion lost a leg to German artillery. In the wake of a world war and during a cold one, West Point attracted many of the country's finest young men, some of whom excelled at football.

With Blaik providing guidance and example, Lombardi flourished. At his first Army practice, Lombardi screamed at players with profanity. Blaik took his new coach aside for a mild reprimand. "Vince, we just don't do it that way at West Point," counseled Blaik. "You can't talk that way to cadets. You can't drive them that way because they're being driven all day." Corrected by Blaik, Lombardi learned to curb his explosive temper and even his sharp tongue.

In Lombardi's first two years at West Point, Army continued to dominate. In 1949, Army was undefeated and finished fourth in the country. In 1950, the Army cadets were undefeated and untied until their final game against a 2-6 Navy team when they were upset 14-2, a loss that noticeably darkened Blaik's mood. But that defeat, even to Navy, would prove an annoyance to Blaik and his Army staff compared to what would shortly convulse West Point. On April 2, 1951, two cadets reported that other cadets had been passing on the questions on identical tests given to different classes over successive days. Army football players were heavily involved. As written, the West Point honor code was unyielding: "A cadet will not lie, cheat, steal, or tolerate those who do." Red Blaik's own son Bob, the team's quarterback, was implicated for failing to report what he knew fellow cadets were doing.

Despite Army's football success, some at West Point believed the emphasis on football was too great and football players enjoyed undue privileges. The cheating scandal provided the football critics with their opportunity. Army politics ultimately drove decisions. The Academy discharged by administrative order 83 cadets, including those like Bob Blaik who had never cheated but failed to report those who had. While roiling West Point, the scandal devastated Army's football team. Only two varsity players remained. Scouring the Academy grounds for cadets with even marginal football talent, Blaik and his coaches did the improbable—Army fielded in 1951 a football team. The Cadets went 2-7, playing hard against opponents like Southern California before succumbing in the season's final game to Navy 42-7. Army's 1952 squad showed improvement, and the 1953 team marked a return to excellence, posting a 7-1-1 record and beating Navy 20-7.

After the 1953 season, the New York Giants, seeking a head coach, tried to hire Blaik. The Army head coach rejected the overtures but touted Lombardi. Concerned that he lacked pro football experience, the Giants instead offered Lombardi a job as the top offensive assistant coach. Lombardi was reluctant to leave West Point and sought a raise. Telling Lombardi that he was already the highest paid Army assistant coach,

Blaik counseled his hesitant assistant to accept the Giants' offer. Lombardi did, returning to his native New York City.

* * * * *

The New York Giants were a talented team. On offense, the Giants in 1954 had quarterbacks Charlie Conerly and Don Heinrich, halfback Frank Gifford, and receiver Kyle Rote. A year later, running backs Alex Webster and Mel Triplett joined the team. The Giants' new head coach, Jim Lee Howell, a former Giant player and Marine Corps drill instructor, did little coaching. He quickly recognized the excellence of his assistants and allowed them to coach. Opposite Lombardi was a cerebral defensive player-coach, Tom Landry, who for two years still played defensive back and in his austere ways resembled Red Blaik.

Lombardi's adjustment was hard. He had never played professional football. Unlike college football, where teams stressed running the football, in pro football, the passing game was the rushing game's equal. The Giant players were older—several like Conerly and Eddie Price had fought in a war—and clearly better athletes than the college players Lombardi had coached. They were not impressed by a coach who often screamed and boasted that he had coached at Army with Red Blaik. In the beginning, Giant players accepted Lombardi with doubt, if not at times with contempt. But Lombardi, smarter and less rigid than his brash and loud ways suggested, turned to his players and asked for their help. Receivers coach Bill Swiacki, an offensive end at Columbia and in the NFL, tutored Lombardi on the passing offense in pro football. Over time, the Giants' offensive players saw that their new coach, if at times combustible, knew football and more important how best to use his players so that they could excel and their team could win.

Confident in his abilities, Lombardi desperately wanted to be a head coach but watched over the years his contemporaries being promoted as he received little interest and grew older. He believed the reason, especially with colleges in the South, was prejudice against Italians. But Lombardi could bitterly recall that he had applied to Notre Dame and never received a response. Geographically, football flourished more in the coal and industrial regions of the Midwest and in the rural South than in Northern cities with large Italian populations that favored other sports. Colleges tended to hire head coaches from their region. And there had been Italian-American head football coaches: Amerino "Moody" Sarno, Lombardi's Fordham teammate, and Aldo Donelli at Northeastern colleges, and Gene Ronzani in Green Bay in the early 1950s. A factor with some college programs may have been Lombardi's bossy temperament and occasional gruffness.

In 1954, Fordham won only one game. After the season ended, its football coach resigned. Fordham, a school for which Lombardi had much affection, contacted Vince about coaching the Rams, and Lombardi and the school's athletic director reached a preliminary agreement. But on December 15, 1954, Fordham's president, Father Laurence McGinley, announced that Fordham was ending its football program.

In 1956, the Giants won the NFL Championship, smashing Chicago in the title game 47-7, and in 1957, the Giants finished second in the Eastern Conference. Both Lombardi and Tom Landry, New York's top two assistants, were receiving notice from other NFL teams needing a head coach. After the 1957 season, the Philadelphia Eagles offered Lombardi their head coach job. But Giants' owner Wellington Mara intervened, advising Lombardi that the Eagles job was a poor one because of questionable ownership and that a better coaching opportunity would come. Mara matched Philadelphia's salary offer of $22,500 per year, and Lombardi stayed in New York. For the New York Giants, the 1958 season proved memorable but disappointing. The Giants won the Eastern Conference with a 9-3 record and then played in the historic 1958 Championship Game, losing in overtime to the Colts in a contest the Giants could have won.

* * * * *

In 1958, Green Bay's place in professional football, though anchored in a long past with notable success, was in jeopardy. The economics of a changing sport and recent failure on the field threatened the franchise. In the postwar years, rising gate receipts and television revenue, with each team having its own television contract, grew the financial divide between teams in major cities and Green Bay. Located in Wisconsin's Brown County with De Pere and Allouez, Green Bay in 1960, with a population of 62,888, was smaller than Kenosha and Racine and only its state's sixth-largest city. The city was known for making toilet paper and other paper products and processing cheese. Though featuring several architecturally distinctive buildings, including the Chicago Commercial Style Bellin Building and the Hotel Northland with its Art Deco trappings, Green Bay's downtown, built on a grid plan, was pleasant but modest with main streets named after presidents and trees. Providing different forms of comfort, the heavily Catholic city was also noted for its many churches and bars. Its main ethnic groups were German, Belgian, Irish, French, and Polish. The 1960 census showed Brown County had a population of 125,082 with only 128 listed as "Negroes"— in Green Bay, only 18 were listed. Of the 12 NFL teams, the league's second-smallest city was Pittsburgh with a population ten times greater than Green Bay's.

In 1957, Green Bay temporarily silenced some skeptics by constructing a second City Stadium. The cost was $960,000. The Packers would no longer have to play games in old City Stadium, a wooden structure seating 25,000 that was used by Green Bay's high schools and that required at one time visiting teams to dress at their hotel and the Packers at adjacent East High School. But the new stadium, built on Green Bay's west side, was still the league's smallest with a seating capacity of 32,150 and smaller by 11,000 seats than Milwaukee's new County Stadium, where other teams wanting a bigger payday sought to play.

On the field, despite a proud history, Green Bay was struggling. In 1921, a Green Bay team, started two years earlier, entered the American Professional Football Association. In 1922, the league was renamed the National Football League. Other cities with teams in the league were Dayton, Akron, Canton, Evansville, and Toledo. Unlike its Midwest counterparts, Green Bay survived lean years, especially those during the Great Depression, and at times flourished. The Packers won five championships from 1929 through 1939 and then a sixth championship in 1944. During their early years, the Packers fielded great players—Curly Lambeau, Johnny "Blood" McNally, Don Hutson, Clarke Hinkle, Cal Hubbard, Mike Michalske, and Arnie Herber.

But in 1948, the Packers began to lose. From 1948 to 1958, Green Bay did not have a winning season, and its combined win-loss-tie record was 37-93-2. After the 1957 season, Green Bay fired its head coach, Lisle Blackbourn, and promoted assistant Scooter McLean with a one-year contract. Known for having lax practices and few curfews and for losing money to his players in card games, McLean lasted one season. The Packers finished 1-10-1, the worst year in their 39-year history.

* * * * *

Unlike every other NFL team, the Packers were a publicly owned nonprofit corporation with nearly 1,700 shareholders. The team was run by a 45-member board of directors with a 13-member executive committee. It was a cumbersome team structure that produced frequent disagreement on what needed to be done. For years, some inside the league thought Green Bay was too small for professional football. With the Packers suffering their worst season, talk that the Packers needed to relocate grew louder. At a perilous moment in the history of the franchise, two men proved critical: Dominic Olejniczak, who provided organizational leadership, and Jack Vainisi, who provided football judgment.

On April 28, 1958, the Packers' board of directors elected Olejniczak as its president. He was a real estate broker and long-time Green Bay politician, who won his first mayoral election by 85 votes and ran city government for 10 years. As Green Bay's mayor, Olejniczak played a leading role in the team's 1950 stock sale to bolster the Packers' finances and six years later in the construction of new City Stadium. Short, unpretentious, and blunt, Olejniczak, with key allies, was determined to change how the team's organization was run. On December 8, 1958, the team's executive board authorized Olejniczak to pick five other executive-committee members for a six-person select committee to plot the team's future. The select committee immediately went to work. On December 15, at the select committee's urging, the executive committee recommended that the board of directors reduce the committee's size from 13 members to seven; that the team hire a general manager, who would have authority over personnel and coaches and answer only to the team's president; and that team president Olejniczak lead the search for a new general manager and head coach.

With his one-year contract expiring on December 31, 1958, Scooter McLean resigned on December 17 as head coach. In the press, as December ended and January arrived, coaching rumors abounded. None involved New York Giants assistant Vince Lombardi. Curly Lambeau was a Green Bay legend, a local kid who starred at East High School and who coached and played for the Packers for 31 years. Still colorful and rakish at 60, Lambeau returned to Green Bay from California and sought the job of general manager. Forest Evashevski, Iowa's fiery football coach whose second-ranked 1958 team had just won the Big 10 title and the 1959 Rose Bowl, was an early favorite for head coach. Deciding to stay at Iowa, Evashevski rejected Green Bay's offer to be head coach and general manager. As late as January 24, 1959, the *Green Bay Press-Gazette* was reporting that Jim Trimble, the coach of the Hamilton Tiger-Cats in Canada, was a leading head coach candidate.

Traveling on January 20 to Philadelphia for the last 26 rounds of the NFL draft held on January 21 and then a league meeting, a Packers contingent led by Olejniczak personally met with Vince Lombardi. In recommendations, the league's elite—Bears owner George Halas, Giants owner Wellington Mara, Cleveland coach Paul Brown, and NFL commissioner Bert Bell—praised Lombardi. A week earlier, Red Blaik had resigned as Army's head coach. It was a job Lombardi coveted, but he quickly learned that Army would hire only a West Point graduate as Blaik's successor. The Green Bay suitors pointed out to Lombardi that despite their recent record, the Packers had talented players; that he would have total control as head coach and general manager; and that Green Bay, the harsh winters aside, was an attractive city in which to raise a family with a low cost of living, country clubs, and good Catholic schools.

On January 26, 1959, Lombardi flew to Green Bay for further discussion. It was the city's 17th day of below-zero weather since the month began. He was offered a five-year contract with an annual $36,000 salary to be the Packers' next head coach. On January 28, shortly after the team's board of directors voted to give the executive committee power to hire the new coach, Olejniczak announced that Vince Lombardi would be the Packers' new head coach and general manager, and that Lombardi would be given "a completely free hand." Two days later, the *Green Bay Press-Gazette*, for its story on the Lombardi selection, ran the headline "Who's That? Lombardi Being 'Introduced' in Packerland." Marie Lombardi, who took delight in her husband's professional success, had misgivings about leaving her native New York to move to a small Wisconsin city. At a Fordham University alumni dinner at New York's Waldorf Astoria Hotel, she sought out Giants owner Wellington Mara, imploring him not to release her husband from his current contract. Mara, who had counseled Lombardi two years earlier to reject Philadelphia's offer to be head coach, gently refused. "Marie, I think Green Bay is the place for him."

* * * * *

Given Green Bay's many losing seasons, a surprising star of the Packers organization was its personnel director, 31-year-old Jack Vainisi, who was known for his competence, long hours, and affability. A Chicago native whose parents owned a neighborhood grocery near Wrigley Field, Vainisi played football at Notre Dame briefly before military service. In the Army, he contracted rheumatic fever, which damaged his heart and ended his days playing football. After graduating from Notre Dame, Vainisi was hired by Green Bay's head coach Gene Ronzani, his former high school coach, to work in the Packers personnel department. At a time when NFL teams relied on college-football preview magazines to prepare for the draft, Vainisi on scouting trips began courting football coaches across the country, enlisting them to scout part-time for Green Bay. Their scouting reports led to Vainisi maintaining over 4,000 folders for college and pro players. Despite their dismal 1958 record, the Packers had promising players. Under Vainisi's guidance, Green Bay had drafted well. In its three drafts from 1956 to 1958, Green Bay picked Paul Hornung, Forrest Gregg, Jim Taylor, Ray Nitschke, Bart Starr, Jerry Kramer, Bob Skoronski, Hank Gremminger, Ron Kramer, and Dan Currie. And in the team's search for a new coach, Vainisi promoted Lombardi and counseled the Giants assistant that to succeed in Green Bay, he would need full power as both head coach and general manager, authority that only George Halas in Chicago and Paul Brown in Cleveland then had.

Jack Vainisi would never see the Packers team that he helped to build play in a championship game. Tragically, on the Sunday after Thanksgiving in 1960, Vainisi suffered a heart attack and died in his bathroom at home. The fire department had to break down the locked door to reach Vainisi's body. He was 33 years old and left behind a pregnant wife and two young daughters. At his funeral, Paul Hornung asked Jack's widow, Jackie, what he could do to help. "Become the type of football player Jack knew you could be," she answered. The following Sunday, Green Bay thrashed Chicago 41-13. Jackie Vainisi received the game ball signed by every Packer player.

* * * * *

Facing reporters after the January 1965 Playoff Bowl defeat, Lombardi promised there would be changes. Days after the game, he traded with the Giants, his old team, for placekicker and punter Don Chandler. In April, seeking more speed on offense, he traded with the Los Angeles Rams for receiver Carroll Dale, dealing linebacker Dan Currie, who had never completely recovered from a major knee injury in 1962. But talented tight end Ron Kramer was demanding a trade to Detroit, where his family lived, threatening otherwise to play out his contract option when he could sign with another team. Defensive back Jesse Whittenton was considering retirement to run an El Paso country club. Guard Jerry Kramer was still recovering from his many surgeries in 1964. And with the Packers roster, age was becoming a concern. By September, nine starters would be 30 or older.

With training camp in July drawing near, Lombardi attended a media dinner at Green Bay's Oneida Golf and Riding Club. Answering questions, he commented that Baltimore, as the defending champion, should be considered the favorite to win the Western Conference in 1965, adding that it would take at least 10 wins to capture the conference crown. But in a Milwaukee television interview days before training camp opened, Lombardi predicted, "The Packers will win it all."

3

Baltimore: The Year of Redemption

He was rich and powerful, and he considered as his due the special privileges given to those rich and powerful. Unlike the Maras in New York and Art Rooney in Pittsburgh and the other NFL owners for whom their franchise was their fortune and whose lives had been long intertwined with professional football, Carroll Rosenbloom, the owner of the Baltimore Colts, came to the sport later in life, already wealthy and accomplished, and he saw more quickly than others what the game was becoming and how big it could become. Driven to win both on the football field and in NFL owners' meetings, Rosenbloom was a formidable owner. When he spoke, the voice was sonorous, the enunciation precise, and the message clear. Those who dealt often with Carroll Rosenbloom knew that he was shrewd and very smooth and most of all determined to get what he wanted.

By birth and upbringing, Rosenbloom was a Baltimorean, but over time, ambition and lifestyle would fray his ties to his native city. His father, a Jewish immigrant from Poland, built a successful textile business making work apparel. At the University of Pennsylvania, Rosenbloom enjoyed sports more than his studies. At Penn, he played football, where his position coach was Bert Bell, a future NFL commissioner. After graduation, Rosenbloom worked in his father's textile business. Carroll's father told him to sell a Roanoke, Virginia subsidiary, Blue Ridge Overalls Company, with lagging sales in the early years of the Great Depression. He instead bought it. For Blue Ridge's denim and khaki clothing, Carroll secured government contracts with the Civilian Conservation Corps and later distribution contracts with retailers like Sears Roebuck and J. C. Penney, turning Blue Ridge into a major success. At age 32, Rosenbloom retired briefly, moving to a large estate on Maryland's bucolic Eastern Shore. But two years later, when his father died, Rosenbloom returned to the family business, and during World War II, Blue Ridge made a fortune selling khaki uniforms to the United States government. In 1959, he sold Blue Ridge for $7 million in cash and $20 million in stock from the acquiring P & R company where Rosenbloom was named a director.

Rosenbloom's business interests and associations were many and at times controversial. He owned and directed large holding companies, Philadelphia and Reading Corporation, and Universal Controls. He was the largest investor in Seven Arts Productions, which produced movies and Broadway plays such as *Funny Girl*. Shortly before Fidel Castro's overthrow of the Batista regime in Cuba, he and a partner bought a Havana casino in a deal involving organized-crime financier Meyer Lansky. His friends included professional gamblers and a close business partner, Louis Chesler, known for his association with Lansky. He was a long-time friend of Joe Kennedy, the father of a president recently slain and of a former United States attorney general just elected to the United States Senate. In New York, where he stayed at his luxury Central Park South apartment in the Navarro hotel, his golf partners were Bill Paley, the founder and head of CBS and the president of New York's Museum of Modern Art, and Dan Topping, president of the New York Yankees.

At times Rosenbloom seemed like a character in a F. Scott Fitzgerald novel, ready for the next gala at East Egg. With his thinning, black hair slicked back, chiseled face, stylish ties and suits, and still athletic frame, a *Sports Illustrated* profile suggested that he looked "like a swinger" with "a hint of Hollywood." He was never one to follow convention or rules written by others. His wife, Velma, and their three children lived on the family's Maryland estate. But for years,

Rosenbloom had in south Florida a second family with Georgia Wyler, a Miami television host and nightclub entertainer, and their two children. Wyler met Rosenbloom in 1957 at a Palm Beach party hosted by Joe Kennedy. Married five times previously, she was blond, shapely, and 20 years younger. Awaiting Rosenbloom's divorce, the two for years intended to marry. Rosenbloom readily admitted that before buying the Colts, he had bet on pro football games. Credible accusations were made, but never conclusively proven, that Rosenbloom, while owner of the team, had bet on and even against the Colts, including a $1 million wager on Baltimore in the 1958 NFL Championship Game.

If Rosenbloom was tepid at first about owning a pro football team, no one after the team finally achieved success on the field questioned his passion to win championships and, in good times, his generosity toward his players. Few in professional sports were more adept at weaving good intentions and self-interest. Always seeking an advantage, Rosenbloom believed wisely that his players, if rewarded, would play better. In 1959, as a postseason bonus for his players, he matched the league's payout for winning the NFL Championship Game, $4,674. Rosenbloom once illegally wrote checks payable to front-office employees with the instruction to cash the checks and give the money to Lenny Moore. But Rosenbloom wanted his players to succeed outside of and after football. He encouraged Colt players to live in Baltimore and sought to find them good jobs and business opportunities. Often with his financial help and guidance, they opened restaurants and started other businesses, and several like Gino Marchetti and Alan Ameche became wealthy. When learning that a player's child or father had special medical needs, Rosenbloom quickly offered to help. Seeing distant and cheap owners in other league cities, many Baltimore players felt fortunate that Rosenbloom was their team's owner, but Johnny Unitas, the Colts' biggest star, never fully trusted Rosenbloom and kept his distance.

* * * * *

Unlike Green Bay's NFL past, Baltimore's experience with professional football was considerably shorter and less storied. In 1947, the All-America Football Conference, the NFL's then-rival league, took over the Miami Seahawks franchise, which was heavily in debt, and sold the team's assets to businessmen wanting to bring pro football to Baltimore. The new team was called the Colts, a nod to the city's horse-racing associations with the Preakness race, Pimlico track, and horse breeding elsewhere in Maryland. In December 1949, the NFL and the weaker AAFC merged with the NFL accepting three AAFC teams: the powerful Cleveland Browns, the San Francisco 49ers, and the Baltimore Colts. On the field and at the box office, the Colts struggled. Baltimore's owner, Abraham Watner, was well known for his 1943 misfortune when a gust of wind blew out of his open office window over $10,000 in cash onto a busy Baltimore street, and he recovered little. At a January 1951 NFL owners' meeting, Watner sold his team's players and equipment to the league for $50,000—Green Bay claimed the helmets. Outraged at their team's dissolution, the Colts' board of directors and the city of Baltimore sued Watner and the NFL, claiming the owner had lacked the authority to sell.

Another woeful franchise was the NFL's Dallas Texans, once the New York Yanks football team. The Texans started in 1952 and played only one year, winning one game and averaging in attendance fewer than 14,000 fans in their four home games in Dallas. Unable to pay their players and $250,000 in debt, the Dallas team owners turned their franchise over to the league. Defending a lawsuit over the Colts' demise and now saddled with a failed franchise, the NFL saw Baltimore as a new home for the Texans team. On December 3, 1952, at a luncheon before the Advertising Club of Baltimore, NFL Commissioner Bert Bell told his audience that Baltimore could claim the Texans franchise if the city sold 15,000 season tickets in six weeks. Baltimore fans bought nearly 16,000 season tickets in four weeks.

Ownership of the new Baltimore franchise remained an issue. Bert Bell had long wanted to bring Maryland businessman Carroll Rosenbloom into the league as a team owner. Bell's relationship with Rosenbloom had begun 20 years earlier at Penn where Bell coached Rosenbloom, and the two were Jersey Shore summer neighbors. On January 23, 1953, Bell, determined that Rosenbloom should own the Baltimore franchise, called Rosenbloom and closed the deal: "Carroll, you're the new owner. I just announced it." The league's terms for Rosenbloom's purchase were generous: $200,000 to be paid over eight years in annual $25,000 installments. Rosenbloom relented, agreeing to own 51 percent of the new franchise if Bell could provide a general manager. Bell recommended Don Kellett, another Penn graduate who had played football in college with Rosenbloom. A man of some ability, Kellett had coached football and basketball at Penn, had done sportscasting, and was managing a Philadelphia television station. Told to hold down expenses and promised as an incentive a percentage of the team's profits, Kellett agreed to become general manager.

* * * * *

In 1960, Baltimore was the nation's sixth-largest city. It had a great university, Johns Hopkins, and a nationally prestigious though stodgy newspaper, the *Baltimore Sun*, with foreign bureaus across Europe and in New Delhi. Venerable banks like Mercantile Bank & Trust and national corporations had their home offices in Baltimore and, along with the city's big law firms, provided civic leadership. Like other long-established cities in the East and Midwest, Baltimore had a heavily Catholic populace and a heavily Protestant business hierarchy, and a common question was where did one go to high school. But unlike its neighbors to the north—Philadelphia, New York, and Boston—and nearby Washington, Baltimore at its core was marked not by flash and pretension but by grit and cultural insecurity. The city was stamped by its large port, shipyards, and steel mills—in the 1950s, the Bethlehem Steel mill in Sparrows Point had employed 30,000. Filled with rowhouses, neighborhood bars, and churches, Baltimore was noted for its riot of distinctive neighborhoods, over 200 in number, many with matter-of-fact names like

Little Italy, Brewers Hill, and Pigtown, Babe Ruth's childhood home. The city had a high number of blue-collar workers with roots in the countries of eastern and southern Europe who did not cheer for a college team and were eager to embrace pro football. "This Baltimore is a big Green Bay," an assistant coach for the AAFC Colts team in 1947 observed.

With its fierce parochial pride and working-class identity, Baltimore embraced the new Colts. Since their AAFC years, the Baltimore Colts had a band, in 1965 numbering 127 volunteer members with majorettes, cheerleaders, and a color guard. The team had a foot-tapping fight song, "Let's Go You Colts," and as a mascot a white horse named Dixie that after touchdowns would circle the football field in Baltimore's Memorial Stadium. The Colts' 1965 media guide listed 11 corrals, non-profit clubs often connected to a tavern or a neighborhood that organized rallies, parties after games to celebrate wins, and trips to away games, but also supported local charities. When the new Colts began playing in Baltimore in 1953, the team averaged in attendance 28,000 per game. That number increased in 1957 to 46,648 and in the 1958 championship year to 53,641. Since 1963, the Colts sold over 50,000 season tickets; for adults, the prices ranged from $42 to $28, and for students, the cost was $14.

And the Colts relished Baltimore's passion. Players frequently visited hospitals and enthusiastically signed autographs, regardless of the number of waiting fans. In late 1957, a prominent fan, "Willie the Rooster," who led stadium cheers and greeted players after games, died at age 37 of a heart attack. Star players John Unitas, Alan Ameche, and Art Donovan, and general manager Don Kellett attended his funeral and served as pallbearers. When the Colts were flying home from New York after their 1958 championship win, authorities at Baltimore's Friendship Airport contacted the team's plane, suggesting a diversion to Washington because 30,000 fans had swamped the airport to welcome their team home. After the plane landed in Baltimore, an ambulance transported into town Gino Marchetti, who had broken his leg at the end of the game. Marchetti would never forget seeing, as the ambulance approached Baltimore, a man in the winter weather standing on the side of the road with a young boy and shining a flashlight on a sign that read "Welcome Home Champs!"

Winning sports teams provide pride and a sense of belonging to the cities and states that they play in and represent, especially those enduring tough times and looked down upon. The Colts' dramatic championship win in 1958 over New York and second championship in 1959 gave Baltimoreans a winner, inflating pride in their city and inflaming passion for their football team. A Colts band member wearing his uniform could be seen each morning raising the American flag and the team's banner. In 1965, Colt players and coaches were still neighbors who sold cars and insurance during the offseason and who attended the same churches and shopped at the same stores. Unitas and Shula, though sitting in different pews, were regularly seen attending Mass at Immaculate Conception in Towson and on game day early morning Mass at Immaculate Heart of Mary in Loch Raven, a short drive to Memorial Stadium.

The reporters covering the Colts became well-known and the broadcasters prominent. The city's leading newspapers were the morning *Baltimore Sun*, the *Baltimore Evening Sun*, and the *Baltimore News American*. Bob Maisel and Cameron Snyder covered the Colts for the *Sun*, the city's newspaper of record, and Paul Menton and Jim Walker for the *Evening Sun*. Both newspapers sparingly gave the Colts front-page attention. But the *News American*, the result of a 1964 newspaper merger, catered to Baltimore's working-class readers with the color and drama found in afternoon tabloid newspapers sold in the biggest cities and covered the Colts exhaustively. On Mondays during football season, the *News American*'s front page would feature prominently a game headline and a game article written by a Colts player or coach. Its sports editor was John Steadman, a veteran Baltimore reporter and a former Colts publicist. The paper also featured N. P. "Swami" Clark, whose lively writing entertained readers. Better known for his deep voice than his angular frame, Chuck Thompson was the Colts' radio and television voice who also did radio broadcasts for the baseball Orioles. Thompson's signature expressions, exclaimed after a touchdown or another big play, were "Ain't that beer cold" and "Go to war, Miss Agnes." The former drew letters from listeners who disapproved of alcohol but doubtless pleased principal sponsor National Brewing. The latter came from Thompson's golfing buddy, who used his unique saying in lieu of profanity on fairways and greens. On Baltimore television, Vince Bagli, known for warmth and authenticity, was beginning his broadcasting career on WBAL.

* * * * *

After one season, the Colts transferred their head coach, Keith Molesworth, to the team's personnel department. In their search for a new head coach, the Colts first sought Blanton Collier, Paul Brown's chief assistant at Cleveland. Brown summarily dismissed Baltimore's inquiries, reporting that Collier did not want to coach the Colts. Baltimore then asked the Browns about another Cleveland assistant, Weeb Ewbank. Determined not to lose to NFL competitors his long-time assistant coaches who were schooled in the precise ways that he ran his football team, Paul Brown responded that Ewbank as well had no interest in the Baltimore job. For the Colts, luck and airline seating intervened. Leaving Montgomery on a flight after scouting the 1953 Blue-Gray game, Colts general manager Kellett was seated next to Charlie Winner, a coach at Western Reserve University who was scouting part-time for the Browns. Winner also was married to Weeb Ewbank's daughter Nancy. Hearing that the Colts had been told that Ewbank was not interested in being Baltimore's new coach, he assured Kellett that his father-in-law wanted to be a head coach and gave him Ewbank's telephone number. Contacted by the Colts, Ewbank agreed to become Baltimore's next head coach. Feeling betrayed, Paul Brown was furious.

Wilbur Charles Ewbank was known as "Weeb"—his younger brother struggled to say Wilbur. Standing only five-foot-seven and weighing 146 pounds, Ewbank was a star in multiple sports at Miami of Ohio. In football, he played quarterback; after Ewbank graduated, his successor at the position was Paul Brown. Joining the Navy in 1943 after years as a high school coach, Ewbank worked under Paul Brown coaching the Great Lakes Naval Station football team. After the war, Ewbank was an assistant coach at Ivy League Brown and head coach at academically prestigious Washington University in St. Louis before joining the Cleveland Browns in 1949 as an offensive line coach.

When named as the Colts' new head coach in 1954, Ewbank predicted a championship in five years. In his early seasons, Baltimore struggled. In 1956, Ewbank's third year, the Colts were 4-7 and playing their final game against the Washington Redskins. Owner Carroll Rosenbloom was known for high expectations, not patience. Before the Redskins game, Cleveland's Paul Brown, still resentful that Ewbank had left the Browns, called Washington's owner George Preston Marshall, urging that the Redskins beat Baltimore so badly that Ewbank would be fired. But Baltimore won 19-17, and Ewbank as head coach survived. Despite disappointing season records, the Colts had reasons for encouragement. In their recent draft selections, the Colts picked in 1954 guard Alex Sandusky, defensive end Ordell Braase, and receiver Raymond Berry as a future pick; in 1955 fullback Alan Ameche, quarterback George Shaw, and offensive linemen Dick Szymanski and George Preas; in 1956 Penn State halfback sensation Lenny Moore; and in 1957 offensive tackle Jim Parker and linebacker Don Shinnick. And in 1956, the Colts during the offseason signed quarterback John Unitas, a free agent cut the year before by the Pittsburgh Steelers in training camp. Replacing an injured George Shaw at quarterback in game four of the 1956 season, Unitas showed how special he one day would become.

Ewbank was short with a cherubic face and an older man's extra pounds. His appearance concealed his coaching talent. The heading for his profile in the team's 1957 press guide read "Professor." Well-organized and meticulous in preparation but simple in presentation, Ewbank was both a skilled teacher and a good judge of football talent. He learned from

Paul Brown that detail mattered—Weeb changed the color of the Colts helmets from blue to white so that Baltimore's coaches, when watching game film, could better see Baltimore players. During games, Ewbank could be overcome by excitement, and sideline decisions were not his strength. But his game-day emotion was offset by his willingness to give Johnny Unitas, for whom no moment was ever too big, free rein of the team's offense.

In 1957, with their young star players maturing, the Colts finished 7-5, their first winning season. With the league's second-best point differential, the difference between the points scored and points given up, they flashed greatness. In the 1958 season, they achieved it, winning in overtime at Yankee Stadium the NFL Championship in an ending so dramatic that NFL Commissioner Bert Bell cried, knowing he had just seen a game that would change the future of pro football. In 1959, the Colts repeated as league champions, easily beating the Giants 31-16 in the title game.

But the 1960 season brought disappointment to the Colts. The turning point was a November game at Wrigley Field against Chicago that Baltimore won 24-20 with the heroics of Unitas and Lenny Moore on a last-second touchdown pass. After their Chicago win, the Colts, at the end of eight weeks, led the Western Conference with four games left. But the Chicago game was so physically brutal that, even with his flair for hyperbole and storytelling, Baltimore defensive tackle Art Donovan, a Pacific Theater Marine, called it worse than World War II. Baltimore lost its next four games and Chicago three of its last five. A rueful Ewbank later remarked that in Wrigley Field that Sunday, Baltimore won a game but lost a championship. In 1961, Baltimore finished 8-6 in the league's new 14-game format, and the Green Bay Packers, winning the NFL Championship, were now the Western Conference's dominant team.

The 1962 season ended Ewbank's tenure as Baltimore's head coach. In Los Angeles for Baltimore's mid-season game against the Rams, halfback Lenny Moore argued with Ewbank at a team meeting that he should not be fined for a curfew violation, maintaining he could not catch a taxi because he was Black. When Ewbank refused to rescind the fine, Moore walked out of the meeting, followed by several Black teammates. To calm suddenly turbulent waters, Carroll Rosenbloom flew from Hawaii to Los Angeles to visit Moore, one of the owner's most prized players. But Moore's defiance damaged Ewbank's standing as head coach.

Two weeks later, in a late November game in Memorial Stadium, the Bears embarrassed the Colts 57-0. The next day, Rosenbloom asked Gino Marchetti, his favorite player, to meet him at the Baltimore Sheraton Hotel. Seeing Marchetti upset over the Chicago loss, Rosenbloom confided, "Now I've got my chance to fire Weeb Ewbank." Asked for head coach suggestions, Marchetti recommended Don Shula, his former Colts teammate and the Detroit Lions' defensive coordinator. Marchetti called Shula the smartest defensive player he had ever seen and compared him to Unitas in his understanding of the game. By happenstance, Baltimore was playing the Lions in Detroit next Sunday. On the Saturday night before the Detroit game, Rosenbloom interviewed Shula to be his next head coach. Lions' head coach George Wilson knew of the interview; Weeb Ewbank did not. When Rosenbloom doubted whether he was ready to be a head coach, Shula offered a challenge: hire me and let me show you. On Sunday, Baltimore lost to Detroit 21-14.

The Colts won their last two games against Washington and Minnesota by a total of 38 points, but their 7-7 finish was not good enough. In the team's offices after the season, veteran linebacker Bill Pellington and general manager Don Kellett joined Marchetti in promoting Shula. Deciding to hire Shula, Rosenbloom fired Ewbank, who had two years left on his contract. Rejecting Rosenbloom's offer to remain with the team in a different capacity, Ewbank signed a three-year, $100,000 contract to coach the AFL's New York Titans, which would soon be rebranded as the New York Jets. But the Don Shula era in Baltimore had begun. With his sturdy build, thick black hair, and assertive jaw, the new head coach looked like an older defensive back eager to play one more year. Signing a two-year contract that paid $30,000 each year, he had just turned 33.

* * * * *

Don Shula always wanted to make his mark. One of seven children, he was the son of Hungarian immigrants. Shula was born early in the Great Depression in Grand River, Ohio, a small town outside Painesville and near Lake Erie that was 27 miles northeast of Cleveland. His father, who had come to America at the age of six, worked in a rose nursery for two or three dollars each day and then as a commercial fisherman. At Painesville High School, Don played basketball, baseball, and eventually football, and ran track. After Shula as a youngster sustained a gashed face playing football, his mother forbade him from playing the sport. As a junior, he forged his parents' signatures on an authorization form for football so he could play.

A former high school coach helped Shula get a one-year football scholarship paying only tuition at John Carroll, a small Jesuit college outside Cleveland, with the promise of a full four-year scholarship if he made the school's team. Shula won his four-year scholarship. During his senior year, Syracuse played a game at John Carroll, and Cleveland Brown coaches attended to scout Syracuse players. Playing in freezing weather, John Carroll, with two fourth-quarter touchdowns, upset Syracuse 21-16. Shula, running for over 100 yards, impressed the Cleveland coaches.

In the NFL draft held in January 1951, a 30-round marathon held over two days, the Browns picked Shula in the ninth round, the draft's 110th pick. Turning down an offer to teach math and coach at a Canton, Ohio high school for $3,750 per year and setting aside any earlier thoughts of entering the priesthood, Shula signed a Cleveland contract paying $5,000 if he made the team. In 1951, the Browns drafted 36 college players. The team had only 33 roster spots. In Cleveland's final exhibition game that year, Browns head coach Paul Brown told Shula that his game performance would determine whether he made the team. Kicked in the mouth by Rams' star receiver Tom Fears, Shula, maintaining his focus, made two interceptions and the team's final roster, one of only two rookies to do so. Shula played two years for the Browns as a reserve defensive back.

In 1953, Cleveland sent Shula to Baltimore in a 15-player trade. Shula learned of the trade when he was reading the newspaper after classes at Western Reserve University, where he was working on a master's degree in education. Arriving in Baltimore, Shula was asked by an assistant coach to help teach and implement the Browns' defense. With the Colts, Shula befriended and shared a house with the team's wildest players—Gino Marchetti, linebackers Bill Pellington and Don Joyce, and defensive tackle Art Donovan. Joyce during the offseason professionally wrestled, and Donovan, the grandson of a middleweight boxing champion and the son of a famed boxing referee, was known for his irrepressible humor and appetite.

To compensate for his lack of speed and limited athleticism, Shula relied on sure tackling, intelligent play, and a passion to master the game's finer points. The Colts' 1957 press guide offered this description: "Smart student of the game and someday should make a successful coach." But shortly after the media guide's release, quarterback Johnny Unitas and receiver Raymond Berry in training-camp drills repeatedly exposed Shula's athletic shortcomings. The Colts cut Shula, who was signed by Washington. He played one year for the Redskins. When Washington that season played the Colts, Shula was assigned to defend Berry, who caught 12 passes for two touchdowns and 224 yards. A Washington newspaper reporter described the Colts' targeting of Shula as "murder." Attending a meeting of Redskin coaches before the 1958 season, Shula inadvertently saw he was listed behind a rookie on the team's depth chart. With an upcoming marriage to Dorothy Bartish, Shula recognized at age 28 that his future in football would be as a coach, not as a player.

Shula in 1958 began his coaching career at the University of Virginia. He coached for one year at Virginia, which finished the season with a 1-9 record, the result of high academic requirements for football recruits. In 1959, Shula accepted an offer from his former Cleveland coach, Blanton Collier, to work as an assistant at Kentucky. A superb teacher, Collier stressed the lessons taught by Paul Brown in Cleveland, especially the importance of detail. After Shula's first year in Lexington, the Detroit Lions called, offering a job as a defensive assistant coach. Shula told Collier his goal was to be an NFL head coach. "If that's your goal," said Collier, "you need to take the job in Detroit."

In 1960, Shula began coaching the Lions, first as the defensive backs coach and later as the defensive coordinator. It was an era of great defenses when quarterbacks standing in the pocket and receivers crossing the middle of the field were hunted and defensive units like those in New York and Chicago were celebrated. On defense, the talented Lions had seven past or future All-Pro players—defensive linemen Alex Karras and Roger Brown; linebackers Joe Schmidt and Wayne Walker; and defensive backs Yale Lary, Dick "Night Train" Lane, and Dick LeBeau. Don Shula brought to the Lions an exhaustive defensive playbook, detailed game plans built on film study, and incisive instruction, and Detroit's defense became one of the game's most feared units.

* * * * *

Returning to the Baltimore team that seven years earlier had cut him, Shula was younger than, and had played with, several Colt players. He had never been a head coach on any level. And he was now working for an owner whose expectations went beyond contention and who fired a respected coach who had won two NFL championships. Shula named two older defensive players, former teammates Gino Marchetti and Bill Pellington, as player-coaches. In contrast to Ewbank's emphasis on simplicity, Shula introduced a thicker playbook with more challenging terminology. And in personality, Shula was a marked change from Ewbank. The new coach was direct and fiery and welcomed confrontation—players always knew where they stood with Don Shula.

Tension between the young head coach and his star

quarterback, Johnny Unitas, quickly surfaced and simmered. When upset, Shula would scream at players. Even the team's 1963 media guide called Shula "a holler guy." It was a trait of some coaches that Ewbank lacked and that Unitas detested. And Unitas had enjoyed a close relationship with Ewbank, who recognized his potential, engaged him closely in developing game plans, and allowed Unitas, once games began, to freely run the Colts offense and reject the few plays Ewbank might send in. For Shula, a defensive coach, the Colts in recent years had relied too heavily on passing. Wanting an offense with better balance by running more, Shula believed that to succeed as head coach, he needed to limit Unitas's nearly total command of the offense. But this was a time when the top quarterbacks insisted that they, not coaches, call plays. "You don't become a real quarterback until you can tell the coach to go to hell," said Unitas. Applauded by nearly everyone for his intuitively brilliant play selection, Unitas believed that he knew more about pro football offenses than Shula and that for the Colts to win, he needed total command. Ironically, Shula wanted Unitas to play more like Green Bay's Bart Starr, and in Green Bay, Vince Lombardi, an offensive coach, wanted a bolder quarterback like Unitas.

Both Shula and Unitas were fiercely competitive and could be obstinate. Open conflict between the two flared early in the 1963 season when Unitas, on fourth down and a half yard, waved off Baltimore's field goal team. A heated sideline exchange ensued. After the game, the head coach, backed by player-coach Gino Marchetti, met his quarterback. "If you're going to show me up like that," Shula told Unitas, "I can't be the coach of the team." And then there was Shula's bluntness in postgame interviews. In a late October game in 1963, the Colts lost to Green Bay 34-20 and played badly; in the first half, Unitas threw two interceptions and completed only three of eight passes. After the game, Shula told reporters that he had considered benching Johnny Unitas, the sport's biggest name. "Yes, if things had continued to go bad in the third period, I would have taken him out," Shula volunteered. "He had a bad first half. There is no denying it."

Though Shula and Lombardi were both intense and

emotional, their coaching methods, shaped by personality and experience, could be different. In Baltimore, the players worked longer but felt less fear and uncertainty than in Green Bay. To motivate, Shula, however demanding and abrupt, did not deliberately humiliate players as Lombardi occasionally could. But like Green Bay's head coach, Shula was intelligent and knew his craft well. Over time, his players saw a young coach who was willing to listen to and learn from what they had to say. Shula and Unitas, their success dependent on each other, would achieve some mutual respect but never mutual affection.

Baltimore had a stable of top assistant coaches like Don McCafferty and offensive line coach John Sandusky, and Shula kept them, making McCafferty, whose calming presence Unitas welcomed, the team's offensive backfield assistant and chief offensive coach. To his credit, Shula also retained long-time defensive assistant Charlie Winner, Weeb Ewbank's son-in-law. Winner's coaching skills were inversely related to his five-foot-six stature, and his early years reflected the Great Depression era in which he grew up. Born in Somerville, New Jersey, Winner won a scholarship to Southwest Missouri State. "I have a chance to go to college, and it won't cost the family anything," he informed his father. "What do you think?" His father replied, "I think you ought to go out and get a job and help the family." The next day, with perhaps $150 in his pocket, Winner boarded a bus for Missouri. After Pearl Harbor, Winner volunteered for the Army Air Forces and served on a B-17 crew bombing Germany. On his 17th mission, his bomber late in the war was shot down over Hamburg, and he became a prisoner of war. Returning home, Winner finished college at Washington University where he played football under Ewbank and then began coaching.

* * * * *

In 1963, the Colts drafted well. Their top two picks were Ohio State offensive lineman Bob Vogel and Syracuse tight end John Mackey. Other selections were tight end Butch Wilson, running back Jerry Logan, and receiver Willie Richardson.

Weighing only 240 pounds, Vogel relied on intelligence and superior technique to play left tackle. His addition allowed the Colts to move Jim Parker to left guard. Vogel, a first-round selection, signed when the two leagues were competing for newly drafted college seniors. His first contract paid $18,500 per year. At a time when the cost of the average house was $19,000, it was an amount he treasured as one more player whose father had worked in coal mines and whose mother at times did not eat at dinner so the children could.

The Colts opened the 1963 season, losing three of their first four games, but Shula remained a steady presence. Baltimore won five of its last six games to finish 8-6. In his second season, Shula in 1964 was ready to fully take control of his team. That year, Baltimore finished 12-2 but was then embarrassed by Cleveland in the NFL Championship Game. After that loss, Gino Marchetti and Bill Pellington, both a player-coach and Shula friend, retired from football. But playing in his 11th and last Pro Bowl Game, Marchetti avenged the perceived slight of Frank Ryan two weeks earlier wanting to run up the score in the 1964 NFL Championship. In an exhibition game played for pride, Marchetti slammed Ryan downward, separating the Cleveland quarterback's shoulder in an action many believed was retaliation.

As the Colts entered the 1965 season, there were other roster changes. The Colts drafted in the first round Duke linebacker Mike Curtis and somehow succeeded in trading away to Detroit the aptly named Joe Don Looney for middle linebacker Dennis Gaubatz. Looney, who ventured to graveyards to read because they were quiet places, was football's most bizarre character. Watching a tag-team event at a wrestling tournament, he jumped into the ring to help an outnumbered wrestler, thinking a riot had broken out. In college, for bad grades and bad behavior, he was kicked out of Texas, TCU, and Oklahoma. But the Giants, seeing a track-star-fast running back who weighed 230 pounds, still picked Looney in the first round in the 1964 draft. When the Giants' summer camp opened, Looney showed a preference for lifting weights at home to loud music rather than attending mandatory team meetings. Within weeks, the Giants traded Looney to the Colts. In Baltimore, looking for the apartment of nurses he had met, Looney knocked down the door to the wrong apartment and terrorized the couples inside, angry that he was not playing more often and that Barry Goldwater had badly lost the 1964 presidential election.

Obtained in a 1964 trade, Lou Michaels would replace Marchetti at defensive end. On offense, though all starters were returning, age in the offensive line was a concern--on opening day, tackle George Preas was 32, guard Alex Sandusky 33, and center Dick Szymanski three weeks shy of 33. But the Colts were a talented team with depth, All-Pro players at the receiver positions and at halfback, and foremost Johnny Unitas. And they still burned with the pain of last year's Championship Game disaster in Cleveland. The Colts' own 1965 press guide described the game as a "nightmarish 27-0 slaughter" and "a searing, shocking defeat." The team's press guide continued: "Now Shula must refit the pieces of his mangled machine. It won't be difficult to drum up incentive for the 1965 season. Everyone knows about that near-miss in Cleveland." For the Baltimore Colts in 1965, there was only one goal: an NFL championship. It would be the year of redemption.

4

The NFL: "The Sport of the '60s"

On an Indian-summer Sunday in October 1959 in a Philadelphia football stadium, an era in professional football ended. On October 11, with minutes left in a game between the Pittsburgh Steelers and Philadelphia Eagles at Franklin Field, NFL Commissioner Bert Bell slumped over lifeless in his stadium seat. He had suffered a heart attack and was pronounced dead minutes later as he was rushed into University Hospital three football fields away. Fittingly, at a stadium where he had played and coached, Bell was watching two teams that he had owned, at least in part, and coached. At the time, he was sitting not in a private box with team and league officials, but in an end zone seat surrounded by fans known for their passion. He was 64 years old.

Bell was a heavyset man who visibly aged during his 14 years as commissioner. For years, his health was poor. In 1954 at Philadelphia's Racquet Club, he collapsed. His physicians counseled him to work fewer hours and stop smoking. In early 1959, he had a mild but portentous heart attack. Given his health scares, Bell was hoping to retire as commissioner after the 1959 season and buy the Philadelphia Eagles, the team he had started and named. A day after his father's funeral, Bell's older son learned from a Philadelphia National banker that his father had been days away from buying the Eagles franchise for $950,000 with the intent of eventually passing the team on to his two sons.

Born in 1895, Bell was the product of a different age. His real name, which he loathed and screamed privilege, was de Benneville. His family was prosperous and prominent in a city known for rigid class gradations. His father was a Pennsylvania attorney general and a University of Pennsylvania trustee who declared that for college Bert would go to Penn or go to hell, his mother could trace her ancestors to a time before the American Revolution, and his brother served as a Pennsylvania Supreme Court justice. Bert Bell attended the finest private schools, including the prestigious Haverford School outside Philadelphia where he enjoyed playing several sports and found football his favorite. Not wishing to test his father's beliefs on eternal damnation, Bell entered Penn where he played football. A world war and military service in France interrupted his college years. After leaving Penn as a student in 1920, Bell coached football as an assistant at Penn for nine years, in the beginning under head coach John Heisman, and then at Temple for three years. He also managed the Philadelphia Ritz-Carlton, owned by his family, and worked as a stockbroker. But Bell was a devotee of saloons and racetracks, a noted bon vivant in Philadelphia until his engagement to a beautiful Ziegfeld Follies dancer and actress, Frances Upton. She conditioned her acceptance of Bell's marriage proposal on his giving up alcohol, a promise he kept.

In the NFL's formative years, the Great Depression and later a second world war challenged franchise survival and threatened financial ruin. From 1933 through 1940, Bell owned the Philadelphia Eagles and for five years was their head coach and general manager. For the next seven years, he and Art Rooney owned the Pittsburgh Steelers. In 1946, the NFL failed to renew Elmer Leahy's contract as commissioner. The league's owners then elected Bell, one of their own, as their new commissioner.

In appearance, Bert Bell projected old-world decorum. He was a stocky man who favored dark double-breasted suits and wore his hair slicked-back with a middle part. In manner, he was the patrician as the common man. For 14 years, the outgoing Bell, devoid of pretense, guided the NFL with a firm hand from his Philadelphia office, featuring paintings and photographs showing family and league history. As commissioner, he relied on his large personality marked by humor and empathy, his friendships with team owners, and the trust and respect he had earned as a competing owner and later as their commissioner. He ran the NFL as though it were a small business. Nurturing his personal relationships with the league's owners, Bell, with his gravelly voice, incurred nearly a thousand dollars each month in long-distance telephone charges. To those questioning his informal ways, he would say "why write when you can call." Sitting at his dining table at home, smoking incessantly and using dominoes, Bell personally drew up 12-game schedules for as many as 13 teams.

Immediately after being named commissioner, Bell had to negotiate among the league's reluctant owners the demand of Cleveland Rams' owner Dan Reeves to move his team to Los Angeles. In Bell's first year, the All-America Football Conference began its challenge to the NFL, fielding eight teams in 1946. After four years of competing against each other and with player salaries increasing, the two leagues agreed to merge, with the NFL accepting three AAFC teams. In his early years running the league, Bell dealt with struggling NFL franchises that would not survive—the New York Yanks, the Boston Yanks, the Dallas Texans, and the early Baltimore Colts. Throughout his years as commissioner, he guided other teams that at times were financially struggling like the Green Bay Packers.

Among his contributions to the fledgling sport, Bell introduced and promoted team parity as necessary for the league's success. At an NFL owners' meeting in 1935, Bell as the Eagles owner proposed a draft of college players so that the league's weaker teams could sign good players. "Gentlemen, I've always had the theory that pro football is like a chain," argued Bell. "The league is no stronger than its weakest link, and I've been a weak link for so long that I should know." In 1936, the NFL conducted its first draft with nine teams picking 81 players over nine rounds. The first player picked was Jay Berwanger, a star halfback at the University of Chicago and the first winner of the award later known as the Heisman Trophy. Berwanger, demanding $15,000 per year, would never play a down of pro football. The Chicago Bears, obtaining his rights from Philadelphia, refused to pay more than $13,500.

As commissioner, Bell had other achievements. He shielded the game's integrity. He mandated that coaches before games list their injured players, guarded for as long as possible the identity of officials assigned to games, and changed the league's constitution to give the commissioner greater authority to punish those betting on games or otherwise engaging in conduct detrimental to the league. He convinced team owners to agree to benefits and other compensation demands made by the newly formed NFL Players Association to ward off antitrust legislation some in Congress were considering and an antitrust lawsuit the association was threatening. And he began efforts to establish a pension fund for players.

But it was during Bell's tenure that pro football's popularity, evidenced by game attendance, television viewers, and team revenue, began to surge. Nearly one-third of the nation watched on television the 1958 Championship Game between Baltimore and New York. After eight minutes of sudden-death overtime, Colt fullback Alan Ameche, "the Horse," crashed into the end zone to give Baltimore the title. "I never thought I'd see a day like today," Bert Bell tearfully exclaimed in the Yankee Stadium press box. *Sports Illustrated* called the overtime thriller the "Best Football Game Ever Played." Measured by how well the game was played overall, it was not—the Giants had only 10 first downs and lost four fumbles, and the Colts turned the ball over three times. The Colt players believed that they should have beaten the Giants handily and that their November 30 comeback win against San Francisco with three fourth-quarter touchdowns was their finest effort in 1958. But measured by how much a game changed the future of its sport, Baltimore's overtime win was the greatest, and Bell sensed immediately what the game would mean to professional football. Ultimately, that was Bert Bell's true legacy as commissioner—he helped to build the league's foundation for the explosive growth that would come next.

* * * * *

Upon Bell's death, Austin Gunsel, the league's treasurer, became interim commissioner until the 12 owners could elect a permanent one. The owners were scheduled to meet in January 1960 at the Kenilworth Hotel in Miami Beach. But in addition to selecting a new commissioner, the NFL's owners at the meeting needed to address the threat of a new and rival football league. After the 1958 Championship Game, Lamar Hunt, a serious man with Texas oil money, approached Bert Bell about NFL expansion to Dallas. Bell rebuffed Hunt's overtures, saying the NFL was not ready to expand. In 1959, Hunt and others like Bud Adams, who had once hoped to own an NFL team, started the American Football League. The AFL was set to begin play with eight teams in 1960. As a response to the AFL challenge, Chicago Bears owner George Halas urged that the NFL expand to Dallas and Minnesota over the next two years. And Chicago Cardinals owner Charles Bidwill Jr., tired of competing in Chicago against the Bears, sought league approval to move his team to St. Louis.

The leading candidate to succeed Bell was Marshall Leahy, the San Francisco 49ers' attorney. An able man with teenage daughters, Leahy refused to move East and would agree to be commissioner only if the league moved its office from Philadelphia to San Francisco. Leahy's condition aroused strong opposition from three owners—Baltimore's Carroll Rosenbloom, Washington's George Preston Marshall, and Philadelphia's Frank McNamee. A supermajority of 75 percent, nine of the 12 owners, was needed to elect a new commissioner. Rosenbloom and Marshall told George Halas that they would oppose expansion if he supported Leahy.

The NFL's owners took seven days and 23 ballots to elect a new commissioner. Leahy repeatedly received eight votes but, with Halas each time abstaining, never the requisite nine. Those opposing Leahy supported, though with limited ardor, interim commissioner Gunsel and later Baltimore general manager Don Kellett. Finally, after 22 rounds of voting, Leahy's supporters looked for a compromise candidate. Several owners suggested Pete Rozelle, the 33-year-old general manager of the Los Angeles Rams who had been a favorite of Bert Bell and had shown unusual skill in marketing the Rams and navigating the tensions between Dan Reeves and his co-owners. On the 23rd ballot, Rozelle was elected with the necessary nine votes. He received a three-year contract paying $50,000 per year. Noting Rozelle's concern over his youth and the job's responsibilities, Paul Brown offered assurance: "Pete, don't worry—you'll grow into it." Rozelle made clear that he wanted to move the league headquarters, though to New York City, not the West Coast. After his election, Rozelle chaired the remainder of the owners' meeting with a structure and formality the owners were not used to seeing.

Pete Rozelle was tall and lanky, and he seemed to always have a good tan. He had perfect manners and an easy smile, and he was by nature genial and gracious. With the powerful owners who hired him, he was respectful and tactful, leading often by suggestion and careful nudging. As the Rams general manager, Rozelle knew the challenges of running an NFL franchise. But he came from the world of public relations and marketing. Unlike so many of the owners who elected him, Rozelle was not tethered to the game's past, and he saw that pro football was perfectly suited to television and an increasingly restless nation entering a new decade. After his election as commissioner, it would be repeatedly said that Pete Rozelle was simply the right person in the right place at the right time. Steelers owner Art Rooney was even more effusive: "He is a gift from the hand of Providence."

* * * * *

Pete Rozelle was born in 1926 in South Gate, California, a small community near the Pacific Ocean located midway between Los Angeles and Long Beach. His parents named him Alvin Ray, but an uncle called him Pete. The Great Depression claimed his father's grocery store. In high school, he played basketball and tennis, wrote for the school newspaper, and contributed to a Long Beach newspaper. After high school and two years in the Navy, Rozelle enrolled at Compton Junior College where he was the student publicity director for athletics and found part-time work with the new Los Angeles Rams football team.

In 1948, Pete Newell, the young basketball coach at the University of San Francisco, attended a basketball tournament at Compton Junior College to scout junior-college players. Newell left the tournament impressed by how well the tournament had been run and particularly by how capable and amiable the young student publicist, Pete Rozelle, was. Months later, when the job of student athletic-news director became open at the University of San Francisco, Newell recommended Rozelle, who won the position and received a full scholarship. In the years after World War II, with military veterans flooding college classrooms, San Francisco's sports teams were enjoying fleeting success. The 1949 basketball team competed in the NIT Tournament. The 1951 football team, with stars like Gino Marchetti, Bob St. Clair, and Ollie Matson, went undefeated but refused to play in the Orange Bowl because of its condition that only the school's White players could travel to Miami for the game.

After graduating from USF, Rozelle became the university's full-time news director until the Los Angeles Rams called. In 1952, the Rams hired Rozelle as the team's publicist to replace Tex Maule, a former Texas sportswriter who was leaving California to work for the new Dallas Texans franchise. The Rams' general manager was Tex Schramm, once a sports editor with the *Austin American-Statesman.* At USF, Pete Newell introduced Rozelle to the coach's long-time friend, Ken Macker, an ambitious young publicist. In 1955, Macker started an international public-relations firm and invited Rozelle to join his new venture as a partner. Rozelle did so and went to work promoting the 1956 Summer Olympics in Melbourne.

Two years later, the Los Angeles Rams franchise was embroiled in fighting between owner Dan Reeves, who was drinking heavily, and his partners. General manager Tex Schramm quit the team in disgust to take a job with CBS Sports. NFL Commissioner Bell believed that Pete Rozelle, with his amiable personality, gift for charting consensus, and past relationship with Reeves and the Rams organization, was the person needed to restore order to the fractious franchise. Bell called Rozelle, imploring him to return to the Rams as general manager. The commissioner then contacted Dan Reeves, demanding that he hire Rozelle. Responding to Bell's call for help, Rozelle returned to the NFL as the Rams' new general manager. With diplomacy, Rozelle managed the team's internecine struggles. And with his background in marketing, he made the Rams off the field even more successful. Rozelle hired a top graphic artist for the team's game programs and yearbooks, and he opened a Los Angeles Rams store to sell team-related merchandise. Known for their large crowds at Los Angeles Memorial Coliseum, the Rams in 1958 were averaging 83,000 per game and drew more than 100,000 against Chicago and Baltimore. Success on the field proved more difficult. After finishing 8-4 in 1958, the Rams won only two games in 1959, and Rozelle failed to sign the team's first-round pick, LSU halfback Billy Cannon, who opted at the last moment to play for the AFL's Houston Oilers.

* * * * *

Upon becoming commissioner, Rozelle took charge. The NFL was no longer a struggling sports league with a romantic past but a sports-entertainment business with a boundless future. Before leaving Miami, the owners on January 28 awarded franchises to Dallas, which would begin play in 1960, and to Minnesota, which would play in 1961. At the owners' meeting in March 1960, the league approved the Chicago Cardinals moving to St. Louis. As Rozelle had promised, the league relocated to New York City, the nation's center of finance, television and print media, and culture. The NFL moved into the General Dynamics Building at Rockefeller Center, a Midtown Manhattan location surrounded by the country's television networks, national magazines, biggest corporations, and top advertising agencies. The new address was an announcement that the National Football League had truly arrived. In May 1962, the NFL successfully defended in a Maryland federal court an antitrust suit filed by the AFL. Weeks later, the league's owners rewarded Rozelle with a $10,000 bonus and a new five-year contract paying $60,000 per year.

* * * * *

In 1950, only nine percent of American households owned a television set. By 1960, a year in which a televised debate decided a close presidential election, nearly 90 percent did. Baseball, a languid sport, remained better suited for radio where vivid descriptions could stroke the imagination of listeners and colorful anecdotes between pitches and batters could entertain. But football, with its speed and violence, seemed made for television. Though driving the sport's popularity, television was still a barely tapped source of future revenue and growth.

In 1960, the NFL as a league did not have a television contract for regular-season games, only a contract with NBC for championship games. Rather, each of the 12 teams had its own contract with different networks—Baltimore and Pittsburgh with NBC, Cleveland with an independent sports network, and the other nine teams with CBS. The contracts paid teams different amounts—Baltimore received $600,000 per year, eight times more than what Green Bay was paid.

Before beginning play in 1960, the new AFL secured a five-year television contract with ABC paying a total of $8.5 million. With a plan radical for its time, the AFL split the television revenue equally among teams so that each AFL team was guaranteed over $200,000 per year, a sum greater than the amount most NFL teams were receiving in television money. Seeing the AFL's television package and steered by Rozelle, the NFL owners returned to the parity concept championed by Bert Bell for so long. In January 1961, they voted—some with lucrative contracts reluctantly—to give Rozelle the authority to negotiate on behalf of the entire league a television contract for regular-season games with all teams sharing equally the television proceeds. In July, a federal court ruled that the CBS contract Rozelle agreed to for all teams violated antitrust law and was illegal. Two months later, Congress passed the Sports Broadcasting Act of 1961, giving the NFL the antitrust exemption that it wanted for television contracts negotiated by the league acting for all teams. In January 1962, the NFL signed with CBS a two-year television contract paying $4.65 million each year for all regular-season games.

In 1964, the television contracts for both leagues were set to expire. With all three networks wanting NFL games, the NFL created a sealed-bid process for a two-year contract for both the regular season and the league championship. The bids were to be opened on Friday, January 24, at 11 a.m. Having broadcast NFL games for the last two years, CBS was clearly the league's preferred partner. Bill MacPhail, head of CBS Sports, had contacts throughout the NFL. Dallas's influential general manager, Tex Schramm, was a former CBS Sports executive. And MacPhail had become one of Pete Rozelle's closest friends—the two even shared a Long Island summer home. For television networks, the NFL was in sports programming the crown jewels. Trailing CBS and NBC in prestige, ABC wanted badly to carry the NFL. Leading ABC's contract efforts was Roone Arledge, a talented 32-year-old producer known for his creativity and dramatic storylines in covering sports. When the bids were opened, it was learned that NBC had offered for two years $20.6 million, ABC $26.4 million, and CBS $28.2 million. Arledge and others at ABC left seething, convinced that the league had leaked information regarding their bid efforts to CBS.

After the bids were opened, Rozelle called Cleveland owner Art Modell, who would deliver the contract news to the other owners. Hearing that the winning bid was $14.1 million, a downcast Modell replied, "I had been hoping for a little more, but hell, Pete, seven million a year isn't half bad. We can make it." "No, Art," said Rozelle, "14 million per year, 28 million for two years." After a pause, Modell responded, "Pete, you got to stop drinking at breakfast."

Leaving the league's offices to celebrate, Rozelle and Bill MacPhail retreated to nearby Toots Shor's, the lively Midtown Manhattan bar and restaurant known for its drinks and the presence of sports celebrities. NBC's vice president of sports, a disheartened Carl Lindemann, returned to his office but saw a note on his desk asking that he call AFL Commissioner Joe Foss. Three days later, with negotiations at times taking place in the limousine of Sonny Werblin, the show-business owner of the New York Jets, NBC and the AFL agreed to a five-year television contract paying the league a total of $36 million. Under the NBC contract, each of the eight AFL teams would receive $900,000 each year, only $100,000 less than what each of the 14 NFL teams would be paid under the new CBS deal. The NBC contract ensured that the AFL would stay and that the war between the two football leagues would continue. And ABC's Roone Arledge went on a buying tear, securing for ABC the television rights to cover college football, the NBA, the PGA golf tournament, and the 1968 Winter and Summer Olympics.

* * * * *

In 1963, the league opened the Pro Football Hall of Fame in Canton, Ohio, and started NFL Properties, a subsidiary that would standardize and promote sports merchandise for all 14 teams. It hired Elias Sports Bureau to manage game and player statistics for the league. And in early 1965, the NFL created another division, NFL Films. Ed Sabol was an accomplished college swimmer at Ohio State who refused to take part in the 1936 Olympic Games in Berlin because he was Jewish. Hating his job selling overcoats in his father-in-law's business, Sabol for fun began filming his son's high school football games with a movie camera given to him as a wedding gift. He turned his avocation into a business venture. In 1962, his company, Blair Motion Pictures, won with a $3,000 or $5,000 bid the rights to do the highlights film for the NFL's 1962 Championship Game. Blair had no experience filming a pro football game, and Pete Rozelle had doubts. Meeting Rozelle at the 21 Club in Midtown Manhattan and using his salesman skills and martinis, Sabol described how his highlights film would be different from what the league had previously seen. One pledge was to film the game with eight cameras, double the number normally used.

Six weeks after the Giants and Packers played for the 1962 Championship on a frigid Sunday in Yankee Stadium, Sabol played his Championship Game highlights film at Toots Shor's for a select audience of media members and NFL and Giants representatives. Titled "Pro Football's Longest Day," Sabol's production proved to be different. The writing by Sabol and narration by sportscaster Chris Schenkel were dramatic. The college march music was exultant. The slow-motion replays of key plays were gripping. When the film ended, Rozelle sought out Sabol, telling him this was the best highlights film he had ever seen. After producing the game highlights for the next two Championship Games, Sabol recommended to Rozelle that the league do a highlights film each year for every team and proposed that the NFL buy his company for $280,000 and hire him to run the new in-house addition for an annual $30,000 salary. At their spring 1965 meeting, the NFL owners agreed.

* * * * *

Andre Laguerre was the most unlikely of sports editors. He was the son of a French diplomat and an English mother with aristocratic lineage. He was married to a Russian princess who counted as a distant ancestor Catherine the Great. And he had dined often with Albert Camus, the French writer who in 1957 won the Nobel Prize for Literature. Born in England in 1915, Laguerre lived for two years in San Francisco where his father served as the French consul. After completing his studies at an exclusive English public school, he opted not to attend Oxford but to immediately begin his newspaper career, covering in 1938 the fateful Munich Conference. In 1940, he served in the French army and at Dunkirk fought his way onto a British ship escaping to England. In London, Laguerre impressed Charles de Gaulle, the imperious head of the Free France government-in-exile, and became his press attaché. After the war, he joined *Time* and headed the magazine's bureaus in Paris and London. In 1955, asked to name the best political reporter in Britain, Winston Churchill answered that, of course, it was Andre Laguerre.

But to the surprise of many, Laguerre's passions included sports, and he covered the 1956 Winter Olympics. In early March 1956, he was named *Sports Illustrated*'s assistant managing editor and moved to New York. In the great magazine empire built by Henry Luce that included *Time*, *Life*, and *Fortune*, *Sports Illustrated* for years financially struggled and drifted, focused too often on the pastimes of the very rich with cover articles on marlin fishing, show dogs, and the Yale-Dartmouth football weekend. In 1960, determined to change the magazine's direction, Laguerre met with Luce, an intellectually restless man who saw journalism as a nearly sacred mission and whom Laguerre admired. In their meeting, Laguerre argued that he needed to take over *Sports Illustrated* as its managing editor. Luce agreed.

Stocky, his hair turning white, with black-rimmed glasses and often a half-knotted tie and a lit cigar, Laguerre made *Sports Illustrated* into a weekly must-read for sport enthusiasts. He restructured the magazine's staff, creating departments based on the sport covered. He recruited outstanding writers like John Underwood, Frank Deford, and Dan Jenkins. Laguerre set high goals and began the emphasis on "fast color" photographs with his teams of photographers and editors using strobe and other specialized lighting equipment to vividly capture sports' drama and excitement. To meet seemingly impossible deadlines, he oversaw the logistical ballets of chartered jet planes and helicopters to receive on time the photographs and stories of epic games and championship fights finished only hours earlier. To his writers and photographers, Laguerre was inspirational. Near tight deadlines, he was composed, much like the great athletes in critical moments whom they covered. And at frequent staff gatherings at a favorite Midtown bar, Laguerre's taste and capacity for Scotch were legendary.

The sport to which Laguerre fixed his star was pro football. In a 1962 memorandum to Henry Luce, he wrote:

> I'm developing a strong hunch that pro football is our sport. We have grown with it, and each of us is a phenomenon of the times. We gave it more coverage last year, but I plan to extend it this fall. It seems that our reader identifies himself more with this sport than golf or fishing. College football is too diffuse and regionalized. Baseball in some quarters is considered old-fashioned or slightly non-U. Horse racing and winter sports have less broad appeal.

Pete Rozelle, introduced to Laguerre by Tex Maule, would say that *Sports Illustrated* "treated pro football like it had never been treated before." But other publications were joining in the chorus of adoration. In the December 21, 1962 issue of *Time*, the magazine's cover featured Vince Lombardi with the banner "The Sport of the '60s" for its NFL cover story. And in January 1964, *Sports Illustrated* named Pete Rozelle, a sports commissioner, its 1963 Sportsman of the Year with the magazine's cover featuring an unusually somber Rozelle against a backdrop of NFL helmets.

In the fall of 1965, the NFL commissioned pollster Lou Harris to do a study on pro football's popularity. Harris reported that as of October 1965, football had replaced baseball as the national pastime and was now America's favorite sport. "It is quite clear," Harris wrote, "that the full potential of NFL football has hardly been tapped."

* * * *

For some time, there were rumors of NFL players keeping company with gamblers and mobsters and betting on games. In late August 1962, visiting the Packers before an exhibition game in Milwaukee, Pete Rozelle invited Paul Hornung, Green Bay's halfback, to join him for coffee. Rozelle asked Hornung whether he knew Abe Samuels and Gil Berkley, two known gamblers. Hornung admitted that he knew both but added that neither had ever asked him to do anything illegal or improper. "You're going to have to watch your associations," warned Rozelle, ending their discussion.

In January 1963, in its march to popularity and prosperity, the NFL faced a gambling scandal. On January 4, the *Chicago Tribune* quoted Bears owner George Halas that the NFL was investigating rumors of a scandal in pro football involving an unnamed player on a Midwestern team. The next day, the *Chicago American* reported that Chicago Bears fullback Rick Casares had passed a lie-detector test on which he was asked whether he had thrown any games. On January 8, Rozelle reached Paul Hornung in Los Angeles, advising that he immediately needed to see the Packer star in New York. Hornung met the next morning with Rozelle and a league attorney in a Plaza Hotel suite in New York. Questioned about gambling, Hornung denied betting on NFL games. After failing a lie-detector test the next day, Hornung finally confessed that through his Las Vegas friend Barney Shapiro, he had bet on NFL games--and even on Green Bay--eight or nine times from 1959 through 1961. Hornung said his biggest bet was $500 but denied ever betting against the Packers. The league later learned that Detroit defensive tackle Alex Karras had made six bets up to $100 on NFL games, including a wager on the Lions playing Green Bay.

The league's gambling investigation, conducted by former FBI agents, took over three months. Some 50 players were interviewed. The league looked into allegations that Baltimore owner Carroll Rosenbloom had bet on NFL games. Its perfunctory investigation of Rosenbloom failed to find conclusive evidence that the powerful owner had made any such wagers. On April 17, 1963, the league rendered its verdict. Rozelle called Hornung and Karras, advising each that he was suspended indefinitely for gambling, but that reinstatement would be considered in 1964. Hornung accepted his punishment and showed contrition. Karras protested he had done nothing wrong and showed defiance. The league then issued a press release, announcing the league's action against the two players for betting on NFL games though stressing that there was no evidence either player had bet against his team or sold information to gamblers. Also, the league fined five Detroit Lion players $2,000 each for wagering small amounts on the 1962 NFL Championship Game and the Lions organization $4,000 for ignoring Detroit police reports of Lion players associating with "known hoodlums" and for allowing unauthorized persons to sit on the team's bench during games.

The public's response was favorable—that the league had thoroughly investigated the gambling allegations and imposed substantial punishment on the guilty players. Dallas general manager Tex Schramm thought that Pete Rozelle, in his deliberate but decisive handling of the gambling charges, truly came of age as commissioner, quelling any remaining doubts inside the league about his youth. But even for Rozelle, there were stumbles.

On Friday, November 22, 1963, President John Kennedy, a friend of so many in the league, was assassinated in Dallas. Hours after the president's death, the NFL had to decide whether to play its Sunday games. With visiting NFL teams scheduled for late Friday flights, Rozelle called for advice Pierre Salinger, a University of San Francisco classmate who had been President Kennedy's press secretary. Salinger recommended that the NFL play, saying the late president loved football and would have wanted the teams to compete. The AFL cancelled its games. Many NFL owners and players did not want to play. Covering the assassination, the tumultuous events that followed, and America's grieving, all three television networks suspended entertainment programming and commercials for four days through the president's funeral on Monday, November 25. But Rozelle, schooled in public relations, ordered the NFL to go forward on Sunday.

For once, Rozelle's uncanny instincts for what the public wanted and for how to act in a crisis moment were missing. A mourning nation, still in shock over a popular president's death, criticized the NFL's decision to play. And Rozelle could not know that two hours before NFL games would begin, the president's alleged assassin, Lee Harvey Oswald, would be gunned down on live television as he was moved from a Dallas jail. As the games were surreally played, with no player introductions and in silent stadiums, Rozelle realized he had just made his biggest mistake as commissioner.

The year 1965 brought Pete Rozelle more personal turmoil and greater professional challenge. The job of NFL commissioner, though financially lucrative and professionally rewarding, exacted a personal price. Rozelle often arrived for work early at the league office. Lunch and dinner were chances to court the executives of the biggest companies whose advertising dollars the NFL wanted and their advertising-agency partners. At home, in his posh Sutton Place apartment on Manhattan's East Side, business telephone calls filled the evening hours and weekends, especially during football season. Over the years, Rozelle's long absences and late nights had taken a toll at home. Rozelle's wife, Jane, started drinking when her husband in the mid-1950s made his long trips to Australia to promote the Melbourne Olympics. In 1963, Jane was hospitalized three times for her addiction. In 1965, she threatened her seven-year-old daughter, Anne Marie, and the child's babysitter with a knife. Rozelle found his wife at a Midtown bar with Anne Marie, his only child to whom he was devoted, on the adjacent stool. He would file for divorce.

* * * * *

With the signing of college seniors, the competition between the two pro football leagues was becoming a war imposing a financial burden too great for all combatants. On January 2, 1965, Joe Namath, the celebrated Alabama quarterback, signed a three-year, $427,000 contract with the AFL's New York Jets. For Jets owner Sonny Werblin, the Namath signing was a uniquely smart investment. Werblin once headed the television division of entertainment giant Music Corporation of America. MCA's clients included Elizabeth Taylor, Jack Benny, Jackie Gleason, Johnny Carson, and Ed Sullivan. Werblin's lodestar was that star headliners determined box-office success. "I believe in the star system," he proclaimed. "It's the only thing that sells tickets." Relishing the chance to sell his flamboyant quarterback, Werblin said, "When Joe Namath walks into a room, you know he's there."

The AFL's New York franchise now had a quarterback with immense football talent and Hollywood appeal who could sell tickets and evening tabloid newspapers and hopefully win games. For its July 19, 1965 issue, *Sports Illustrated* featured on its cover Joe Namath in his Jets uniform with the lights of Broadway as a backdrop and the banner "Football Goes Show Biz." For their upcoming 1965 season, the Jets sold 35,000 season tickets, a 24,000 increase from the year before. But the Namath contract, the amount unprecedented, was a tipping point, the moment when both leagues realized that their pursuit of the top college players was now a runaway train.

In a May 1965 *Sports Illustrated* article titled "The New National Football League (?)," Dan Jenkins reported on the many rumors of the two leagues merging. "Everyone knows," Jenkins wrote, "that pro football is going to achieve that peace someday." Pete Rozelle dismissed talk of a merger. "I'll tell you how talk like this gets started every year," he said. "The other league starts it." But seeing one another in South Florida where they had winter homes, pro football owners like NFL owner Carroll Rosenbloom and AFL owner Ralph Wilson had already begun discussing the possibility of a merger. Strangely, in the war between the two leagues, Rozelle, known for judgment and consensus, wanted to fight and win, and increasingly, his owners, led by Rosenbloom, wanted peace. NFL team owners believed that the AFL, with a new television contract, its own stars, new stadiums, an exciting brand of football, and announced expansion to Miami, was now too popular and too established to fail. With player contracts soaring, NFL owners now recognized that the time had come to seek some form of rapprochement with the other league. Merger proved the rare instance where the NFL owners would act despite Pete Rozell's disapproval. In his May article, Jenkins predicted an agreement as early as December and certainly within two years. As the summer of 1965 arrived, with team training camps scheduled to open, football fans welcomed the excitement of a new season. Those also interested in the business of professional football wondered how negotiations between its millionaire owners might fundamentally change the sport.

5

Preseason: "This Is a Man's Game"

They played football when young for fun and then later for status with classmates and teenage girls. But many who excelled in the sport grew up in a world shaped by a 12-year-long depression and a world war, and in hard regions where a coal miner's life seemed destiny or on tough streets in big cities where only the moment, not the future, mattered. Football was their escape—a chance to go to college, to leave home, and to chart in life a different path. In late July, NFL and AFL training camps opened. Hundreds of young men reported to small colleges removed from the cities where professional teams played, ending offseason jobs and college studies to make a pro football team roster and prepare for the 1965 season.

Since 1958, Green Bay held training camp in De Pere, Wisconsin, at St. Norbert College, a small Catholic school run by the Norbertine order. With a population of roughly 12,000, De Pere was a pleasant town on the banks of the Fox River 10 minutes by bus from the Green Bay team facilities where the Packers would practice. On July 21, camp opened with rookies and some veterans reporting.

On the first night with all players present, Vince Lombardi made his traditional comments on team, character, pride, total effort, and of course winning—a chain of platitudes and clichés when given by most speakers but inspiration and powerful injunctions when delivered with Lombardi's fervor.

Packer players saw that the offseason had not diminished Lombardi's anger over finishing second the last two seasons and especially their play in 1964. Lombardi's need to win bordered on the pathological. His message that the Packers would win in 1965 was an unconditional edict.

For veteran players, the training-camp schedule remained an unpleasant constant: early breakfast, the first of four bus rides to and from Green Bay's practice field, morning practice beginning at 10 with laps and intense calisthenics, a light lunch at St. Norbert, afternoon practice at three with helmets and shoulder pads, a return to De Pere and a hearty dinner, a 7:30 meeting to receive new plays and review film of yesterday's practice, and then 90 minutes or two hours of free time before curfew at 11. The practices and evening meeting each lasted 90 minutes.

Two dreaded practice routines were the nutcracker drill and the grass drills. Commonly called the Oklahoma drill and popular throughout pro football, the nutcracker drill was an individual test—a defensive player stood in a five-yard space between huge blocking bags and tried to stop a running back led by an offensive lineman. Lombardi's grass drills were group torture—all players running furiously in place with Lombardi shouting the knees should be higher, dropping to their stomachs when Lombardi yelled "down," and then jumping up and running again when the head coach commanded "up." Though practices were scripted to the minute, the duration of the grass drill and the number of repetitions seemed solely dependent on Lombardi's mood, which was often surly. At one practice, rookie Bill Curry counted 78 reps. One player heard a coach boast that the record was 164 repetitions. Players threw up breakfast and even fainted. Defensive tackle Hawg Hanner once collapsed and was hospitalized with heat exhaustion. But Vince Lombardi insisted his teams would be the best conditioned. By September, they often were.

* * * * *

Their names evoked violent collisions on hard fields on wintry Sundays. Fittingly, Packers Jim Taylor and Ray

Nitschke played respectively fullback and middle linebacker, positions that demanded and celebrated toughness. Both were known for giving teammates no quarter in training-camp practices. Both came to football from childhoods marred by traumatic times that included a parent's death.

Jim Taylor was driven by hardship endured as a youngster and later by the universal acclaim Jim Brown received as football's greatest fullback. Born in Baton Rouge, Louisiana, he was 10 when his invalid father died. To help support the family, Jimmy delivered newspapers in both the early morning hours and the afternoon. Until his junior year, he was too small to play high school football. A poor student, Taylor flunked out of LSU as a freshman but later re-entered after attending a Mississippi junior college. At LSU, he played fullback and linebacker and did some placekicking for coach Paul Dietzel. In the 1958 draft, Green Bay picked Taylor in the second round, the 15th player selected that year. The Packers scouting report on Taylor was generally favorable:

> I think Jimmy Taylor is a fine pro prospect. He is 6' tall and 200 lbs. Has fine speed for 50 yards—5.5. He runs the 100 in 10.1. He has very fine hands and is a good short pass receiver. He is lazy in his blocking, but could be a good one. Very sound of body and legs and has never been hurt. Married and has 1 child. He is the type that will make a better pro than college player. Good extra point man. He is not a baseball player and needs money. He is the type that will play as long as he can. Not too smart. Just what you are looking for in brains. I think he is cut out to be the remaining HB on a pro team.

As a rookie, Taylor at times struggled to remember play assignments. But he became his team's best-conditioned athlete, a rock-hard 215 pounds and ahead of his time in his devotion to lifting weights. Though smaller than some at his position, Taylor with his thick frame, determined gaze, and crewcut looked like a fullback. And he certainly played like one, running low to the ground with quickness and vision and always willing to attack defenders. Many defensive players in the league, like Art Donovan and Ordell Braase, thought he was football's most punishing runner. On runs past the line of scrimmage, Taylor looked for defensive backs to run over. "You've got to sting 'em," he once explained. "I figure if I give the guy a little blast, he might not be so eager to try and stop me next time." In a 1964 magazine article, quarterback Bobby Layne, who embodied the excesses of pro football in the 1950s, listed Taylor as one of the 11 meanest players in the sport. In a November 1965 *Sports Illustrated* article, Baltimore linebacker Dennis Gaubatz said, "Anybody who says he ain't been run over by Taylor ain't played against him."

Taylor's most memorable game was perhaps the 1962 NFL Championship when Green Bay beat the Giants 16-7. It was a cruel day at Yankee Stadium when the temperature dropped to 17 degrees, icy winds reached 30 miles per hour, and television crews used bonfires to keep cameras working. Embarrassed by the Packers in the 1961 Championship Game, the Giants defense targeted Taylor, hitting him late with elbows and knees. In the first quarter, Giants middle linebacker Sam Huff, who relished his tough-guy image, led with his helmet to hit Taylor in the head. The Packer fullback badly bit his tongue and swallowed blood throughout the game. At halftime, Taylor received stitches for a gashed elbow.

In the second half, at the bottom of a player pile, Taylor saw what he believed was Huff's exposed calf and bit the player's leg. On the sideline, the assailed Giant, tackle Dick Modzelewski, complained to Huff, "Sam, I tell you, Taylor bit me like a dog." "I warned you," Huff answered, "that guy ain't human." The battle between Taylor and Huff raged. Once in the huddle, Taylor urged Starr to call his number on a running play. Receiving the handoff, Taylor ran as fast as he could straight towards Huff. Before returning to the huddle, Taylor taunted the linebacker, "Is that as hard as you can hit me?" Taylor carried the ball 31 times, gaining 85 yards and scoring the game's only offensive touchdown. After the game, Huff saluted Taylor's effort: "No human being could have taken the punishment he got today."

Beginning in 1960, Taylor every year gained over 1,000 yards rushing and was voted to the Pro Bowl. Overshadowed by Jim Brown and at times by his teammate Paul Hornung, he still four times made an All-Pro team. Taylor's best year was 1962 when he led the NFL in rushing with 1,474 yards, beating out Jim Brown, and was named the NFL's Most Valuable Player. Upset that Brown was universally hailed as the game's top fullback, Taylor every Monday morning during the season checked Cleveland's box score to see how the Browns' fullback had done. On the few occasions the Packers played against Cleveland, Taylor welcomed the chance to upstage Jim Brown and usually did.

As a youngster, Taylor saw his family's financial despair. As a player, he saw Vince Lombardi as general manager resist his players' salary demands in often bitter contract negotiations but repeatedly receive hefty salary increases in new contracts. More than other players, Taylor seemed preoccupied with money, and he proved successful in his business ventures. Among the Packer veterans, he especially resented the big sums that NFL teams were throwing at just-drafted college players. Like Max McGee, Taylor could playfully, if not as artfully, taunt Lombardi. In coping with his head coach, McGee used humor, usually good-natured, that caused even Lombardi to laugh. At a time when players smoked in locker rooms, Taylor, knowing Lombardi hated cigar smoke, liked to puff on a cigar when his head coach approached.

Football and marriage saved Ray Nitschke, Green Bay's middle linebacker. At six-foot-three and 240 pounds, with a strong upper body and short legs, Nitschke was the heart and literal center of the Packers defense, calling out his team's defense based on the offensive formation he saw. Nitschke was born outside Chicago. When he was three, his father, returning from a union meeting, was killed in a car accident. At 10, he was washing dishes in a restaurant to help his family. When he was 13, his mother died at 41 from a blood clot, and Ray was raised by older brothers who were not much older than he was. Big and bitter, he looked for fights on Chicago's streets. In high school, he excelled in baseball, football, and basketball, though not in his studies. His high school coach, former Notre Dame player Andy Puplis, called Nitschke the meanest kid he had ever coached. In college at Illinois, where he played fullback, linebacker, and even quarterback, an assistant coach described him as "vicious." As a junior, refusing to wear a helmet with a facemask, he lost four teeth when on a kickoff an Ohio State player with his helmet hit him in the face. With the loss of teeth, the hulking Nitschke, who became bald early, looked even more menacing.

In 1958, Green Bay drafted Nitschke in the third round. In a small city where seemingly everyone knew the Packer players and what they did, stories of Nitschke drinking heavily and brawling in bars spread. Arriving in Green Bay in 1959, Vince Lombardi showed limited tolerance for Nitschke's misconduct and at one time considered cutting him before being reminded by his assistant coaches of how talented a player he was.

Before the 1961 season, Nitschke married Jackie Forchette, a young woman from a Michigan Upper Peninsula farm who had been reluctant to date Ray because of his reputation. In private life, marriage transformed Nitschke, giving him a contentment and sense of belonging he had not known for years. Nitschke stopped drinking. The couple in 1963 adopted a young boy and planned to adopt a second child. But on the field, Ray Nitschke did not change. Even his teammates in practice feared his deadly forearm. In an early game, rookie Bill Curry, injured on a kickoff return, lay on the field; Nitschke ordered him to stand up and hustle to the sideline, adding that first-year players had not earned the right for help in leaving the field. In an age of great middle linebackers like Joe Schmidt, Bill George, and Sam Huff, Nitschke was named in 1964 first-team All-Pro.

* * * * *

The centerpiece of the Packers camp and offense was the Green Bay power sweep, a play introduced first and practiced daily that Lombardi modeled on the single-wing sweeps run by Jock Sutherland's Pitt teams in the 1930s. Grounded in years under Red Blaik at West Point, Lombardi's system was execution—his core principle was that plays flawlessly run could not be stopped and would break opponents. In June 1963, a young junior college coach, John Madden, attended a coaching seminar at the University of Nevada at Reno where Lombardi spoke on his power-sweep play. After finding a seat in the last row of the meeting room, Madden was amazed over what he heard. For eight hours, with passion and clarity, Lombardi talked about a single play, breaking down the responsibility of each of the 11 offensive players and his options depending on which of several different defenses was being played and the response of the defensive players.

Lombardi's friend Tim Cohane, the former Fordham publicist, called Lombardi's power sweep "complex simplicity." Its success required teamwork, intelligence, and uncommonly high execution made possible only through relentless repetition and demanding practice. The power sweep contained variations and could be run by different backs from different formations. But the quintessential sweep play in Green Bay was Right Red 49—"right" referred to the play's direction to the right or tight end side of the offense, the color "red" to the formation where the halfback lined up behind the left tackle and the fullback behind the right tackle, the first number four to the halfback who would be carrying the football, and the second number nine to the hole the greatest distance from the center on the right side of the offense where the ballcarrier should run.

Halfback Paul Hornung was perfectly suited for the power sweep, which required patience and vision by the runner rather than speed—Zeke Bratkowski quipped that Hornung was just fast enough and slow enough. And with Hornung, a former Notre Dame quarterback, running to his right, defenses had to respect the halfback's option to pass, which Hornung occasionally did with success. As the play was designed, the tight end's block of the left outside linebacker, pushing him inside or outside, determined the runner's path and often the play's success. The right offensive tackle would chip the left defensive end and then seal off the middle linebacker. The fullback would follow the right offensive tackle blocking the left defensive end. And the right guard, left guard, and even left tackle then pulled to the right looking for defenders to block. The power sweep was a dance of behemoths, on the blackboard a ballet with its intricate structure, but on the field more jazz dance with each player deciding in a fraction of a second what to do and whom to block depending on how defensive players were positioned and what their own teammates were doing.

* * * * *

Continuity distinguished the Packers' coaching staff. Like Lombardi, three assistant coaches were returning for their seventh year in Green Bay: Phil Bengtson, the team's chief defensive coach who was known for his teaching skills and quiet demeanor; offensive backfield coach Red Cochran; and defensive backs coach Norb Hecker. In 1962, Tom Fears, in his time one of the game's great offensive ends, was added as the receivers coach. Only Ray Wietecha, coaching the offensive line, was new.

But with players, the year 1965 was one of change for Green Bay. The Packers would have at least seven starters, five on defense, who were not members of their 1962 championship team. After the 1964 season, Lombardi traded for placekicker Don Chandler and receiver Carroll Dale. Before camp opened, defensive halfback Jesse Whittenton and offensive tackle Norm Masters announced they would be retiring. Signed as a free agent in 1958, the instinctive Whittenton started in Lombardi's first year and was leaving football to return to his native Texas after he and a cousin bought an El Paso country club. The Packers were moving receiver Bob Jeter, because of his speed and athleticism, to defense. "He's too good to sit on the bench," said Lombardi on the eve of training camp.

At tight end, Ron Kramer played out his option, signing with Detroit. Behind Kramer on the 1964 depth chart was Marv Fleming, an 11th-round draft pick in 1963. To strengthen the tight end position, Green Bay in mid-August traded with the Washington Redskins for the rights to Bill Anderson, an assistant coach at the University of Tennessee who left the NFL after the 1963 season but wanted to play pro football again. Dave Robinson, talented and recovered from his knee injury in 1964, would be replacing left outside linebacker Dan Currie, whom Lombardi had traded to Los Angeles for Dale. And at the team's urging, defensive tackle Dave Hanner retired as a player late in preseason, though he remained with the Packers as a defensive line assistant coach. Called Hawg and known for chewing tobacco, the once Arkansas farm boy had been one of the team's most popular players. His replacement was Ron Kostelnik, a sturdy second-round pick in 1961 from the University of Cincinnati whose Ukrainian grandparents had settled in Pennsylvania coal country.

* * * * *

Professional football was a violent game. Vince Lombardi joked that ballroom dancing was a contact sport and football a hitting sport. The violence was part of the game's appeal. In a time when concussions were common and players with a head injury were expected after a few downs to return and play, the NFL only slowly adopted rules to reduce the sport's danger and reluctantly enforced the few it had. Both the horse-collar tackle, when a defender pulls on the collar of the jersey to bring the runner down, and the clothesline tackle were legal. Until 1962, a defender could legally grab the ball-carrier's face mask. In 1955, *Life* published a pictorial article titled "Savagery on Sunday." Two of the players cited sued the magazine for defamation and received modest awards at a 1958 trial. But the article quoted a Lions defensive tackle, Bob Miller, that defenses targeted opposing quarterbacks. "We're not trying to hurt anyone, but it's no secret that star pro passers are a bad insurance risk," Miller confessed. "They get hit even after they get rid of the ball."

More candid was Giants linebacker Sam Huff. Playing in the nation's media capital and as adept at self-promotion as he was at playing football, Huff was the subject of both a November 1959 *Time* magazine cover story and a 1960 CBS documentary titled "The Violent World of Sam Huff," which was narrated by Walter Cronkite. "You rap that quarterback every chance you get," said Huff in the *Time* article. "He's the brains of the outfit. If you knock him out clean and hard on the first play of the game, that's an accomplishment. For that matter, we try to hurt everybody. We hit each other as hard as we can. This is a man's game." For play some considered questionable, Huff added, "You get penalties when you get caught and touchdowns when you don't."

* * * * *

Success at quarterback in the NFL required exceptional athletic ability, intelligence, and of course toughness. The Baltimore Colts had such a quarterback. In appearance and demeanor, Johnny Unitas seemed the most unlikely of sports legends. Yet Bronx-born Art Donovan, Baltimore's defensive tackle through the 1950s and early 1960s, believed that in his era, the two greatest professional athletes were New York Yankee star Joe DiMaggio and Johnny Unitas. Both were iconic athletes who off the field shunned the spotlight and, at decisive moments on the field, embraced it. Compared to other professional football players, Unitas had a modest frame. He was listed at six-foot-one and probably weighed after games and demanding practices less than 190 pounds. He was gangly with stooped shoulders, long and dangling arms, big hands, and a bow-legged gait. His smile was toothy and crooked, and he was known for his crew cut and high-ankle black shoes. He threw passes with an exaggerated over-the-top motion. Pointing out Unitas to Frank Gifford before a 1956 exhibition game, New York Giant quarterback Charlie Conerly said, "Look at that goofy son of a bitch."

The awkward physical features masked remarkable athletic talent. But in a violent game known for broken bones and concussions when quarterbacks were not protected but were singled out for late hits, what elevated Unitas was his physical and mental toughness. Rams defensive tackle Merlin Olsen thought that Unitas, when rushed, would intentionally hold the football longer than he needed to hold it, an act of defiance to show rushing defenders he could not be intimidated. Unitas's pain threshold was high. He played often with jammed fingers and a sore right arm. Unitas showed no emotion as trainers during games would pop dislocated fingers back into place, and he refused to take any medication for pain, even aspirin. In game six of the 1958 season, a Green Bay defender, Johnny Symank, intentionally jumped with his knees onto Unitas who was lying on the ground, breaking three ribs and puncturing a lung. Unitas missed two games and played the rest of that season with a nine-pound, rubber-lined aluminum brace, leading Baltimore to its first championship.

But a November game in 1960 against the Bears at Wrigley Field burnished the legend of Johnny Unitas. Colts receiver Alex Hawkins believed that football game was the most savage he had ever seen. Baltimore defensive tackle Art Donovan compared it to his war experience as a Marine in the Pacific. Throughout their long history, the Chicago Bears were known for their tough and even brutal play. With defenders like Doug Atkins, Bill George, Earl Leggett, Joe Fortunato, and Richie Petitbon, the Bears aggressively blitzed Unitas, several times sacking him and repeatedly knocking him down. With less than a minute to play, Chicago led 20-17, but the Colts had the ball and entered Bears territory. Retreating to pass, Unitas was held by linebacker Bill George, and then Doug Atkins—the six-foot-nine, 280-pound Bear defensive end no offensive lineman wanted to anger—slammed his shoulder and forearm into Unitas's face, splitting the bridge of the quarterback's nose and mangling his face. "Well, kid, that's about it for you today," Atkins taunted. "Not just yet, it ain't," replied Unitas.

Unitas waved off the backup quarterback trying to enter the field. Sickened by the sight of his quarterback's battered face covered with blood, Jim Parker nearly vomited on the field. Parker would later say that to stem the bleeding, Alex Sandusky scooped mud and grass from the field and shoved it up Unitas's nose. Raymond Berry recalled that it was Unitas himself who slowed the bleeding with stadium turf. A newspaper photograph showed Baltimore's team physician and trainers on the field treating Unitas's bashed face. As they wiped blood off Unitas's face, Bears' fans chanted, "Take him out! Take him out!" With 17 seconds remaining, on fourth and 14 from the Chicago 39, Unitas stood behind his center and then retreated. Running a play called 66-Take-Off, Lenny Morre darted 10 yards, faked an inside move, and raced to the right corner of the end zone. Nearly 50,000 Chicago fans were on their feet howling. Unitas threw a perfect strike to Moore in the end zone for the winning touchdown. Walking off the field, the battered quarterback in a rare display of emotion thrust his arms upward. "Never in his career with the Colts has Unitas taken such a physical beating and never has he been more glorious," wrote the *Baltimore Sun's* beat reporter Cameron Snyder. A stunned George Halas, saying his Bears despite the loss had played their finest game of the year, was more succinct: "The Colts didn't beat us—Unitas did." Having watched the final touchdown, a Chicago fan wondered, "We knew he was good—now, is he human?"

To students of history watching Unitas play a sport replete with martial references and seeing his courage, tactical daring, and leadership by deed, there were traces of Trafalgar and the Nelson Touch. On and off the field, the stoic Unitas, though always blunt when he spoke, typically said little and scorned bravado. Yet at a time when television was finally capturing pro football's excitement, Johnny Unitas was the biggest star in a game nearly bursting with star players. By the ultimate yardstick used by football players to judge one another and to measure greatness—how one played in the biggest moments in the biggest games against the best players—Johnny Unitas stood alone, for no other quarterback ever in a game's final minutes seemed so oblivious to the pressure of a fading clock and charging defenders and so certain to find a way to win.

* * * * *

John Constantine Unitas fittingly came from a region filled with steel mills, coal mines, and football fields. He was a Pittsburgh kid. Both parents were born in Lithuania. His early years saw family drama, tragedy, and sacrifice. His father, Francis, ran a business shoveling and delivering coal. In an affair, his father impregnated his sister-in-law. When

John was five, Francis, at the age of 38, died of renal failure induced by years of digging coal. The country was still mired in the Great Depression. For the Unitas family, difficult times became harder. John's mother, Helen, took over the coal-delivery business and in the evening cleaned offices for three dollars per night. With an uncle disabled from decades of working in coal fields, the family of six moved into a two-bedroom house in Mount Washington outside Pittsburgh. Helen Unitas preached to her four children not to ask for luxuries and liberally defined what was a luxury. Taking accounting classes at night, Helen found a city government job as a bookkeeper.

Growing up, Johnny Unitas was skinny, shy, and socially awkward. An indifferent student, he struggled in the classroom but stood out in football. Playing at 140 pounds for St. Justin High School, John beat out Dan Rooney, the son of Steelers owner Art Rooney, as the first-team quarterback for Pittsburgh's All-Catholic League. Despite his high school football accomplishments, Unitas's poor grades and frail frame limited his college choices. The University of Pittsburgh wanted to sign Unitas, but he failed the school's entrance exam. A priest at St. Justin arranged a visit to Notre Dame. The assistant coach overseeing the workout, Bernie Crimmins, showed no interest, telling Unitas that he was too small to play major college football. Finally, the University of Louisville offered a conditional scholarship with head coach Frank Camp promising Johnny's mother that her son would graduate and attend Mass weekly.

Louisville football was an undistinguished mid-level program. But Unitas, tutored in the fundamentals of playing quarterback by assistant coach Frank Gitschier, started as a freshman. In his four years at Louisville, the Cardinals won 12 games and lost 21, and Unitas played both quarterback and defensive back, and even returned kicks. As a senior, he played with a fractured ankle.

In the 1955 NFL draft, the hometown Pittsburgh Steelers picked Unitas in the ninth round with the 102nd pick. At a time when NFL rosters were limited to 33 players, Unitas in training camp was listed fourth on the team's depth chart behind veteran quarterbacks Jim Finks, Ted Marchibroda, and Vic Eaton, who also played defense and punted. In camp practices, Unitas impressed owner Art Rooney's two sons, Dan and Tim, but not Pittsburgh's coaches. Both sons raved about Unitas's accuracy and complained to their father that the coaches were not even giving Unitas an opportunity to compete—15-year-old Tim wrote that Unitas was the best passer not only in camp but perhaps in the entire league. Unitas did not take a snap in exhibition games. Predictably, he was cut, prompting the quarterback to angrily protest to head coach Walt Kiesling that he had never been given a chance. When released, Unitas was given $10 for bus fare home from the Steelers' camp in St. Bonaventure, New York, 220 miles from Pittsburgh; newly married, he hitchhiked home to save the money.

Steelers owner Art Rooney later called Cleveland's Paul Brown to recommend Unitas. Brown, whose 1955 roster was set, suggested a tryout before the 1956 season. Unitas found a construction job on a pile-driving crew working six days each week. But on Thursday nights, he played semi-pro football for the Bloomfield Rams, competing on a hard clay field at times for three dollars per game with free beer at a local pizza restaurant. In the spring of 1956, a football fan wrote to the Baltimore Colts that the Bloomfield team had a quarterback the Colts might want to consider. In May, Weeb Ewbank worked out Unitas and was struck by how he threw a football, especially the exaggerated way that Unitas followed through with his passes, snapping his wrist and turning over his fingers much like a baseball pitcher throwing a screwball. The Colts signed Unitas to a $7,000 contract for 1956 contingent on his making the team.

As the 1956 season began, Unitas backed up second-year quarterback George Shaw, an Oregon All-American who was the first pick in the 1955 draft. In Shaw's rookie season, Bears linebacker George Connor smashed Shaw in the face with his shoulder, breaking Shaw's face mask and knocking out four teeth. A year later, again against Chicago, Shaw suffered a serious knee injury, and Unitas entered the game. Unitas's first extended play in pro football was inauspicious—an interception and a fumbled center exchange resulted in Chicago touchdowns, and the Bears won 58-27. But the next week, Unitas led the Colts to a 28-21 win over Green Bay. Weeks later, when an equipment manager asked Gino Marchetti about Shaw returning, Marchetti replied, "He's never going to be the quarterback again—Unitas is the quarterback." In 1957, the Colts had their first-ever winning season, and Unitas in his second year led the NFL in passing yards, passing touchdowns, and passer rating. From 1957 through 1964, Unitas was named six times to an All-Pro team, every year to the Pro Bowl, and twice as the NFL's Most Valuable Player. In 1958 and 1959, he led Baltimore to NFL championships.

* * * * *

Vince Lombardi stressed winning in preseason. He believed winning was a habit and, even in practice and in exhibition games, created expectations. From 1960 through 1963, Green Bay won 22 exhibition games, losing only to the College All-Stars in 1963. But in 1964, its 3-2 preseason mark presaged disappointment in the regular season. On the eve of Green Bay's first exhibition game in 1965, Lombardi applauded his team's effort in training camp. Speaking at the annual Meet the Packers luncheon, the head coach called his current team his best conditioned ever. "This is by far the best camp I've ever had since I have been with the Packers. There is more spirit, more determination, more everything than I have seen since I have been with the Packers."

Green Bay played its first exhibition game at newly named Lambeau Field against the New York Giants. Having won the NFL Championship in 1956, the Giants, flush with talent, remained a contending team but lost the NFL Championship Game five times from 1958 through 1963. In 1964, the Giants finished last in their division with a 2-10-2 record, their first losing season in 11 years. Some stars of past years—Charlie Conerly, Kyle Rote, Sam Huff, and Rosey Grier—had retired or been traded. Aging stars like Andy Robustelli, Y. A. Tittle, and Frank Gifford returned for a final season they should not have played. Giants fans were questioning their young head coach, Allie Sherman, a Brooklyn native.

The Packers won easily 44-7. The game's biggest play was Tom Brown's 92-yard punt return. After the game, Lombardi told reporters, "I've got to say I'm satisfied because of the score," before citing his displeasure with the kickoff and punt coverage teams. On August 21 at the 16th annual Midwest Shrine game played in Milwaukee before 47,066 fans, the Packers led Chicago 21-0 at halftime and beat the Bears 31-14. Lombardi seemed unimpressed by his team's performance. Except for the coverage teams, the Packers' one deficiency against the Giants, he saw no improvement from the prior week's performance. Bears coach George Halas was more laudatory: "The Packers are in mid-season form right now."

On a hot Saturday night in Dallas a week later, the Packers fell to the Cowboys 21-12. Dallas played with regular-season intensity. Defended by Herb Adderley, Dallas receiver Buddy Dial had an outstanding game, including a 46-yard touchdown catch. Meeting with reporters two nights later after review of the game film, Lombardi, despite the loss, noted, "We actually played a little better game than I thought." In their fourth exhibition game, the Packers soundly beat Cleveland 30-14, leading the Browns 23-12 in first downs and 376-230 in total yards. For Green Bay, the biggest highlight was Willie Wood's 56-yard punt return.

In their final exhibition game, Green Bay defeated St. Louis 31-13, providing some consolation over their Playoff Bowl loss to the Cardinals in January. But Jim Taylor left the game with an injured ankle. A sellout crowd of 50,858 attended. With Don Hutson and Curly Lambeau's son on the field, the game was a celebration. City Stadium, its most recent renovations complete, was formally dedicated as Lambeau Field.

* * * * *

Curly Lambeau, with his vibrant personality and rich past, was a Green Bay legend. He was a local kid who starred at Green Bay's East High School and at Notre Dame under Knute Rockne. Beginning in 1919, Lambeau played for or coached the Packers for three decades—from 1920 through 1929, he was both their star halfback and head coach. Lambeau was married three times; his second wife was a former Miss California. On June 1, 1965, Lambeau at age 67 suffered a fatal heart attack as he was picking up his date, the founder of Green Bay's Golden Girls cheerleaders who was 34 years younger.

Shortly after Curly's death, the *Green Bay Press-Gazette* urged that City Stadium be renamed after Lambeau. Public support for the name change was overwhelming, and the Green Bay City Council would unanimously agree. Though George Halas was an honorary pallbearer, Vince Lombardi did not attend Lambeau's funeral. Until the day before the City Council's vote, the Green Bay Packers were silent on renaming the stadium. The reason was that Vince Lombardi opposed the name change.

In late July, the Packers 1965 yearbook, largely edited and co-published by Art Daley, appeared. Daley was the Packers beat reporter for the *Green Bay Press-Gazette.* The yearbook was not a team publication. Its cover was a color photograph of Lombardi and Lambeau shaking hands in 1961 when Lambeau was elected to the Wisconsin Athletic Hall of Fame. At the time, a reluctant Lombardi had to be coaxed to be photographed with Lambeau. Seeing the yearbook, Lombardi phoned Daley, calling it the worst ever and angrily hanging up. Hearing earlier about the cover, Lombardi had wanted to see the yearbook before it was published, and Daley refused, citing Lombardi's evident desire to edit the publication's content.

For three months, Lombardi refused to speak to Daley. Finally, in late October, Lombardi ended his petulance, telling Daley he did not like the spotlight taken away from him and his team. Self-interest and on occasion friendship drove Lombardi's relationship with the press. As a New York Giants assistant coach wanting favorable newspaper coverage in his quest to be a head coach, Lombardi was friendly and solicitous to reporters. In Green Bay, he remained cordial to some New York and national writers but could be indifferent and even curt to local reporters whose positive coverage of the Packers seemed assured.

* * * * *

On July 25, the Baltimore Colts opened camp at Western Maryland College in Westminster, a Maryland town with a picturesque main street located an hour northwest of Baltimore and east of the Antietam battlefield, and 10 minutes from the Pennsylvania state line. Nearly a century old with a Methodist affiliation, Western Maryland featured a hilly campus with red brick buildings and a sunken football field. Don Shula's training camps were hard and physical. Baltimore practiced twice each day for longer periods than Green Bay did. Shula too favored the Oklahoma Drill with its primal face-off. Summoned in an early practice to begin the Oklahoma drills, linebacker Don Shinnick, pointing to the other side of the field, shouted to fans at the practice, "Come on, here's where the blood is!"

On offense, a concern was whether the age of the several starters would finally begin to diminish their performance. Two linemen, George Preas and Alex Sandusky, were nearing retirement. Unitas and Berry were 32, and Lenny Moore, spectacular in 1964 after a disappointing 1963 season, would shortly be turning 32.

On defense, Shula's concern was not age but the retirements of Bill Pellington and Gino Marchetti. At the critical middle linebacker position, Pellington provided ferocity, experience, and play-calling skills. Marchetti was acclaimed as the best defensive end to ever play. Baltimore's exhibition games showed that the team had found capable replacements for both. In June, Baltimore traded for linebacker Dennis Gaubatz, giving Detroit Joe Don Looney and a draft pick. An eighth-round pick in 1963, Gaubatz, a Texan, had played for Paul Dietzel at LSU where he had been a defender on the Tigers' Chinese Bandits unit, named after the ferocious fighters in the popular "Terry and the Pirates" comic strip. Mentored for two years by Detroit's Joe Schmidt, Gaubatz was noticeably faster than Pellington, instinctive, and ready to start.

Distinguished by his thick black hair, elongated chin, and stout frame, defensive end and placekicker Lou Michaels had experience and a reputation. His father worked in Pennsylvania's coal mines, and the family changed its name from Majka. In the 1958 NFL draft, he was Los Angeles's first-round pick, the fourth player selected overall. Off-field confrontations plagued Michaels, who was particularly formidable after drinking Scotch. The Rams traded Michaels after he battled with some success nine Los Angeles police officers, and Pittsburgh in 1964 sent the combative lineman to Baltimore after he broke a teammate's jaw in a fight. After his car hit a Baltimore lamp post in an early-morning accident in October 1964, Michaels resolved to drink more beer and less whiskey. But he was a talented, two-time Pro Bowl defensive end.

On August 14, the Colts opened the preseason beating St. Louis 22-10 in New Orleans, which was seeking an NFL franchise. The night was especially humid, and the crowd, 75,229, was especially large. Baltimore's defense stood out, giving up only three points and intercepting four passes. After the game, Shula praised both Gaubatz and Michaels. "I was particularly pleased with our hitting," said the head coach. "Gaubatz made tackles all over the field, and when our boys tackled, the Cards stayed tackled." His two defensive assistants, Charlie Winner and Bill Arnsparger, concurred in Shula's assessment of their defense's play. Coaching Baltimore's defensive line, Arnsparger played at Kentucky's Paris High School under Blanton Collier. After serving in the Marines, Arnsparger attended college at Miami University in Ohio and coached under Woody Hayes at Miami of Ohio and Ohio State, under Collier at Kentucky, and then at Tulane. "You don't need monsters to stop a running game," Arnsparger said. "We have enough size. What counts is the 'pop' we can deliver."

In past years, the Colts' defensive line featured All-Pro players like Gino Marchetti, Art Donovan, and "Big Daddy" Lipscomb. With tackles Billy Ray Smith and Fred Miller, and ends Michaels and Ordell Braase, Baltimore's defensive front remained the foundation of the team's' defense. No one was bigger than 245 pounds. But each one was quick, prized teamwork, and cherished the game he played. Smith, a third-round pick in 1957, was a Golden Gloves boxing champion. Miller, a seventh-round selection, was a sharecropper's son who grew up in a small North Louisiana town and went to LSU; in frame and style of play, he reminded NFL guards of Green Bay's Henry Jordan. Overshadowed by Marchetti for years, Braase was eager to prove he was not just a steady contributor, but a Pro Bowl defensive end.

In the St. Louis game, Unitas strained his right elbow and in practice threw only short passes. In its second exhibition game, Baltimore, again showing a strong defense, beat Detroit 23-3. Gary Cuozzo replaced Unitas, and rookie linebacker Mike Curtis broke his nose. Playing against Pittsburgh in game three of the preseason, Baltimore won easily 38-10, but center Dick Szymanski broke his left forearm. He was fitted with a cast from his wrist to his forearm and was expected to miss a month. Two days after the game, Baltimore traded with Pittsburgh for center Buzz Nutter, who had played for the Colts years earlier in their championship years.

The Colts went undefeated in preseason, one of only two NFL teams to do so. In its fourth exhibition game, Baltimore in Norfolk beat Washington 33-23. But the Colts suffered more injuries. Running from the pocket, Unitas was kneed in the head; groggy and dizzy, he left the game. And Jerry Logan strained his knee. The preseason ended with the Colts beating Philadelphia 33-14 and Unitas playing.

* * * * *

In the 1960s, the country was changing. Driven by ratings and advertising dollars from the biggest companies, television trod carefully. In 1965, Lucille Ball and Red Skelton were popular stars; *Bonanza* was the top show; and newer shows like *Gomer Pyle U.S.M.C.* and *Bewitched* were hits. The *Sound of Music* filled movie theaters. But film and especially music, needing a smaller audience for success, would soon prove eager to probe the bounds of what was socially acceptable. Politically, a distant war in Vietnam was dividing the country.

The war dominated each day the front page in major newspapers and national news broadcasts. Large protests against the war were becoming common with 25,000 marching in Washington on April 17.

And the demand for equality by Black Americans, simmering for generations, was reaching a crescendo moment. In 1964, Congress passed the landmark Civil Rights Act, prohibiting discrimination in public places, and riots, usually sparked by a police encounter, erupted in New York's Harlem, Philadelphia, Rochester, and other cities. In January 1965, the AFL moved its All-Star game from New Orleans to Houston when Black players, experiencing problems catching cabs and entering nightclubs, voted to boycott the game. In March 1965, John Lewis and Martin Luther King Jr. led dramatic marches in Selma, Alabama, for the right to vote. In August, Congress approved the Voting Rights Act. Five days after President Johnson signed the legislation, rioting swept through the Watts neighborhood in Los Angeles.

In racial equality, the NFL, reflecting the country, had a sordid past. In 1961, 13 NFL teams had only 83 Black players, and the Washington Redskins had none. Many Black players believed that teams had a ceiling of seven or eight Blacks, who largely played running back, wide receiver, and defensive back. Historically, exhibition games in the South presented logistical challenges and ugly moments. At a 1959 exhibition game in Dallas between the Colts and the Giants, the teams' planes had to stop before reaching the terminal for Black players to board special buses because Blacks could not enter the airport terminal. The night before the game, Black players for both teams, staying at a rundown motel lacking television and radio in a Black neighborhood, met and nearly decided to boycott the game. Raymond Berry later apologized to his Black teammates for what they had endured. Playing in Miami the next week, the Colts stayed in one hotel, but Black players experienced problems with taxi service.

In Green Bay, a small city with few Blacks, Lombardi abhorred bigotry. He warned his players often that those showing racial or ethnic bias could not play for him and told

Green Bay restaurants and clubs that those refusing service to the team's Black players would be classified off-limits for all players. In the early years, housing was a concern. In 1961, Willie Davis, Herb Adderley, and Elijah Pitts settled for a one-bedroom house where the two rookies slept on a couch and a kitchen cot. But Lombardi worked hard to find suitable housing in Green Bay for his team's Black players. In 1964, Elaine Robinson and Ruth Pitts with their children moved to Green Bay for the season. They were the first wives of Black players to do so. After a Jacksonville exhibition game requiring his players to stay in different hotels, Lombardi refused to ever again separate his team. For games in 1961 and 1962 in Columbus, Georgia, the Packers found housing in the officers' quarters at the Fort Benning military base.

Bypassing the training-camp custom that players elected their team captains, Lombardi named defensive end Davis as a defensive captain. Small at 240 pounds but quick and tenacious, Davis had twice been voted first-team All-Pro. But given the times, the Green Bay coach surely knew the importance of naming a Black player as a team captain.

Willie Davis and his story were inspirational. He was born in Claiborne Parish in rural North Louisiana. His father, working as a sharecropper, was paid 50 cents per day on a farm patrolled by armed guards and abandoned the family when Willie was eight. His mother, Nodie Davis, escaped with Willie to Arkansas where his grandparents lived. From his mother, high school coach and science teacher Nathan Jones, and Grambling football coach Eddie Robinson, Davis learned the importance of hard work and education for success in life.

Drafted by Cleveland in 1956, Davis was too small to play in Paul Brown's defense. In 1960, Green Bay traded for Davis. He was reluctant to leave Cleveland and considered quitting football. Lombardi zealously recruited Davis, telling him that the Packers believed he could be a great player and had sought the trade. Knowing extreme poverty and discrimination, Davis remained uncommonly positive in outlook. In camp, thinking that Bill Curry could help the team, Davis approached the discouraged rookie and offered encouragement. When Lombardi is raging at you, Nitschke is busting you, and you think you can't take it any longer, Davis said, "Just look at me—I'll get you through it." In the offseason, competing against students from the country's best colleges, Davis attended the University of Chicago to obtain his master's degree in business administration.

In Baltimore, a major city that was 12 times bigger than Green Bay and that had a large Black community, there seemed on the field no racial divisions. But Black players were not seen at restaurants and clubs favored by their White teammates and particularly disliked Westminster, the team's choice for training camp, where some restaurants and theaters refused to admit Blacks until legally compelled to do so. Even in Colts-crazed Baltimore, the legacy of segregation could prove stronger than football stardom. In 1963, Lenny Moore, Jim Parker, and rookie John Mackey entered a Baltimore tavern whose front window featured posters of Moore and Parker. They were refused service. When leaving the bar, Mackey claimed the pictures.

* * * * *

With the 1965 season for the NFL and AFL about to begin, *Sports Illustrated*'s "Pro Football 1965" preview issue arrived in mid-September in mailboxes and at newsstands. Reviewing the AFL, Edwin Shrake picked the Buffalo Bills and San Diego Chargers as conference winners. With quarterbacks Jack Kemp and Daryle Lamonica, tight end Paul Costa, and a terrific offensive line, Buffalo was called the AFL's best, perhaps three players away from competing with the NFL's top teams. The Chargers, coached by Sid Gillman, had an explosive offense with quarterback John Hadl, receiver Lance Alworth, and running backs Paul Lowe and Keith Lincoln.

In the NFL, Tex Maule picked Cleveland to win the Eastern Conference, trailed by Dallas, St. Louis, Washington, Philadelphia, New York, and finally Pittsburgh. Though prohibitive favorites in the East, Cleveland had a July scare involving star fullback Jim Brown, who reported a week late to his team's training camp in Hiram, Ohio. A 1965 *Time* cover story described Brown as "flashy, arrogant," and "casually discreet." Both claiming the entitlements of a pro football star and driven by anger over racism, Jim Brown was indifferent to criticism by others and welcomed controversy. "I do what I want," said Brown in the magazine profile. In a Cleveland courtroom, he faced criminal charges that he had slapped repeatedly and sexually assaulted 18-year-old Brenda Ayers, who admitted that on other occasions she had slept with Brown. At trial, Brown, who was married, testified the allegations were baseless, and his attorneys argued shakedown. On July 22, after deliberating for 80 minutes, a Cleveland jury found Brown not guilty. Yet, even in the early 1960s when sportswriters looked past the nighttime escapades and misdeeds of the athletes they covered, Brown's public pursuit of women with rumors of abuse drew attention.

Athletically, Jim Brown was a prodigy. Leaving college, he was six-foot-two and weighed 230 pounds with a 45-inch chest and thighs as big as his 32-inch waist. Weeks after he was born on St. Simons Island in Georgia, his father abandoned the family. When Jim was two, his mother moved to Great Neck, New York, to work as a domestic servant, leaving her son in a great-grandmother's care. At eight, he traveled alone by train to join his mother on Long Island. At Manhasset High School, Brown earned 13 letters in five different sports. Playing football at running back, he averaged as a senior 14.9 yards per rushing attempt. Playing basketball in his final year, he averaged 38 points per game—he set a state record by scoring 53 points in a game, and three nights later he broke it by scoring 55 points.

At Syracuse, Brown proved exceptional in every sport he played. In basketball, as a sophomore reserve, he was his team's second-leading scorer and top rebounder. As a senior, he refused to play on the team, convinced he was not starting because Syracuse refused to start more than two Black players. In lacrosse, Brown dominated against opponents markedly slower and 60 pounds lighter. His lacrosse coach was Roy Simmons, whose intelligence and decency Brown relished. At Ernie Davis's funeral in May 1963, with Syracuse football coach Ben Schwartzwalder and Cleveland coach Paul Brown standing nearby, Jim Brown loudly introduced Simmons to his Cleveland Brown teammates as "my favorite coach of all time."

Picked sixth by Cleveland in the 1957 NFL draft, Jim Brown in his first year showed he was as good as any runner in the history of the sport. In Cleveland, Brown provided leadership and an activist's perspective to the team's other Black players, which created divisions before Blanton Collier became head coach. When Brown did report to training camp in July, he was 29 years old and had other interests. He had recently appeared in a movie, *Rio Conchos*, a Western starring Richard Boone and Stuart Whitman. Hollywood was a new world to conquer. Though playing as well as he had ever played, Brown told others that at most he might play two more seasons.

* * * * *

In the more formidable Western Conference, Maule favored Green Bay to win, followed by Baltimore, Minnesota, Los Angeles, San Francisco, Chicago, and Detroit. Maule confidently predicted that Green Bay would successfully replace departing starters. "After a two-year period of reverses and rehabilitation, the Green Bay Packers are bigger, younger and probably stronger than ever before. The Packers are ready to return to the top, both in the West and the league." With the Colts, he seemed uncertain, predicting that they would finish second or even third in the conference depending on how well those replacing Gino Marchetti and Bill Pellington played. But surely the new season would be exciting. Quoting an unnamed major league baseball owner, Maule wrote that "pro football has become the glamour sport."

6

September: The Season Begins

For the first time in 17 years, the Green Bay Packers would be opening the season on the road. Their opponents were the Pittsburgh Steelers, a team mired in decades of mediocrity and disappointment. Entering the league in 1933, the Steelers, called the Pirates in their first seven years, had a cumulative record of 148-214-16. In 32 seasons, they had never won a championship of any kind and had only eight winning seasons. Two weeks before their first game, the Steelers were looking for a new head coach.

Pittsburgh's head coach for eight seasons was Buddy Parker, a laconic and moody Texan. As Detroit's young head coach in 1952 and 1953, he won league titles. But in August 1957, at the annual preseason "Meet the Lions" banquet before 500 fans and team officials, Parker, the program's last speaker, walked to the lectern and announced without warning that he was quitting. "Sometime in every football coach's career, there comes a time when he reaches a situation which he can't handle. I've just arrived at that point. Tonight, I'm getting out of the Detroit Lions' organization. I've had enough." The resignation shocked the crowd, especially the team president whom Parker on the dais had been sitting next to.

Returning to coaching in Pittsburgh, Parker produced four winning seasons. But the Steelers in 1964 finished 5-9 and had little talent because of their head coach's penchant for trading away draft picks for aging players. Shortly after the Steelers lost their fourth straight exhibition game, Parker told team owner Art Rooney that he was quitting as head coach. The Steelers promoted assistant Mike Nixon to be their new head coach. Stories circulated that Parker told Rooney, "I can't win with this bunch of stiffs." In their season opener at home, the Steelers were 14-point underdogs.

On opening day, September 19, a heat wave gripped the eastern United States. Pitt Stadium could have been a football field in South Carolina on a hot August afternoon—the temperature hit 94 degrees, and the humidity was high. Sweat drenched the players in uniform and fans in the stands. The Steelers wore their traditional white pants and black helmets with the distinctive one-sided Steelers logo introduced in 1962.

The first half was surprisingly competitive. Playing hard for their new coach, the Steelers looked inspired and aggressively rushed Bart Starr. After a scoreless first quarter, Pittsburgh kicked two field goals after long drives and took a 6-0 lead. With less than two minutes remaining in the half, Steelers quarterback Bill Nelsen threw a sideline pass intended for Roy Jefferson. Packer cornerback Herb Adderley stepped in front of the Steeler receiver. Intercepting Nelsen's pass, he ran 34 yards down the right sideline for Green Bay's first score. But Pittsburgh quickly moved the ball 60 yards downfield and kicked its third field goal, ending the half with a 9-7 lead. Braving the heat, 38,000 Steelers fans stood and applauded.

During halftime, Lombardi berated his offensive players for their ineffective play but made few changes. In the second half, Green Bay scored on its first six possessions. On their first series, the Packers drove 79 yards, and Starr threw a 31-yard touchdown pass to tight end Marv Fleming. Adding two field goals, Green Bay led 20-9 at the end of the third quarter. In the final period, Adderley had his second interception, and Ray Nitschke had his team's third interception. Green Bay won 41-9. Green Bay had no turnovers, and Pittsburgh had four. In the second half, Pittsburgh had only 64 yards of offense. Starr was outstanding, completing 17 of 23 passes for two touchdowns.

After the game, Lombardi was thankful that the game had two halves. Packer players attributed their second-half comeback to superior conditioning. "The heat? It was like this every day at training camp," exaggerated Herb Adderley. "Coach Lombardi worked us hard in it, and it made us a little mad, but you saw how it paid off today." But the reason for the Packers' surge was superior depth and overall talent. On Tuesday, after reviewing the game "movies," Lombardi offered little praise. Aside from turnovers leading to points, Lombardi said, "We were no ball of fire on defense." He added, "Outside of Bart Starr, who had a good game, we did little on offense." Asked whether Pittsburgh wilted in the second half because of the hot weather, Lombardi responded, "We wilted in the first half."

* * * * *

Favored by six and a half points, the Colts opened the season at home at Memorial Stadium against the Minnesota Vikings. Seating 60,000, Memorial was one of the NFL's most feared venues for visiting teams. Because of their rowdiness and passion, Colts fans proudly called it the "World's Largest Outdoor Insane Asylum." But months earlier, the Houston Astrodome opened. On the eve of the game, Carroll Rosenbloom proposed that Baltimore build a domed stadium that could be used by both the Colts and Baltimore's baseball Orioles. "You just don't trust a man with good intentions," Rosenbloom told the *Baltimore Sun's* skeptical sports editor, Bob Maisel. "How long can we expect people to battle a parking problem, then sit in the open on wooden benches with no backs, while they have domes and theater chair seats all around us?" Located between East 33rd and East 36th Streets in northern Baltimore, Memorial Stadium, with pillars obstructing sightlines, had been constructed decades earlier but upgraded repeatedly. Its most notable feature was the memorial spanning the height of the stadium exterior at the home plate entrances that honored those fallen in two world wars and that ended with the wording "TIME WILL NOT DIM THE GLORY OF THEIR DEEDS."

The Vikings, entering the league as an expansion team in 1961, predictably struggled in their first three years. But in 1964, they were the NFL's surprise team, finishing 8-5-1 and tying Green Bay for second place in the Western Conference. In its 1964 season opener, Minnesota shocked Baltimore 34-24. Minnesota's quarterback was Fran Tarkenton, who was known for his wild scrambles that several times each game excited Viking fans, embarrassed defensive linemen, and produced big plays. For the cover of its September 13 pro football preview issue, *Sports Illustrated* chose an art print that showed Tarkenton sprinting with the football while looking downfield to pass. The magazine's NFL preview called the Vikings the league's "most exciting team" and a "half inch away" from winning the West. Young talent coursed through Minnesota's offense. Halfback Tommy Mason from Tulane, the first pick in the 1961 draft, and Bill Brown, a 228-pound Illinois fullback, had won postseason honors. Paul Flatley from Northwestern was a tall and productive receiver, and Nebraska's Mick Tingelhoff was the league's best center. On the Vikings' defense, Carl Eller, Jim Marshall, Roy Winston, and Lonnie Warwick were promising players, but Minnesota's defensive backfield was suspect.

It was the hottest September 19 in Baltimore in 69 years. As in Pittsburgh, the temperature at kickoff was 94 degrees. A "Turkish bath," reported the *Baltimore Sun.* The Colts' offensive line coach, John Sandusky, was convinced that "it must have been 120 sometimes down on the field." Safety Wendell Harris, who played college football at LSU, called it the hottest game he had ever been in.

Minnesota struck first. On the game's third play from scrimmage, Larry Vargo intercepted a Unitas pass at midfield. Two plays later, Tarkenton, as he was being hit, threw a 36-yard touchdown pass to Hal Bedsole, and Minnesota led 7-0. After the Colts' first turnover, the teams traded interceptions. Blitzing linebacker Rip Hawkins, the Vikings aggressively rushed Unitas. As the first quarter ended, Minnesota kicked a 34-yard field goal for a 10-0 lead.

In the second quarter, the Colts mounted a long drive. Lenny Moore scored on a one-yard plunge behind blocks by

Jim Parker and Bob Vogel, narrowing Minnesota's lead to 10-7. A minute later, Jerry Logan, leaping high, intercepted Tarkenton and ran 38 yards down the sideline for a Baltimore touchdown. At halftime, the Colts led 14-10 and changed their pass protections to give Unitas more time.

Early in the second half, a Minnesota field goal cut Baltimore's advantage to 14-13. The Colts answered. Unitas hit Jimmy Orr for a 52-yard pass and then a nine-yard touchdown throw. The third quarter ended with another Minnesota field goal, but Baltimore still led 21-16. In the final period, the Vikings' sloppy tackling showed fatigue. "We wore them out," said Jerry Hill. Capping an 80-yard drive, Unitas threw a 31-yard touchdown pass to tight end John Mackey, who carried Vikings safety Ed Sharockman into the end zone, putting the Colts ahead 28-16. Finishing a 52-yard drive, Baltimore scored again on Hill's eight-yard touchdown run. The Colts won 35-16.

Despite two early interceptions, Unitas completed 14 of 22 passes for 224 yards and two touchdowns. After early success, Tarkenton struggled for Minnesota, completing only 10 of 24 attempts. The Colts showed discipline when rushing Tarkenton. "We preached containment to the defense all week," said Shula. "The runs he did get were right up the gut after we closed off the outside to him." Baltimore cornerback Lenny Lyles shut down Vikings receiver Paul Flatley until the game's final minutes and made several tackles for a loss. He received his team's game ball. Substituting liberally, Don Shula thought the day's heat and humidity helped the Colts, who held training camp in muggy Maryland rather than temperate Minnesota.

Always candid and often caustic, Vikings head coach Norm Van Brocklin was critical of his team's play. "Unitas hit his receivers," said Van Brocklin, wet with perspiration. "Our guy didn't hit his. We had people open all day." Also, the Minnesota coach singled out defensive halfback George Rose: "Orr looked like he was eating his lunch out there."

* * * * *

In Week Two, the Packers would host the Colts in Milwaukee. In his game preview, Art Daley in the *Green Bay Press-Gazette* predicted that unlike their "picnic" in Pittsburgh, the Packers on defense would be challenged. "Johnny Unitas, given little protection," he wrote, "is nothing short of murder" with his quartet of remarkable targets—Raymond Berry, Lenny Moore, John Mackey, and Jimmy Orr. Since his first season, 1956, Unitas played with both Berry and Moore. Vince Lombardi preached perfection to his players seeking excellence. Raymond Berry pursued perfection expecting to achieve it. Though Berry did not stand out in high school and college where many pro football players because so talented easily excelled, no player could have accomplished what Berry did without serious athletic ability. In his first 10 seasons, he led the league three times in both receptions and receiving yards, and twice in receiving touchdowns. He was named three times first-team All-Pro and twice second-team. But Berry was a football savant. Through obsessive preparation and practice, he turned catching a football into a science.

Raymond Berry—his father, a high school coach and math teacher, was Ray—grew up in Paris, Texas, a town of roughly 16,000 northeast of Dallas near the Oklahoma state line. He did not start on his high school football team until he was a senior when he finally weighed 150 pounds. After high school, the only school offering Berry a scholarship was the Schreiner Institute, a Texas junior college. After playing one year at Schreiner, he received a trial scholarship from SMU where he not only played football but, in field events, competed in the high jump and broad jump. By his final college year, Berry stood six-foot-two and weighed 180 pounds, and he played both receiver and linebacker. As in high school, Berry would not start at SMU until his senior year, but he was voted a co-captain because of how hard he worked and how much he was respected. Limited by a T-formation offense that favored the run, Berry caught only 32 passes in his three years at SMU. When Berry was a junior, Baltimore picked him in the 20th round as a "future" pick.

With his earnest demeanor and eccentric ways, Berry seemed different from many who played professional football. Hours after battling the Giants in Yankee Stadium in November 1958, Berry wearing thick glasses appeared as a regular contestant on the CBS television show *What's My Line*. Emblematic of its time, the Sunday-night game show featured four panelists, witty and dressed in evening gown or black tie, who through their questions tried to guess the occupation of guests—the "celebrity guest" that night for whom the panelists wore blindfolds was French actor Charles Boyer. By nature, Berry was fastidious. At training camp, he adorned a normally spartan dorm room with plants and rugs and arranged his belongings as though awaiting a military academy inspection. He washed his football practice pants so they would not shrink. On long road trips, he carried his own weight scale to precisely monitor his weight.

With poor eyesight, he wore especially large and uncomfortable contact lenses. He had a weak sacroiliac joint; when it was out of place, one leg was shorter. To compensate, Berry wore a four-inch-wide back brace. Unlike other players, he did not during the offseason sell insurance or work in a bank, choosing instead to improve his football skills and remain in top physical condition. His rigorous program consisted of push-ups, sit-ups, and pull-ups; drills running backwards and sideways; and isometric exercises. To strengthen his large hands, Berry constantly squeezed Silly Putty, developing exercises for each finger.

But in the study of his craft, Berry had no equal. In his contract negotiations with the Colts, Berry insisted that the team provide him with a movie projector. Watching game film, Berry graded himself on every play and studied the game's other receivers and defensive backs. Like a botanist writing a college textbook, Berry sought to dissect and categorize every facet of playing wide receiver. He catalogued 12 different types of short passes and seven types of long passes based on how the ball was thrown—the scoop, the toe dance, the wrong shoulder—and after regular practices had his quarterbacks throw him each type of pass. He had at least six different ways to run every pass route. Though not fast, Berry understood that how a receiver used his speed was more important than how fast he could run in a straight line. Early in his career, with the help of receivers coach Bud Shaw, Berry honed an arsenal of fakes and moves to create separation from defensive halfbacks. He practiced recovering balls he fumbled, though entering his 10th season in the NFL, he had fumbled only once.

During the season, Berry spent Mondays watching game movies, so that on Tuesday he could give Unitas a list of passing plays that he thought would work against their next opponent. Each year, he kept in thick binders his copious notes and play diagrams for each opposing team played and players competed against. After nine years of pushing themselves in practice drills and playing together in 105 NFL games, Berry and Unitas knew exactly what each other on the field wanted and was going to do.

For Lenny Moore, the road to professional football began in Reading, Pennsylvania. In a family with 12 children, he grew up in a house without indoor plumbing and with little heating that squatted between an alley and railroad tracks. Sports offered fame and a path to a different life. At Reading High School, Moore scored 22 touchdowns as a senior and was called "the Reading Rocket." At Penn State, where his coaches were empathetic Rip Engle and the more demonstrative Joe Paterno, he set records. As a junior, Moore rushed for eight yards per carry, and he twice led the team in interceptions.

In 1956, Baltimore drafted Moore in the first round, the ninth pick overall, and he was the league's Rookie of the Year. In his first six years, he was named first-team All-Pro four times. Colt teammates like Raymond Berry thought he was the best all-around athlete they had ever seen. Fast and elusive with a receiver's soft hands, Moore played both halfback and flanker and became known for big plays and touchdowns.

Athletically gifted, Lenny Moore did not have to practice as hard as other players. Some teammates noticed. Halfback Tom Matte believed that Moore, wanting to avoid practices, highlighted minor injuries that miraculously improved at the end of game week. In 1962, Lenny Moore was older, and serious injuries began. That year in an exhibition game in Pittsburgh, Moore, sliding out of bounds, hit his knee on a protruding spike and fractured his kneecap. In 1963, losing his helmet, he was kicked in the head and suffered a concussion. He missed seven games. Baltimore's management openly questioned Moore's dedication to his sport, the severity of his injuries, and his willingness to play with pain. Long outspoken over the racial discrimination he had experienced, Moore charged that the Colts in doubting his return from injuries were guilty of a double standard based on race and became bitter.

After the 1963 season, the Colts tried to trade Moore, but other teams showed little interest. Moore was a favorite of owner Carroll Rosenbloom, who prized production and wins on Sunday rather than hard running on Thursday. Summoning Moore, Shula, and general manager Don Kellett to his hotel suite for a meeting, Rosenbloom turned to Moore and asked, "Lenny, do you want to play for the Colts in 1964?" Moore said quickly that he did. "Fine," the Baltimore owner announced, "I just wanted to hear it from you. The meeting is over." Healthy, his pride pricked, and fully committed, Moore in 1964 was the league's Comeback Player of the Year, running and receiving for 1,056 yards and scoring 19 touchdowns. Again, he was named first-team All-Pro. But as the 1965 season began, Moore was nearly 32. The Colts were hoping he had another great season left.

* * * * *

On September 26, in Week Two, Green Bay and Baltimore, considered by many the league's two best teams, met in Milwaukee at County Stadium. Though only the season's second game, the teams and their fans understood that its outcome could decide in December the Western Conference. The *Baltimore Evening Sun* called it a "showdown" game. On game day, a *Green Bay Press-Gazette* headline blared that "Win Over Colts a 'Must' in Packers Drive for Division Crown." Press coverage was heavy—there were 13 Baltimore newspaper reporters alone. In 1964, Baltimore won both games against the Packers, 21-20 in Green Bay and then 24-21 in Baltimore. For Green Bay, Jim Taylor would not play, and Lombardi juggled his offensive line, moving Forrest Gregg to left guard in place of Fuzzy Thurston and starting Steve Wright at right tackle. The Packers were favored by three points.

In contrast to last week's heat, game day was chilly and dark with temperatures near 40 degrees and winds gusting to 20 miles per hour. In the first quarter, Unitas connected with Jimmy Orr on a 57-yard pass to the Green Bay 26. Beaten on the play, the boisterous Herb Adderley told Orr, "From now on, I'm going everywhere you go." Green Bay held, and the Colts kicked a 26-yard field goal for a 3-0 lead.

Early in the second quarter, Unitas tried handing off to Tony Lorick. During the exchange, the ball squirted loose. The Packers recovered the fumble at the Colts' 39. Though Green Bay reached the Baltimore two-yard line, the Packers settled for a short field goal, tying the game 3-3. But Green Bay's defense would score. Rushed hard, Unitas began running to his left and threw to his right, trying to force a sideline pass to Jimmy Orr. On a dead run, Adderley intercepted. Bobbling the ball for 10 yards, the Green Bay cornerback ran down the sideline 44 yards for the game's first touchdown and Green Bay's first lead 10-3. In a celebration rare for the era, Adderley after scoring threw the football far into the end zone crowd. Near the end of the first half, Baltimore, running the football with success, threatened. On third and 18 at the 26-yard line, Unitas threw to Raymond Berry. The Colt receiver made a fingertip catch near the goal line. Running to his left, Jerry Hill scored from the one. As the first half ended, the teams were tied 10-10.

Ferocious hitting causing turnovers dominated a scoreless third quarter. Sacked by defensive end Ordell Braase, Starr limped to the sideline with an injured ankle. He was replaced by Zeke Bratkowski. Paul Hornung injured his shoulder and left the game. When the fourth quarter began, the game was still tied. With 13 minutes remaining, Chandler kicked a 41-yard field goal to give the Packers a 13-10 lead. Minutes later, Unitas threw a short touchdown pass to Berry.

Baltimore led 17-13. The scoreboard showed 8:30 left in the game.

Green Bay mounted a drive but was stopped on downs at the Baltimore 32. Just three minutes were left. The Colts needed only to run out the clock. But Lenny Moore, fighting for extra yards, fumbled. The football popped upward into the arms of safety Willie Wood. With the ball at the Baltimore 37, Green Bay had one more chance. Huddling on the field, Bratkowski asked receiver Max McGee for a play. The veteran urged a corner pattern to the end zone. McGee made an inside fake, as though he were running a post pattern, and then cut to his left. On the fake, Lenny Lyles stumbled. McGee caught a 37-yard touchdown pass, his only reception of the game. The Packers took the lead 20-17 but may have scored too quickly. The game clock read 2:34.

Though playing with a strained right shoulder, Unitas quickly marched the Colts 35 yards to the Green Bay 37. Baltimore needed only a field goal to tie the game. There were 53 seconds left. Unitas passed to Tom Matte for 15 yards, but the Colt halfback, tackled violently, fumbled at the Green Bay 22. Herb Adderley covered the loose ball to seal the win for the Packers. It was Baltimore's fifth fumble of the game.

Statistically, Baltimore should have won, outgaining Green Bay 309 to 184 in total net yards and 197 to 78 in rushing yards. Colt Billy Ray Smith loudly proclaimed the better team did not win. His teammates agreed. Baltimore's defense, quick and penetrating, was outstanding, holding Green Bay's offense to 13 points despite six Colt turnovers, sacking Packer quarterbacks six times, and recovering three fumbles. But the story of the game was Baltimore turnovers—two Unitas interceptions on passes he knew he should not have thrown and four lost fumbles, including two in the final three minutes of the game. "We just gave the game away, that's all," grumbled Don Shula. His owner, Carroll Rosenbloom, agreed, saying, "We blew it."

After the game, Lombardi praised Baltimore's defense as better than its 1964 defensive unit with Marchetti and Pellington. "I think we saw two superb defensive football teams out there today," said Lombardi. "I believe the fumbles resulted from the high tension. Both teams were real high and were hitting hard." Reflecting on the Packers' 1964 season, Lombardi added, "We lost a couple like that last year."

* * * * *

Even after two games, it was clear that the Packers defense was the team's strength and that the left side of the Green Bay defense—defensive halfback Herb Adderley, defensive end Willie Davis, and linebacker Dave Robinson—was the defense's strength. Against Baltimore, Herb Adderley was superb—two interceptions, one for a touchdown for the second consecutive week; a fumble recovered in the game's final moments; and the shutting down of Jimmy Orr after a first-quarter reception. He was named the NFL's Defensive Player of the Week.

An extraordinary athlete, Herb Adderley exuded self-confidence. On the field, he aggressively challenged and taunted receivers. Some called him arrogant. Born in Philadelphia, he was raised by his mother and a maternal grandmother and found sanctuary from his tough surroundings at Enon Baptist Church and a local boys' club. A brother, one year older, was convicted of murder during a robbery when he stole a purse containing $3.75. At Northeast High School, Herb became one of the great players in Philadelphia prep history. He was named All-City in basketball, football, and baseball. Playing football as a senior, he scored 28 touchdowns in eight games. Adderley in later years would find amusing the *Philadelphia Daily News* highlighting his holding Wilt Chamberlain to 48 points in a high school basketball game. When Adderley's high school coach reproached the reporter over the story's prominence in the newspaper, the writer responded that Chamberlain, a foot taller and two years older than Adderley, had scored 90 points in a game the week before. Wanting to escape Philadelphia, Adderley signed with Michigan State where he was an All-Big 10 halfback. In Green Bay, among the team's Black players, he seemed especially sensitive to signs of racial prejudice and could be outspoken on racial issues. He once knocked out a Rams receiver who called him a racial slur, earning him a game ejection and league fine, which Lombardi paid.

In the 1961 draft, Lombardi, seeing Lenny Moore as a comparison, picked Adderley in the first round. As a rookie playing offense, Adderley struggled, particularly as a receiver running pass routes. Lombardi asked Emlen Tunnell, the veteran safety he had brought to Green Bay from the Giants, to see why Adderley, so physically talented, was underachieving. Tunnell reported that Adderley wanted to play defense. In the Thanksgiving Day game against Detroit in 1961, defensive halfback Hank Gremminger was injured and could not return. As the Packers were entering the field at the end of halftime, Lombardi told Adderley that he would be replacing Gremminger. "You're the best athlete we've got. Go out and do the best you can." Thrust into a position he had played sparingly in college, Adderley competed gamely and made an interception that led to a Packer touchdown.

For the cornerback position, Adderley was big at six feet and 205 pounds. In 1962, defensive backs coach Norb Hecker worked with Adderley before and after practices, stressing his new position's fundamentals—lining up in the proper stance, jamming receivers, using a sideline to limit a receiver's routes—and later teaching its subtleties. That year, Adderley started and starred. From 1962 through 1964, he intercepted 16 passes and earned All-Pro honors every year. Adderley was not the first of dominant cornerbacks whom quarterbacks tried to avoid, but he quickly became one of the few like Detroit's "Night Train" Lane who were.

Playing behind Willie Davis at left outside linebacker was Dave Robinson. Home for Robinson, the youngest of eight, was Mount Laurel, New Jersey. As a high school freshman, Robinson played football against his school's big rival on Thanksgiving Day. Hours after the game, Robinson visited his father, Leslie, in the hospital. Leslie made his youngest son promise that he would work hard and stay busy and out of trouble by playing sports. Leslie Robinson died days later. Robinson kept his promise. At Moorestown High School, Robinson played and stood out in multiple sports. As a student, he scored high on his college admissions tests, especially in math, and received scholarship offers from dozens of colleges, including Penn and Columbia. He chose to attend Penn State where he played football and studied engineering.

At Penn State, Robinson experienced a college game and a society still warped by race. In 1959, Penn State and Alabama were picked to play in the first Liberty Bowl game in Philadelphia. Because Penn State had Black players, the Southeastern Conference pressured Alabama to withdraw from the game. The teams finally agreed to go forward with Penn State allowed to play one Black player, senior tackle Charlie Janerette. Robinson could not dress out or even stand on the Penn State sideline for the game.

When Robinson was a junior, Penn State traveled south to Jacksonville to play Georgia Tech in the 1961 Gator Bowl. Before the game, he was told by coaches that he would not start or play in the first series so that the team could honor a senior backup player. Robinson played most of the game. On the field, the hitting was clean. Before the game, Tech head coach Bobby Dodd had warned his players competing against Black players about dirty play. After the game, the Penn State coaches told Robinson he did not start because of death threats made against Robinson that the school had received. In one letter, the anonymous writer claimed to be a former Army sniper and warned that he would shoot "the big black bear" if Robinson were introduced. A year later, Penn State returned reluctantly to the Gator Bowl to play Florida. The Nittany Lions protested that they deserved a bigger bowl game against a better opponent. The Florida players, upset over Penn State's complaints, wore on their white helmets the Confederate battle flag. Florida upset Penn State 17-7.

In the 1963 draft, Green Bay picked Robinson in the first round—Penn State assistant coach Joe Paterno scouted for the Packers and urged the team to pick him. But the AFL's San Diego Chargers also drafted Robinson. His future wife, Elaine, wanted to live in a city with warm weather. Robinson was about to sign with San Diego when told by the Chargers' Al Davis that the team, after signing two other high picks, had just run out of money. Robinson signed a $45,000, three-year contract with Green Bay. In college, Robinson, at six-foot-three and 245 pounds, played tight end and defensive end. The Packers, seeing his athletic ability—he had recorded a 42-inch vertical jump—moved him to outside linebacker. After the 1964 season, Robinson had knee surgery, but when the 1965 season began, he was healthy and was ready to play football.

* * * * *

In Green Bay, the Packers prepared for their next opponent, the Chicago Bears, who had lost their first two games. But games against Chicago over four decades had at times been legendary and seemed nearly always close and physical. The three Packers injured in the Baltimore game—Starr, Hornung, and Dowler—were running well in practice and appeared ready to play.

Behind three teams in the Western Conference standings, the Colts readied to play the San Francisco 49ers, who with an explosive offense won their first two games. But Unitas against Green Bay had injured his right shoulder. Though he was throwing in practice, questions lingered as to whether Unitas would play against San Francisco. As September ended, NFL teams had played only two games, but the Baltimore Colts in the Western Conference could not afford a second loss and a 1-2 record after three weeks.

Western Conference – September 30, 1965							
	W	L	T	PCT	PF	PA	PD
Detroit	2	0	0	1.000	51	29	22
Green Bay	2	0	0	1.000	61	26	35
San Francisco	2	0	0	1.000	79	41	38
Baltimore	1	1	0	.500	52	36	16
Los Angeles	1	1	0	.500	30	48	-18
Minnesota	0	2	0	.000	45	66	-21
Chicago	0	2	0	.000	52	82	-30

7

October: The Race Tightens

Age had wizened his face and reduced his frame, but at 70, George Halas, head coach and owner of the Chicago Bears, was still ornery, profane, and fiercely competitive. On the sideline, dressed in a business suit with a hat and dark glasses, Halas was an animated, scowling curmudgeon, barking orders to officials and challenges to opposing players. In the game of professional football, he was there at the beginning and already a member of the Pro Football Hall of Fame, selected in its inaugural class in 1963.

Born in Chicago, Halas was the son of Bohemian immigrants. At the University of Illinois, where he studied civil engineering, he was an outstanding athlete, a star in football, baseball, and basketball. Halas played a dozen games for the New York Yankees, but a hip injury and foremost the challenge of hitting a curveball ended his hopes of success in major league baseball. He began playing professional football for the Hammond Pros and the Decatur Staleys.

In 1920, Halas, representing the Staleys, and 15 other team representatives met in Canton, Ohio, at Ralph Hay's Hupmobile showroom to form the American Professional Football Association. Some sat on running boards. Before leaving, they elected Olympic gold medalist and football star Jim Thorpe as their president. In 1921, Halas moved the Staleys from Decatur to Chicago. A year later, he renamed his team the Bears, and the APFA was rebranded as the National

Football League. Playing pro football for 11 years, he owned and coached the Bears for two generations during which he survived the Great Depression and a world war, and saw years of small crowds, competing leagues, and failed franchises. The Bears, Packers, and Cardinals were the only three original teams that would survive. Halas not only played and coached, but also sold tickets and wrote press releases. For years, meeting payroll jostled with winning games as the bigger challenge. Like other front-office executives of his time, he relished his reputation for being miserly and unyielding in contract negotiations. As a league patriarch, Halas expected deference from the league office and game officials, whom in past years he had tried to select for his games.

The Bears were the NFL's most storied franchise. Playing in the Midwest in the country's second-largest city, they had over the years great players—nine Bears were selected for the Pro Football Hall of Fame in its first three years, including Bronko Nagurski, Red Grange, and Sid Luckman. After the Chicago Staleys won the APFA championship in 1921, the Bears won six NFL titles from 1932 to 1946. The 1940 Championship Game proved historic when the Bears embarrassed Washington 73-0. Just three weeks earlier, the Redskins had beaten the Bears 7-3. After the game, Halas complained that on the last play, the officials should have called defensive pass interference against the Redskins. Washington's showman owner, George Preston Marshall, called the Bears "crybabies" and "quitters." But in the championship game, Chicago quarterback Sid Luckman executed perfectly the modern T-formation offense as reconstructed by Clark Shaughnessy. Football coaches across the country adopted the new T-formation with a back in motion as a true receiving target and the center snap to the quarterback who could run, pass, or pitch or hand off to a running back. When Shaughnessy was head coach at the University of Chicago, he began advising George Halas as a Bears consultant. Shaughnessy was an ascetic football innovator with the bearing of an athletic Anglican rector and a weakness for milkshakes. On offense, he prized deception and movement. For inspiration and instruction, Shaughnessy sought lessons from military history and tactics and even had a Chicago professor translate German General Heinz Guderian's 1937 book on tank warfare, *Achtung-Panzer!*

Given their lofty expectations, the Bears after their 1946 title struggled. In 1956, Halas stepped down from coaching but returned two years later. In 1963, behind a great defense, the Bears edged out Green Bay for the conference title and beat the Giants 14-10 for the NFL championship. But a season later, Chicago tumbled. The year began tragically when running back Willie Galimore and receiver John Farrington were killed in a car accident in the early days of training camp. The Bears finished sixth in the Western Conference with a 5-9 record.

In 1965, Chicago's defense featured capable, if not All-Pro, veterans in every unit—ends Doug Atkins and Ed O'Bradovich, tackle Earl Leggett, linebacker Joe Fortunato, cornerbacks Bennie McRae and Dave Whitsell, and safeties Richie Petitbon and Rosey Taylor. The Bears offense returned fullback Ronnie Bull, halfback Jon Arnett, flanker Johnny Morris, and tight end Mike Ditka. And in its recent draft, Chicago selected with the draft's third and fourth picks Illinois linebacker Dick Butkus and Kansas halfback Gale Sayers.

The Bears began the new season slowly. They lost their first two games on the road to San Francisco 52-24 and then to Los Angeles 30-28. On Sunday, the Bears, who shared Wrigley Field with the baseball Cubs, would be playing their third consecutive road game. Their opponent was the team that was Chicago's natural archrival based on history and geography and that George Halas wanted to beat more than any other team--the Green Bay Packers.

* * * * *

After two games, the Packers' defense had forced 10 turnovers, and Green Bay was undefeated. The Bears badly needed a win. The Packers expected a physical battle. Games against Chicago always were. Packer veterans Bart Starr and Max McGee remembered their 1960 game in Green Bay against Chicago, which the Bears won on a last-second field goal, as the toughest they had ever played.

On a sunny but chilly afternoon at Lambeau Field, it was a game of two halves. In their first possession, the Bears reached the Green Bay eight-yard line. Ron Kostelnik raced through a crease in the Bears' line and grabbed Bill Wade's arm before the quarterback could hand off. Wade fumbled, and Henry Jordan recovered. George Halas screamed that Kostelnik must have been offsides. The Packers mounted a 14-play drive. Paul Horning scored on a one-yard dive, and Green Bay led 7-0.

On Chicago's next offensive play, Wade wanted to pass. Kostelnik again stormed into the Chicago backfield, hitting Wade's right arm as the quarterback was throwing downfield. The ball wobbled. Linebacker Lee Roy Caffey intercepted the pass and ran 42 yards for a touchdown. As the first quarter ended, the Packers were ahead 14-0. In the second quarter, Green Bay began a drive at its own two-yard line and scored largely on two plays. After Jim Taylor's juggling 41-yard catch, Starr threw a 48-yard touchdown pass to Bob Long. Though Dick Butkus blocked Chandler's extra-point attempt, the first half ended with Green Bay leading 20-0.

At halftime, George Halas replaced Bill Wade at quarterback with Rudy Bukich, who had a quicker release. On their opening drive in the second half, the Bears moved easily down the field. Bukich threw a six-yard touchdown pass to Johnny Morris, but the Bears were called for offensive holding, negating the score. The penalty was questionable. On fourth down, Chicago had the ball at Green Bay's 10-yard line. Bukich threw into the end zone for Andy Livingston. The pass fell incomplete, and the Bears turned the ball over on downs. Paul Hornung then caught Starr's pass at midfield and was finally tackled at the Chicago 17 for a 61-yard gain. Green Bay kicked a field goal and seemed comfortably ahead 23-0.

But the Bears refused to quit, driving 80 yards with big runs by Andy Livingston and Sayers. At the Green Bay six, Sayers tried to run inside and then darted to the outside, racing past every Packer to the end zone. With a quarter remaining, Chicago trailed 23-7. The Bears threatened again but were stopped at Green Bay's five-yard line when Lee Roy Caffey knocked the ball loose from Bukich on fourth down. With seconds left in the game, Sayers caught a 65-yard touchdown pass. The final score was 23-14.

Though the Packers won, Vince Lombardi was irate and could be heard screaming. He ordered reporters standing outside his team's locker room to move to a more distant location and kept waiting a television reporter expecting to interview the winning coach. When Lombardi finally appeared, Lee Remmel in the *Green Bay Press-Gazette* noted that he was "wearing a dark scowl." The coach berated his team's second-half effort. "I guess we felt we had a couple of touchdowns and we could take a vacation." Still in a foul mood on Monday, Lombardi criticized even Packer fans for being too quiet.

The Bears made key mistakes against a good football team—they were stopped twice on downs near the Green Bay goal line, had two costly turnovers, and had a touchdown called back on a disputed holding penalty. But statistically, Chicago dominated—the Bears had 23 first downs to Green Bay's 14. After Chandler's third-quarter field goal, the Bears outgained Green Bay 229 yards to 49. Despite the loss and the 0-3 start, George Halas's tone was uplifting: "I told the boys at halftime that the score up there was a phony." Halas added, "This could be the real beginning of a good ball club. We've got that offense going now, and the defense is taking shape." Indeed, in the second half at Lambeau Field, Chicago's season turned. Its play was a message to other teams that, despite their record, the Bears were a dangerous team and should not be counted out. And certainly, a reason for optimism was Gale Sayers, who finally received meaningful playing time and rewarded Halas with 184 yards running and catching passes. "Sayers put on one of the finest performances ever seen by a rookie here," wrote Art Daley in the *Press-Gazette*. Asked about Sayers, Max McGee, always quick with insightful humor, answered, "That guy can run faster than anyone else in the league—backwards."

* * * * *

San Francisco, Baltimore's next opponent, was originally a member of the All-America Football Conference and entered the NFL in 1950 with two other AAFC teams when the two pro football leagues merged. After going 7-6-1 in 1961, the 49ers had three straight losing seasons. But in 1965, after two games, the 49ers were undefeated. The reason was arguably the league's most talented offense, which in two weeks scored 79 points. Quarterback John Brodie, picked third in the 1957 draft before Jim Brown and Len Dawson, was known for both his talented arm and inconsistency. In its September NFL preview, *Sports Illustrated* called Brodie "a beautiful passer who tends to come apart in important games." The team had two powerful 220-pound running backs—rookie Ken Willard and veteran John David Crow. North Carolina's Willard was selected second in the 1965 draft ahead of Butkus and Sayers. Crow, who played at Texas A&M for Bear Bryant, was the second pick in the 1958 NFL draft and had been named several times to Pro Bowl teams. Brodie's receivers were Bernie Casey, tight end Monty Stickles, and Dave Parks, all first-round picks. A big and strong Texan, Parks was the first player picked in the 1964 draft; as a rookie, he averaged nearly 20 yards per catch and scored eight touchdowns. And the 49ers had a solid offensive line, anchored by Walt Rock and Howard Mudd. The Colts playing at home were favored by 12 points, but their defense would be challenged. Confident in their offense, the 49ers believed that they would win if their defense held Baltimore to 20 or fewer points.

On a windy Baltimore afternoon at Memorial Stadium, the Colts jumped out to an early 10-0 lead. On the opening kickoff, San Francisco attempted an onside kick. Alex Hawkins recovered for the Colts, and Baltimore kicked a field goal. Later in the first quarter, Lenny Moore made a leaping 42-yard catch at the San Francisco three-yard line and then scored on a run around right end.

Midway through the second quarter, Brodie threw to Bernie Casey at the sideline. Bobby Boyd jumped in front of Casey, intercepting the pass; he ran down the sideline 17 yards for a touchdown, putting Baltimore ahead 17-0. San

Francisco finally scored when Lenny Lyles misjudged a long pass, allowing Dave Parks to catch a 53-yard touchdown. With 29 seconds left in the second quarter, Unitas threw a one-yard flare pass to Moore for his second touchdown. At the half, Baltimore seemed in charge 24-7. But on the last play of the first half, Lenny Lyles sprained his knee and could not return. He was replaced by Alvin Haymond, a second-year player who was 25 pounds smaller than Dave Parks.

In the second half, the 49ers targeted backup cornerback Haymond. Parks caught a 45-yard touchdown pass, reducing Baltimore's margin to 24-14. In the fourth quarter, the teams exchanged field goals before John David Crow on an option play threw long to Parks. The 49er wideout outmuscled Alvin Haymond for the ball and stumbled into the end zone for a 46-yard touchdown. Baltimore's lead was cut to 27-24. With three minutes left, Unitas, under a heavy pass rush, was hit as he tried to throw the ball out of bounds. San Francisco cornerback Jimmy Johnson intercepted the wayward pass. The 49ers suddenly had the ball at midfield and a chance to win. But the Colts defense held, and Baltimore held on.

Even in defeat, Dave Parks, catching nine passes for 231 yards and three touchdowns, was voted the Associated Press's Offensive Player of the Week. Bobby Boyd held Casey to only one catch, scored a touchdown on an interception, and made several key tackles. He was named Defensive Player of the Week. "I'm always pleased when we win," noted a grim-faced Don Shula, "but I must admit I'm disappointed in some of our play. We had chances to blow the game open in the third period, but we didn't do it." The Baltimore defense limited the 49ers to 15 first downs and 39 rushing yards but gave up too many big passing plays. In the Colts locker room, Unitas, with a badly sprained right shoulder, could not shave with his right hand. After the game, 49ers head coach Jack Christiansen admitted that Unitas's shoulder injury shaped his team's aggressive defensive game plan. "We always try to kill the quarterback," he said.

* * * * *

Five days after playing the Colts in Baltimore, the 49ers again flew across the country for a Week Four game against Green Bay. Still upset over his team's second-half play against Chicago, Lombardi pushed the Packers in practices during the week. He ordered full-team drills on Tuesday, usually an easy day. On Sunday, the early October weather was sunny and 60 degrees. The Lambeau Field crowd, admonished by Lombardi days earlier for being too tame, was lively.

On its third series of the game, Green Bay faced fourth down and four at its own 45 and prepared to punt. Having seen on game film that the 49ers' punt return team retreated quickly to block for a return, punter Don Chandler began running to his right and gained 27 yards. Chandler, who had played halfback at Florida a decade earlier, later delighted reporters by repeating Max McGee's quip that the punter's jaunt "was the only run in football history where television broke off for a minute commercial and came back for the finish of the play." He added that if he had not made a first down, "I would have kept running right into the dressing room." After Chandler's dash, Bob Long faked an inside move and darted to the corner of the end zone, catching Starr's 23-yard touchdown pass. At the end of the first quarter, Green Bay led 7-0.

In the second period, the Packers were called for defensive pass interference at their one-yard line. San Francisco, stopped for no gain on three straight runs, finally scored on fourth down on Brodie's pass to tight end Monte Stickles, tying the game. Adding two field goals, the Packers were ahead at halftime 13-7.

In the second half, Green Bay showed it was the better team. With 5:41 left in the third period, Starr threw a nine-yard touchdown pass to Marv Fleming, finishing a 10-play drive. On the third quarter's last play, Taylor gained 35 yards running the Packers' power sweep, and Green Bay had the ball at the 49ers' two-yard line and a 20-10 lead. On the next play, Paul Hornung, running behind Fuzzy Thurston, scored. And Don Chandler produced more heroics. Standing in his own end zone, Chandler punted. Pushed by the wind, the ball trickled into the San Francisco end zone for a 90-yard punt. Shutting down one of the league's hottest offenses, Green Bay won 27-10.

After the game, Lombardi seemed content and even saluted the Green Bay fans for their support. Though declining to say the Packers had played a "complete game," he conceded that this was "our best overall effort of the season." On Monday, he applauded his team. "We had determination," said Lombardi, praising his team's goal-line defense. Against the 49ers, Bart Starr was typically productive with 17 completions in 27 attempts and two touchdowns. His lone interception was his first in 298 throws. In his postgame comments, San Francisco's head coach Jack Christiansen praised Starr: "He is so close to Johnny Unitas as anyone I've seen in running an offense, picking flaws in the defense and calling the right plays at the right time."

* * * * *

Baltimore's next opponent was undefeated Detroit at Memorial Stadium on October 10. Baltimore center Dick Szymanski would be returning. In their first three games, the Lions on defense had been outstanding with 11 interceptions and 12 quarterback sacks. But Baltimore, with better balance, was favored by nine points.

Playing for the third time at home with over 60,000 fans filling Memorial, the Colts exploded in the first half. On Baltimore's first series, Unitas hit Jimmy Orr on three straight passes, including a 17-yard touchdown. On their second series, the Colts in five plays scored with Unitas completing his next three passes to Orr, whose 32-yard touchdown catch pushed the Colts ahead 14-0. In the second quarter, after Wendell Harris intercepted Milt Plum, Jerry Hill muscled through Lion defenders for a six-yard touchdown run. Unitas later threw a 35-yard touchdown pass to John Mackey, who caught the ball near his knees at the Detroit 10 and then ran into the end zone. At the half, Baltimore led 31-0.

Though the Lions scored eventually in the third quarter, the game after two quarters was over. The final score was 31-7.

The Baltimore defense held the Lions to 155 total net yards and intercepted Detroit quarterbacks four times. Completing 18 of 24 passes for 319 yards and throwing three touchdowns, Unitas was named the league's Offensive Player of the Week, and the *Baltimore Sun* reported that incredibly he received his first game ball as a Colt. Guarding Jimmy Orr, Detroit defensive halfback Bobby Thompson played soft coverage, hoping to prevent big plays downfield, and gave up both short passes and big plays. Catching nine passes for 167 yards and two touchdowns, Orr credited his success to "skullduggery and John Unitas." Both Orr and Thompson raved over Unitas's ball placement. Unlike last week's narrow win over San Francisco, Don Shula offered only praise with perspective. "It was an almost perfect offensive and defensive effort in the first half." He added, "In the second half, Detroit played better. You can't expect to crush a team with the good defense Detroit has."

On their front page on Monday, both the *Baltimore Sun* and the *Detroit Free Press* featured the Los Angeles Dodgers tying their World Series with the Minnesota Twins but failed to mention Sunday's Colts-Lions game. With its best-of-seven drama, the World Series attracted the country's attention, and many newspapers in major league baseball cities still favored in their sports coverage baseball with its 162-game schedule and unrushed pace.

* * * * *

In Week Five on October 17, Green Bay played the Lions at Detroit. For 13 straight years through 1963, the Packers played in Detroit on Thanksgiving Day. It was a holiday tradition the Packers were eager to forsake. The bad blood between the Packers and Lions lacked the long history, though not the intensity, of Green Bay's rivalry with Chicago. In recent years, defense was the Lions' strength and pride. Older Packers still remembered their sole loss in 1962, a beating in Detroit on Thanksgiving Day when Starr was sacked nine times, Green Bay turned the ball over five times, and the *Green Bay Press-Gazette* wrote that the "Lions seemed to be in a frenzy." The Packers had come to expect Detroit's best game, especially from star defensive tackle Alex Karras who repeatedly professed his hatred of Green Bay. Though the Lions were just routed by Baltimore, their record was still 3-1. With a win on Sunday, Detroit could move into a tie for first place in the conference. Both teams had injured players. For the Packers, Ray Nitschke could not play, and Lee Roy Caffey was moved to middle linebacker.

The game was a sellout. On a cloudy afternoon when the temperature reached 68 degrees, nearly 57,000 fans jammed Detroit's Tiger Stadium. Once called Navin Field and then Briggs Stadium, the old stadium was shorn of comfort but replete with history. The baseball Tigers with Ty Cobb began playing in 1912 at the Corktown neighborhood field where Babe Ruth hit his longest home run, Lou Gehrig battling a dreaded disease finally missed a game and ended his streak of 2,130 consecutive games, Joe Louis defended his heavyweight boxing crown, and the Lions won two NFL titles.

In the opening minutes, Tom Brown intercepted a Milt Plum pass tipped by Willie Wood. The early turnover was one of Green Bay's few highlights in the first half. Starting at the Detroit 30-yard line, the Packers lost yards, and Chandler kicked a 49-yard field goal for a 3-0 lead.

In the next nine minutes, the Lions scored three touchdowns. Ending an 80-yard drive, Milt Plum pitched a 14-yard touchdown pass to tight end Ron Kramer, the former Packer, in the corner of the end zone. On Green Bay's next series, defensive tackle Roger Brown deflected Bart Starr's pass. The ball flopped upward to linebacker Wayne Rasmussen. With three Lions leading the way, Rasmussen ran 36 yards for a touchdown, and Detroit led 14-3. And then Terry Barr, a step ahead of Doug Hart, caught a long Plum pass over his shoulder at the Green Bay five and scored for a 55-yard touchdown. As the half ended, the Lions led 21-3. Running past Lombardi to the locker room, Detroit's defensive tackle Alex Karras taunted the Packers' coach with the score, yelling, "What do you think of that, you big fat wop!"

With his players, Lombardi in triumphant moments could be critical, proclaiming loudly their few failings, but in difficult ones encouraging. At halftime in the Green Bay locker room, he refrained from angry rebukes, and the Packer coaches made their game adjustments. Just before his team re-entered the field, Lombardi was reassuring: "You're all Packers, and you've got your pride. Stay in there, and things will work out for you."

After intermission, the Packers began using three wide receivers and putting their halfbacks in motion to slow Detroit's pass rush. Seeing Detroit cornerback Jimmy Hill limping after a second-quarter groin injury, Starr began throwing to the receiver Hill was trying to cover. Hill's history with Green Bay was a notorious one. In 1963, when then playing for the St. Louis Cardinals, Hill knocked Starr hard out of bounds on the Cardinals sideline. The quarterback fell awkwardly. Trying to brace for his fall, Starr fractured his right hand, and his foot inadvertently hit the defender. Hill then punched Starr in the face while he was lying on the ground.

In the third quarter, Starr completed on the first play from scrimmage a 19-yard pass to Bob Long and on the second play a 62-yard touchdown to Long down the left sideline. The score was now 21-10. On Green Bay's second series, Starr threw a 31-yard touchdown pass over the middle to Tom Moore, cutting Detroit's lead to 21-17. On the Packers' next series, on a third-and-two play with Lion defenders expecting a run, Starr threw his third touchdown pass of the quarter, a short toss to an open Carroll Dale who raced down the field for a 77-yard score. After three quarters, Green Bay led 24-21.

With five minutes remaining, Detroit defensive back Bruce Maher was penalized for hitting Marv Fleming late. When a Lions' assistant coach ran onto the field to protest, a second 15-yard penalty was called against the Lions. The Detroit fans, as enraged as Maher, loudly booed and delayed the game for five minutes. With 2:33 left, the Packers still led by only a field goal but had the ball on Detroit's four-yard line. Starr called a bootleg. Faking a handoff, he ran untouched around right end for the game's final score. Trailing by 18 points at halftime, the Packers won 31-21.

"This was the Packers' finest hour," wrote Art Daley in the *Green Bay Press-Gazette*. In the first half, the Lions outgained Green Bay 209 yards to 71; in the second half, the Packers had 301 yards to Detroit's 87. Leading the comeback, Starr completed 15 of 23 passes for 301 yards and three touchdowns and ran for a fourth touchdown. After the game, smiling broadly, Lombardi said simply, "The Packers have pride," citing a venerable virtue stressed on day one of training camp and throughout the season. The Packers' head coach lauded his quarterback's poise and play: "Starr had himself a great, great game." In the victors' locker room, Bart Starr admitted, "That's probably the best half I've ever had."

* * * * *

Bart Starr's climb to becoming the quarterback of the Green Bay Packers had been steep, hindered by a quiet temperament that obscured his drive to excel and marked by doubters and at times self-doubt. He was born in Montgomery, Alabama, and named Bryan Bartlett. He was the older of two boys. His father Ben, part Cherokee, was a hard man—his parents died when he was young, and he dropped out of school before finding a home in the Army National Guard. The father visibly favored Bart's younger brother Hilton, called Bubba, who was aggressive and outgoing and seemed fearless. When Bubba was 11, running through a field, he cut his foot on a dog bone, caught tetanus, and died three days later. A week later, the father, then a noncommissioned officer in the Air Force, left home to start a tour in Japan. Bart was 13. Over time, Bart's father, twisted by tragedy, would tell his older son that he could never do what Bubba would have done because he lacked his brother's courage.

Despite his father's misgivings, Bart was an accomplished athlete. At Montgomery's Sidney Lanier High School, he was named an All-State quarterback and was recruited by nearly every SEC school. Because his girlfriend Cherry would be attending Auburn University, Bart chose the University of Alabama in Tuscaloosa, only hours from Auburn. The high point of his college years was his elopement with Cherry. A different college experience was a brutal club initiation.

Starr was so severely paddled that he was hospitalized and suffered a permanent back injury that would later disqualify him from military service. In football, Starr as a sophomore started as Alabama's quarterback and finished second in the nation in punting behind Georgia's Zeke Bratkowski. But in his senior year, a new head coach favored younger players, Starr played little, and the Crimson Tide lost every game. In the 1956 draft, the Packers picked Starr in the 17th round. Johnny Dee, Alabama's head basketball coach and a football assistant, had recommended Starr to Green Bay personnel director Jack Vainisi, his former Notre Dame teammate.

In his first three years in Green Bay, Starr occasionally played quarterback and frequently watched Green Bay lose. The 1959 season brought a new coach, Vince Lombardi, who immediately impressed Starr with his discipline and drive to win. Lombardi was less impressed by Starr. Questioning whether Starr was assertive and confident enough to be his quarterback, Lombardi confided in *Green Bay Press-Gazette* beat reporter Art Daley that Starr seemed "so prissy." In his first year, Lombardi traded with the Chicago Cardinals for quarterback Lamar McHan, who had a strong arm and a brash personality. In 1959, McHan started the first seven games before he injured his leg against Chicago. Replacing McHan, Starr produced better passing numbers, and Green Bay won its last four games, finishing with a 7-5 record. But Starr's play did not quell Lombardi's doubts.

In 1960, after the Packers lost their season opener, Lombardi benched Starr for McHan. But completing only four of 16 passes in the season's fifth game against Pittsburgh, the volatile McHan, leaving the field, threw his helmet at Lombardi's feet. "Vince, send someone else in," McHan yelled in a tirade with profanities. "These guys aren't playing for me." Replacing McHan, Starr led the Packers to a comeback 19-13 win. At a Green Bay area supper club that night, McHan, drinking heavily, accosted Lombardi. He stuck his finger in the coach's chest and called him a "dago." With only two quarterbacks on the roster and the Packers fighting for a championship, Lombardi would not trade McHan until the

1960 season ended. But in the days after the McHan confrontation, Lombardi summoned Starr to his office. "After the way you brought us back yesterday, you're my quarterback," Lombardi said. "And I'm not changing again." That season, Green Bay won the Western Conference but narrowly lost to Philadelphia in the Championship Game.

In 1961, Lombardi still questioned Starr and tried to trade for Dallas quarterback Don Meredith. But that season, Starr silenced those doubting his toughness and leadership. In an early-season game against Chicago, Bears linebacker Bill George intentionally hit Starr with his forearm, knocking him to the ground and splitting open his upper lip with the gash extending to his nose. Standing over the prone quarterback, George loudly taunted, "That ought to take care of you, Starr, you pussy." Jumping to his feet, Starr responded with a rare obscenity and pointed his finger at the linebacker. "Bill George, we're coming after you!" he shouted. Bleeding badly, Starr refused his teammates' pleas to get medical attention on the sideline and led the Packers down the field for a touchdown and a 24-0 win.

The Packers finished the 1961 season 11-3 and embarrassed the New York Giants 37-0 in the NFL Championship Game. Attending the game was Bart's father, Ben. After the game, Ben Starr hugged Bart. "I was wrong, son," he whispered. So ultimately was Vince Lombardi. Starr was selected to the Pro Bowl each year from 1960 through 1962, and nearly every season, he ranked high in the statistical categories for quarterbacks, especially with his high completion percentage and few interceptions. Starr could be cautious, more reluctant certainly than Johnny Unitas to throw to tightly covered receivers downfield. But what made Starr special was his total command of Lombardi's offense and game plans achieved through preparation and practice, his astute calling of plays in the huddle, and his reading of defenses and making of audible calls as he stood behind the center. Reserved and sensitive, Starr was different in personality from his boisterous head coach. Favoring Sunday services at Green Bay's First United Methodist Church and shunning beers after practice, he was distant off the field from some teammates. But through what he did on the football field, he earned the respect of his head coach, his team, and opposing players, especially his Baltimore counterpart, Johnny Unitas.

* * * * *

With a 3-1 record, Baltimore traveled to Washington to play the Redskins in Week Five. Entering the NFL in 1932 as the Boston Braves, the Redskins in 1937 moved to Washington. George Preston Marshall, their long-time owner, suffered a serious stroke in 1963. A shameless promoter with a colorful personality and a notorious defender of segregation, Marshall had long refused to have Blacks playing for his Redskins, the team representing and playing in the nation's capital. After the 1961 season, the United States Department of the Interior in the new Kennedy administration told Marshall that unless the Redskins agreed to integrate, they could not play at newly built District of Columbia Stadium, located on land owned and controlled by the federal government. Needing a stadium, Marshall finally relented. In 1962, the Redskins traded their rights to recently drafted Ernie Davis to Cleveland for Bobby Mitchell. Though successful in the 1930s and early 1940s, Washington had not won an NFL championship since 1942 and had not had a winning season since 1955. With Marshall's health poor since his stroke, the Redskins were an organization in transition.

Winless in four games, Washington overall did not have enough talent or good coaching. But the Redskins could score points with quarterback Sonny Jurgensen, halfback Charley Taylor, and flanker Bobby Mitchell. Washington's 1964 draft was sensational with the Redskins picking Taylor high in the first round and Iowa safety Paul Krause in the second. In the voting for Rookie of the Year, Taylor finished first and Krause second. At six-foot-three and 210 pounds, Charley Taylor in his first year ran and caught passes for 1,569 yards and 10 touchdowns. He was voted second-team All-Pro.

Krause was one of Michigan's most legendary high school athletes. Playing at Flint's Bendle High School, he earned 14 letters in four sports and once scored 78 points in a basketball game. The six-foot-three Krause roamed passing lanes like a Yankee center fielder. As a rookie, he led the league with 12 interceptions and made first-team All-Pro. Paul Brown in Cleveland used Bobby Mitchell more as a running back than a receiver. The Redskins used Mitchell as a receiver. With his speed, he flourished. Mitchell led the league in receiving yards in both 1962 and 1963 and in receiving touchdowns in 1964.

At quarterback, Washington had Sonny Jurgensen, whose real name was Christian Adolph III. Known for his mop of reddish blond hair, Jurgensen hailed from Wilmington, North Carolina. He attended Duke where he played quarterback, punted, and set a school record for making interceptions as a defensive back. As a young player in Philadelphia, Jurgensen for three years watched Norm Van Brocklin play quarterback. In 1961, Jurgensen finally played and threw 32 touchdowns, and he was nearly named the league's Most Valuable Player. But the Eagles began to struggle. Predictably, Jurgensen became a target of Philadelphia's notoriously demanding fans. In 1964, the Eagles traded Jurgensen to Washington largely for quarterback Norm Snead. Not quite six feet in height, Jurgensen did not have a resume with championships, he drew criticism for his active nightlife, and his play could be unconventional—he once completed a long pass thrown behind his back in an exhibition game. But having played too often on poor teams with mediocre coaches, Sonny Jurgensen was perhaps the most underappreciated player in professional football. In touch, placement, and the beauty of tight spirals, Sonny Jurgenson threw a football as well as any other quarterback playing professional football.

The Colts were favored by 13 points. On a pleasant autumn afternoon with temperatures in the high-50s, over 50,000 fans packed District of Columbia Stadium, located only two miles from the nation's Capitol building. The team's new president was Edward Bennett Williams, the country's preeminent trial lawyer. Covering a Redskins game, *Sports Illustrated* noted that "[t]he team is impressive socially, if not athletically," and recorded as spectators Supreme Court justices, cabinet secretaries, and Congressional chairmen, clad in suits and ties.

In the early minutes, Sonny Jurgensen's touchdown pass to Bobby Mitchell was called back for offensive holding, and Washington missed a short field goal. With a 34-yard touchdown pass to John Mackey, the Colts led 10-0 at the end of the first quarter.

In the second quarter, after Unitas completed a 58-yard pass to Mackey, Tony Lorick scored on a 12-yard run for a 17-0 Baltimore lead. Still playing for an injured Lenny Lyles, Alvin Haymond intercepted Jurgensen's sideline throw and ran 30 yards for a touchdown, putting the Colts ahead 24-0. At the end of the first half, Jurgensen, eluding Dennis Gaubatz and Billy Ray Smith, scored on an improbable 27-yard touchdown run. But at intermission, Baltimore led 24-7.

Owning the second half, Baltimore scored two more touchdowns and held Washington scoreless. The Colts won 38-7. The score reflected more Washington's mistakes than outstanding Baltimore play. In the *Baltimore Sun,* Cameron Snyder wrote that the Colts proved that a team can win by 31 points "and not look good." But after five games, the Colts were 4-1, and Baltimore's defense had 19 quarterback sacks. For his play in Week Five, defensive end Ordell Braase was named the Associated Press's Defensive Player of the Week.

* * * * *

The Dallas Cowboys were Green Bay's next opponent. Though talented, the young Cowboys were 2-3, having lost their last three games. An expansion team in 1960, the Cowboys in their first five seasons struggled; their combined record was 18-46-4. But with patience and creativity, general manager Tex Schramm, head coach Tom Landry, and chief scout Gil Brandt were constructing a team that one day would contend. For years, aided by an IBM engineer from India, Dallas sought to use computers to evaluate college players for the NFL draft and was beginning to slowly integrate computer results in its player grades. But in late-round picks involving little risk, Dallas wisely prized potential and selected in 1964 track star Bob Hayes and Navy quarterback Roger Staubach, who faced a four-year military commitment during the Vietnam War.

Quarterback Don Meredith had a sore arm, and the Dallas offense was struggling. After five games, Green Bay led the league in scoring defense, giving up only 71 points, three points fewer than Baltimore. But the Dallas Cowboys ranked fourth in that key category, surrendering only 87 points. Dallas coach Tom Landry was building the NFL's next great defense, featuring youth and quickness with linemen Bob Lilly and George Andrie, linebackers Lee Roy Jordan and Chuck Howley, and defensive backs Cornell Green and Mel Renfro. A storyline in the game was the rivalry between Lombardi and Dallas coach Landry. With the Giants in New York, the two coaches had been colleagues but also ambitious rivals who were dramatically different in temperament, background, and coaching approach. They remained personally distant. In creativity, Landry was Lombardi's match. To counter Lombardi's offense with its zone blocking and ballcarriers running not to a designated hole but to "daylight," Landry designed his intricate flex defense that placed two defensive linemen off the line of scrimmage and stressed defenders maintaining lanes.

Played in Milwaukee at County Stadium, the October 24 game delighted only those who savored defensive football. In the *Green Bay Press-Gazette,* Art Daley called it "a throwback to grandpa's day when a single touchdown or a field goal was a day's work." There were 18 punts and 14 quarterback sacks. Starr completed four of 19 passes for 42 yards. Green Bay managed only seven first downs, and its longest play was a 17-yard pass.

At the end of the first half, Green Bay led 3-0. In the third quarter, with the Cowboys near their own end zone, Henry Jordan knocked the football out of Don Perkins' hands. Willie Davis, who had 12 tackles, recovered the loose ball at the Dallas seven. On the next play, with Jerry Kramer clearing his path, Jim Taylor swept around right end for the game's only touchdown and final score. The Packers won 13-3. Turnovers were the difference—five by Dallas and none by Green Bay.

Facing reporters after the game, Lombardi was at first philosophical and then petulant. The glow of last week's second half in Detroit was gone. "I don't give a damn about statistics as long as we win," said the Green Bay coach. Asked by a reporter whether the Packers were "lucky" to win, Lombardi abruptly ended the postgame conference. Dallas coach Landry chose to applaud his defense. "This is as good a defensive game as we have played."

* * * * *

In Lombardi's earlier years at Green Bay, the Packers' offense emphasized the game's fundamentals and power football, and the running backs and offensive line provided their team with points and its identity. In 1965, Green Bay's most consistent and deepest offensive unit was its wide receivers. At the receiver positions, the Packers stressed height and size. But seeking more speed, the team drafted Bob Long in 1964 and later traded for Carroll Dale.

The oldest and easily the most colorful in the receiver grouping was Max McGee, whose intelligence Lombardi respected and whose brittle ego he recognized. McGee used a quick wit to amuse his teammates and fend off his demanding head coach. Criticized by Lombardi in a film session for dropping an easy pass, McGee retorted, "Coach, you can get anybody off the street to make that catch. You pay me to catch the hard one." McGee was Paul Hornung's best friend and roommate. Both were known for their late hours, playboy pursuits, and daring in breaking team curfews. Raised in Texas, McGee was a football star at Tulane. Military service interrupted his football career in the mid-1950s when he flew planes in the Air Force. Though six-foot-two and 205 pounds, McGee was a reluctant blocker but a dangerous runner after the catch. At 33, he was a declining player. With his widow's peak, he looked even older. Carefree compared to his teammates, McGee saved his best efforts for the biggest games.

In lifestyle, McGee's opposite was Boyd Dowler, the team's leading receiver. His father was a teacher and coach. In high school, Dowler was an All-State performer in three sports and set a Wyoming state record in the high hurdles.

For college, he chose nearby Colorado, in part for its excellent track program. At Colorado, he played quarterback in Dallas Ward's single-wing offense, led his conference in receptions as a junior, made 10 interceptions playing defensive back, and punted averaging 43.6 yards per kick. In track, he competed in the high hurdles and ran on the school's 440-yard relay team. Selected by Green Bay in the third round in the 1959 draft, Dowler was named Rookie of the Year in Lombardi's first season as head coach. With his long strides, he lacked quickness but not speed. At six-foot-five and 220 pounds, he could physically dominate small defensive halfbacks and could play tight end as well as flanker and wide receiver. Vince Lombardi believed that Dowler, playing in an offense whose foundational play was the power sweep, was the most underrated receiver in the NFL.

* * * * *

With the Los Angeles Rams traveling to Memorial Stadium, the Colts announced that Sunday's game would be their 12th consecutive sellout. But in the days before the October 24 contest, Baltimore's owner, Carroll Rosenbloom, disclosed that he was hiring an architect for a new Baltimore stadium and that he planned to meet with the Baltimore Orioles owner about the stadium project. In the week's practices, the Colts looked tired. Both Lenny Moore and Lenny Lyles were injured and not expected to play. Though wearing a pad on his arm, Dick Szymanski was ready to start at center after his preseason fracture.

Los Angeles had a 1-4 record, and the Colts were favored by 17 points. The Rams once played in Cleveland and in 1946 moved to California. In the late 1940s and early 1950s, they featured offensive stars like Bob Waterfield, Norm Van Brocklin, Tom Fears, and Elroy "Crazylegs" Hirsch, and played in five Championship Games, winning the title in 1951. But the Rams had not had a winning season since 1958, and their once huge crowds at the Los Angeles Coliseum had thinned by half. On offense, Los Angeles could score points with quarterback Bill Munson throwing to receivers Tommy McDonald and Jack Snow and handing off to halfback Dick

Bass. But the Rams' real strength was football's most imposing defensive line with Deacon Jones, Merlin Olsen, Rosey Grier, and Lamar Lundy. On average, they were 30 pounds bigger than Baltimore's offensive linemen.

Against the Rams, the Colts proved they could come back to win. Los Angeles controlled the first quarter. On the first play from scrimmage, Munson completed a 42-yard pass to a waiting Jack Snow, who with a better throw would have easily scored a touchdown. The Rams settled for a field goal and a 3-0 lead. In the second quarter, Unitas found Berry standing alone near the goal line for an eight-yard touchdown pass and later ran 18 yards on a bootleg play for Baltimore's second touchdown. Baltimore led 14-3. But at the end of the first half, the Rams drove 66 yards and scored on Munson's short pass to Tommy McDonald, cutting the Colts' lead to 14-10.

Early in the second half, McDonald made a leaping seven-yard touchdown catch in the end zone, giving Los Angeles a 17-14 lead. Kicking a field goal, the Rams were ahead 20-14 as the third quarter ended. But the Colts dominated the fourth period. Running behind Jim Parker, Tom Matte crashed into the end zone from the one, and Unitas threw a 15-yard touchdown to Jimmy Orr, who, pushed out of the end zone, landed on top of a baseball dugout. "I saw a pretty girl there I wanted to get a look at," he later explained.

With 34 seconds left, the Colts led 28-20, but Unitas found Orr again for a 25-yard touchdown throw. On the sideline, Los Angeles's head coach, Harland Svare, and a Rams assistant made threatening gestures towards Baltimore's coaches. Leaving the field, Svare confronted Shula.

Baltimore won easily 35-20 and outdistanced Los Angeles in most statistical categories—26 first downs to 13 and 356 total yards to 226. Though sacked five times and hit constantly, Unitas completed 18 of 27 pass attempts for 251 yards and threw three touchdowns. In his *News American* column, John Steadman wrote, "Unitas can do more with less than any quarterback who ever played the game of football."

After the game, Baltimore's veteran offensive linemen praised the Rams' defensive front. Tackle George Preas struggled against Deacon Jones and marveled at his quickness. Praising Merlin Olsen's strength, guard Alex Sandusky said Olsen several times "picked me completely off my feet." In the Rams' locker room, head coach Harland Svare was still angry over Baltimore's last touchdown. The game headline in the *Baltimore Evening Sun* read "Last TD, Not Colts' Win, Irks Ram Coach." And the Los Angeles coach complained about the crowd noise at Memorial Stadium and his team's nine penalties. For excessive fan noise when the visiting team had the ball, an NFL rule allowed officials, after warnings, to take timeouts from and even penalize for delay of game the home team. Svare argued that in Baltimore visiting offensive players often could not hear their quarterback's snap counts. Worse, he charged that in Baltimore and Chicago, fans intimidated NFL officials. For criticizing its officiating crews, the league fined Svare $1,000.

* * * * *

For their final game in October, Week Seven in the 1965 season, the Colts traveled to San Francisco for a rematch with the 49ers. After their first encounter four weeks earlier, receiver Dave Parks boasted, "We should have won it. We will next time." Though their record was 3-3, the 49ers were averaging 33 points per game, and Parks was the league's second leading receiver with five touchdowns. The Colts were six-point favorites.

The game was played on a chilly afternoon in Kezar Stadium with seagulls engulfing the stadium and 45,827 fans attending, the 49ers' biggest crowd of the year. In the first half, the league changed hands four times. John Brodie threw touchdown passes to Bernie Casey and fullback Ken Willard, who also rushed for a score. The 49ers led 21-10. With 4:47 remaining in the second quarter, the Colts began an 82-yard drive. With less than a minute left before halftime, Baltimore's Tony Lorick caught a screen pass and ran 31 yards for a score. But San Francisco was still ahead 21-17.

In the third quarter and early in the fourth quarter, Baltimore kicked a field goal, and Unitas threw two touchdown passes to Jimmy Orr. The Colts seemed comfortably in charge

34-21. The 49ers would suffer greater misfortune. Linebackers Dennis Gaubatz and Steve Stonebreaker hit John Brodie as he was running near Baltimore's goal line, separating the quarterback's shoulder. But Brodie's replacement, George Mira, threw a three-yard touchdown pass to John David Crow, slicing Baltimore's lead to 34-28. There were still three minutes remaining. The 49ers forced the Colts to punt. The scoreboard clock read 1:24. San Francisco had one last chance to win. With Mira at quarterback, the 49ers drove 66 yards to the Baltimore 16, but only three seconds were left. On the game's final play, Billy Ray Smith hit Mira from behind, knocking the ball loose and preserving a Baltimore win.

The Colts looked uninspired, and the 49ers played hard. John Mackey praised their hard hitting: "I think they are the toughest team we play." And playing against a top offense, Baltimore's defense struggled, giving up 26 first downs and 443 total yards of offense. Despite two wins, both Don Shula and owner Carroll Rosenbloom expressed relief that the Colts would not be playing San Francisco again. Fortunately, for Baltimore, Johnny Unitas was again superb. Though harassed often by 49er defenders Dave Wilcox and Charlie Krueger, he completed 23 of 34 passes for 324 yards and four touchdowns.

* * * * *

Against Dallas, the Packers looked flat and were fortunate to win. In Week Seven, their opponent in a return match was the resurgent Chicago Bears, though at Wrigley Field. A Chicago writer wrote that the Packers were "incredibly inept, incredibly lucky, and incredibly still unbeaten." For an Art Daley story, a *Green Bay Press-Gazette* headline asked, "How Good Are the Packers?" Daley concluded they "were just as good as they had to be." The Packers were winning with great defense, holding opponents to a league-best 12 points per game and leading in turnover differential.

On Sunday, Green Bay was playing a team that some believed was the most dangerous in football, outscoring opponents in its last three games 114 points to 53. Rudy Bukich replaced Bill Wade at quarterback in game three against Green

Bay. Playing at 35 with his fourth team, he was suddenly in statistical rankings the league's leading passer, throwing 12 touchdowns and only one interception. Because of their terrible start, the Bears trailed Green Bay by three games in the Western Conference standings. Underscoring the game's importance to the Bears, coach George Halas closed his team's practices. "We play Green Bay next Sunday," he explained. "And I'm not telling anybody anything."

The Packers arrived in Chicago as slight favorites. On a cool and sunny day, a sellout crowd of 45,664 jammed Wrigley Field. It was a typical Chicago Bears game where quarterbacks did not run out of bounds and defensive players targeted running backs and receivers lying on the field. On the game's opening drive, Bart Starr ran 33 yards down the right sideline to the Chicago 14 where defensive back Roosevelt Taylor violently knocked Starr out of bounds. The shaken quarterback briefly left the game. The Packers made a first down at the Chicago three-yard line. On fourth down, Jimmy Taylor dove over the line for a one-yard touchdown. Green Bay took an early 7-0 lead.

In the first minute of the second quarter, Chicago kicked a 24-yard field goal, making the score 7-3. In the quarter's final minutes, disaster struck Green Bay. Starr's pass hit Bear Earl Leggett's helmet and bounced into the hands of Doug Atkins. Chicago had the ball at the Green Bay 43. Four plays later, receiver Jimmy Jones turned around Doug Hart and caught a 13-yard touchdown pass. Moments later, Starr overthrew Boyd Dowler and was intercepted again. In the space of 84 seconds, the Bears scored their second touchdown when Gale Sayers ran 10 yards around right end untouched. Chandler kicked a 43-yard field goal with a minute remaining in the half, but Chicago still led 17-10.

The Packers would not score again, and the Bears would score twice more. In the third quarter, returning a punt, Gale Sayers with the ball in his left hand ran down the sideline, stepping high and exploding past Packers. He cut to his right between two Packers who collided. Sayers was finally tackled at the Packers' 15-yard line for a 62-yard return. Defenders on the field constantly misjudged how fast he was. Three plays later, slanting off left tackle, Jon Arnett scored from the Green Bay two. The Bears led 24-10. In the final quarter, after eight straight Arnett runs, Ronnie Bull on a pitch play turned the left corner and broke tackles for a four-yard touchdown run. Trailing by three touchdowns, Lombardi replaced ailing quarterback Bart Starr. Losing 31-10, the Packers retreated from the field to their locker room. Bear fans near their walkway screamed curses and insults.

In the second half, Green Bay's offense gained only 58 yards and could advance no further than its own 35-yard line. Playing with a sore shoulder and ribs after Rosey Taylor's first-quarter takedown, Bart Starr passed for only 94 yards and threw three interceptions. "I shot at him pretty hard, hoping I could sting him a little," exulted Rosey Taylor in the jubilant Bears locker room. "I guess I succeeded." After the game, Packer Jerry Kramer thought his team had played too cautiously, unlike the Bears who "had nothing to lose" and played "loose." "They were jumping around and strutting out there like crazy." But both Lombardi and Chicago tight end Mike Ditka told reporters that the current Bears team with its explosive offense was better than the 1963 Chicago team that won an NFL championship.

With Chicago's critical win, the Packers and the Colts were both 6-1 and tied for first place in the Western Conference. A *Press-Gazette* headline read, "Pick Champion in the West? Could Be Pack, 4 Others." The Bears, Detroit, and Minnesota were only two games behind, and Chicago would play Baltimore twice. And as Art Daley wrote, the 49ers were only three games back and could contend if they found "a defense to match their high-geared offense." In the race for the Western Conference, seven games remained.

Western Conference – October 31, 1965							
	W	L	T	PCT	PF	PA	PD
Baltimore	6	1	0	.857	217	122	95
Green Bay	6	1	0	.857	165	105	60
Chicago	4	3	0	.571	211	168	43
Minnesota	4	3	0	.571	229	218	11
Detroit	4	3	0	.571	134	146	-12
San Francisco	3	4	0	.429	227	192	35
Los Angeles	1	6	0	.143	119	228	-109

8
November: The Colts Surge

In Chicago, the league's two hottest teams would play on November 7. Baltimore had won its last five games and Chicago its last four, driven by its first-year stars, Dick Butkus and Gale Sayers. The two were competing for Rookie of the Year honors. Offering historical perspective with a fondness for former Bear players, George Halas called Butkus and Sayers "the two best rookies since 1940 when we signed George McAfee and Bulldog Turner." Others in the league thought they were the best first-year players who had ever played.

On a team known for decades for tough defense, Dick Butkus in his first year became, for many, football's most feared defender. Like the Packers' Ray Nitschke, the linebacker to whom he would often be compared, Dick Butkus was Chicago tough—in high school, Butkus was so physically dominant that his coaches would not let him scrimmage against his teammates. At birth, Butkus weighed 13 pounds and six ounces. Growing up on Chicago's South Side, he was the youngest of eight children and shared a small bedroom with four brothers. His father, a Lithuanian immigrant, worked as an electrician and his mother in a laundry. At Chicago Vocational High School, he played fullback as well as linebacker and one year made 70 percent of his team's tackles. Playing linebacker and center at Illinois, he was named as a junior the Big 10's Most Valuable Player and finished as a senior third in the Heisman Trophy voting, predictably behind two quarterbacks, Notre Dame's John Huarte and Tulsa's Jerry Rhome.

In the 1965 NFL draft, after the Giants and the 49ers picked respectively fullbacks Tucker Frederickson and Ken Willard, Chicago drafted Butkus third. At the 1965 College All-Star Game, the annual event where the country's best graduating seniors played the defending NFL champions, All-Star coach Otto Graham thought Butkus was the best All-Star player he had seen in his 10 years of coaching the team. Covering the game for *Sports Illustrated*, Dan Jenkins singled out Butkus: "Though he guessed wrong frequently, he was everywhere, recovering nicely and slamming ballcarriers, even Jim Brown, around like toys." Before playing against Butkus, Vince Lombardi questioned his accolades. "That Butkus guy, number 51, he doesn't look as good as I've heard," he told his team. "Looks like he's just a big stiff that will end up as a defensive tackle." Showing his players the film from Green Bay's second game against Chicago, Lombardi highlighted a play where Butkus knocked over two Packer blockers and drove Jimmy Taylor backwards. Stopping the projector, Lombardi confessed, "I was wrong about that guy."

On the field, Butkus was a typhoon. His hulking presence reeked of unchecked fury. At six-foot-three and 245 pounds, he was as big as offensive tackles. In a ritual during warmups before games, to ratchet up his level of hate, Butkus would search for opposing players smiling or joking, and then tell himself they were laughing at him. The helmet seemed too small for Butkus's head, to be pinching his face, and his upper body too big for stumpy legs. Crowding the line of scrimmage, growling and cursing loudly, his eyes burning with rage, Butkus would explode on the center's snap, knocking aside offensive linemen as he aimed towards whoever had the football. And Dick Butkus wanted not just to tackle and stop the ballcarrier but to physically punish him, launching his shoulders and big torso into the runner's chest and head, and driving him backwards and then into the ground, often with one arm twisting his neck and one hand reaching for the football. He paired remarkable instincts with ferocity. Though not fast, Butkus seemed nearly always at the right place as though he had known the play that had been called.

If his Chicago teammate Dick Butkus captured the game's primal essence, Gale Sayers epitomized the sport's sublime. Off the field, Sayers was modest, his voice containing a trace of a stammer. The son of an automotive mechanic, he was born in Wichita and raised in Omaha; one brother was a star sprinter. In high school in Omaha, Gale Sayers excelled in football and track and field, setting a Nebraska state record in the long jump. At the University of Kansas, he was named to All-American teams as a junior and senior and won the sobriquet "the Kansas Comet." Though lacking Jim Brown's strength and Jim Taylor's lust for contact, Sayers was not a small scatback—he stood six-feet and weighed 198 pounds. Football scouts and coaches marveled over his speed, vision, instincts, and body control. He was a rocket with poetic grace. His runs in the open field rivaled George Balanchine's best work in the New York City Ballet. For a halfback so elusive, he ran not with kinetic escapes from side to side but with a sparseness of movement that was decisive and elegant. His cuts to avoid defenders were made seemingly at full speed. His stops were sudden. His acceleration through narrow creases was explosive. In the open field, with a gliding stride that looked effortless, he pulled away from defensive halfbacks, once confident with the angle they had. Often as he ran towards the goal line, yards ahead of everyone else, he looked backward, not to taunt opponents but to signal to his blockers to relent and not draw an unnecessary penalty.

And Sayers did more than run with the football after handoffs. He caught passes, returned punts and kickoffs, and could even pass. Every time he stepped on a field, he was targeted by defenses and coverage teams, and players who normally rested on the bench crowded the sideline to watch. Every 10 times he touched a football, he scored a touchdown. In 1965, with magic on the field that changed games and permanently engraved the memory of anyone who saw him play, Gale Sayers in his first year was the most exciting player in football.

* * * * *

Though playing Chicago at Wrigley Field, the Colts opened as two-and-a-half point favorites. By Sunday, the gambling line was even. After their torrid October ending with an easy win over Green Bay, the Bears and their fans were confident. On Sunday, the *Chicago Tribune* ran a playful headline for its game preview: "Bears Try to Stop Colts Today (or Is It Vice Versa?)." As expected, the game would be physical and marked by controversy.

The first quarter was scoreless. Marred by questionable officiating, the second quarter was eventful. When John Mackey and Bears safety Richie Petitbon battled over a Unitas pass, the officials ruled a Baltimore completion. Petitbon protested that he had caught the ball and would say that on the next play, Mackey admitted that Petitbon had made the interception. Later, the game officials ruled that linebacker Joe Fortunato had stolen the ball from Tony Lorick for an end zone interception. Both calls were suspect.

Still in the second quarter, Unitas threw a 37-yard touchdown pass to Mackey, who ran over Petitbon and past Dave Whitsell and Bennie McRae for the score. On another series, Chicago defensive end Dick Evey threw Johnny Unitas to the ground late. Fifty pounds smaller, Unitas swung at Evey, punching him in the chin. The big lineman wobbled to the Chicago bench and drew a penalty for unnecessary roughness. On the sideline, Chicago coach Halas wailed in protest. Asked after the game about Evey's departure, Unitas said, "I guess he got some sand in his eyes." Adding a field goal, the Colts led at halftime 10-0. Baltimore dominated the first half, outgaining Chicago 202-71 in total net yards.

In the third quarter, both teams would score. Unitas threw a 49-yard touchdown to Tony Lorick for a 17-0 Colts lead. But on the next series, Chicago marched 86 yards with Rudy Bukich finding Jimmy Jones on a 19-yard touchdown throw. Midway through the quarter, Doug Atkins knocked down Unitas, who left the game with back spasms. Replacement quarterback Gary Cuozzo threw an end zone pass that Chicago cornerback Whitsell tipped and that Raymond Berry held briefly before he fell out of bounds with the ball squirting loose. The back judge ruled Berry had caught the pass for a touchdown. The Bears howled that the call was wrong. Their Wrigley Field fans with thunderous booing stopped play for 10 minutes. The *Chicago Tribune* reported that Berry held the ball "no longer than a first kiss." After the game, Berry admitted surprise over the touchdown call. But the Colts led 24-7.

The Bears made a fourth-quarter run, scoring two touchdowns to narrow Baltimore's lead to 24-21. They would have one last chance, getting the ball back with 1:20 left but no timeouts at their own five-yard line. Lou Michaels ended the game, tackling Bukich in the end zone for a safety. Baltimore won 26-21.

In its Monday editions, the *Baltimore Sun* for the first time in 1965 gave a Colts game front-page coverage. Beginning his game article in the *Baltimore Evening Sun,* Jim Walker wrote: "The Colts kicked the ball to Gale Sayers, ran plays at Dick Butkus, threw passes in the direction of Bennie McRae and gambled on fourth down." He added: "Such things they weren't supposed to be able to do against the resurgent Chicago Bears, who suddenly believed they were the best team in football after their upset victory over the Green Bay Packers."

After the game, George Halas railed against the officials: "The calls in the second quarter were a comedy of errors." Baltimore's defense held the Bears to 77 rushing yards and intercepted Bukich twice. The *Baltimore Evening Sun* called the contest the year's "most bruising game." For the Colts, the win proved costly—Don Shinnick fractured his arm, Wendell Harris aggravated an ankle injury, Guy Reese hurt his knee, and Unitas could barely walk.

* * * * *

In Week Eight, Green Bay hosted Detroit at Lambeau Field. In the days before the game, Vince Lombardi, after flirting with the new Atlanta franchise about becoming its head coach and general manager, signed his third contract extension in four years with Green Bay. His new contract ran for eight years through January 1974.

Coming off a 31-7 win against the Rams, the Lions were

now 4-3 after three straight October losses. Both teams had players battling injuries. Despite bruised ribs, Starr would start. For the Lions, receiver Terry Barr with an injured knee would not play. Though kicked in the face in his last game and nursing a broken nose, defensive tackle Alex Karras would. The son of a Greek immigrant who became a physician and died young, Karras was a maverick. On and off the field, he was a throwback to the wild days of pro football in the 1950s and to Bobby Layne, his first Lions quarterback. In Detroit, Karras was warned about his associations with mobsters, and in 1963, he along with Paul Hornung was suspended for a year for betting on NFL games. Smaller than the Cowboys' Bob Lilly and the Rams' Merlin Olsen, the league's other top defensive tackles, Karras relied on quick hands and feet, violent slaps to the helmets of opposing guards, and a passion to punish quarterbacks.

On a raw November afternoon in Lambeau Field, the Packers learned that other NFL teams had pride. Remembering their second-half collapse against Green Bay three weeks earlier, the Lions' defensive players came to play for four quarters. Favored by as many as 13 points, Green Bay scored only once. The game headline in the *Green-Bay Press-Gazette* read "Packers Offense Collapses Again; Lions Win 12-7" with the subhead "Bays Limited to -58 in 2nd Half."

The Packers struck first. At 2:42 in the second quarter, on an 11-play drive, Jim Taylor scored on a one-yard run, and Green Bay led 7-0. The Lions returned the ensuing kickoff 62 yards to the Green Bay 35. Feeling no pressure in the pocket, George Izo threw a 27-pass to Pat Studstill, pushing the ball to the Packers' five-yard line. On fourth and one, with 15 seconds left in the first half, Joe Don Looney muscled his way into the end zone, tying the game 7-7.

The two offenses in the second half continued to stumble and commit turnovers--for the game, Green Bay turned the ball over three times and Detroit four times. With 4:51 remaining in the fourth quarter, the Lions kicked a 13-yard field goal for a 10-7 lead. Twenty-eight seconds later, Roger Brown sacked Starr in the Green Bay end zone for a safety and a 12-7 Detroit win.

In the second half, the Packers offense never reached midfield and lost yards on 12 of its 25 non-kicking plays. For the day, George Izo, the winning quarterback, completed six of 14 passes for 67 yards and threw three interceptions. With Jerry Kramer out, injured Fuzzy Thurston playing little, and Dan Grimm manhandled by Alex Karras, the Packers offensive line cratered. Intent on stopping Green Bay's passing offense, the Lions sacked Starr 11 times for 109 lost yards—nine times in the second half. After throwing, he repeatedly was hit. In a pileup of players, Karras twisted Starr's ankle. "What's the matter, boy," Karras taunted, "can't you take it." Karras and Wayne Walker thought the Lions on defense played even better than they did in their memorable 26-14 win over an undefeated Packers team in their 1962 Thanksgiving game. Detroit middle linebacker Joe Schmidt called the win "the best game we've played" since he entered the league in 1953. We remembered, Lions coach Harry Gilmer gloated, "the second half of that other ball game," the Lions' breakdown against Green Bay in October.

"It looks like a funeral procession," said Lombardi facing reporters after the game. "They overpowered our line." Asked about offensive line changes, Lombardi answered, "I haven't the slightest idea, unless you've got somebody. Have you got somebody? You saw what I've got."

* * * * *

After eight weeks, in total offense or yards gained, Green Bay was ranked last in the league. On Sunday, playing Los Angeles, Green Bay would be returning to Milwaukee where three weeks earlier its offense against Dallas began to flounder. After reviewing on Monday the Detroit game film, Lombardi questioned whether Starr was "bothered by mental fatigue." "We're not a relaxed offensive team," said Lombardi. "We're too tense on offense." The Packers coach noted that veteran offensive linemen Gregg and Skoronski had played well, but at right tackle Steve Wright had struggled. Though its record was 1-7, Los Angeles presented Green Bay with its suspect offensive front a glaring match-up challenge—the

Rams' hulking defensive line that dominated football's trenches and relentlessly attacked quarterbacks.

On Sunday in Milwaukee, the temperatures were near freezing, neither team scored a touchdown, and the Packers barely won. In the game's early minutes, the Rams on offense achieved their high-water mark. Tom Moore fumbled the opening kickoff. Three plays later, the Rams kicked a 35-yard field goal to lead 3-0. Missing field goal attempts in the second quarter, Los Angeles would not score again. With three minutes left in the second quarter, Don Chandler kicked a 22-yard field goal. At halftime, the game was tied 3-3.

In the third quarter, Lombardi, desperate to give the Packers' offense some spark, benched Bart Starr for Zeke Bratkowski. Both offenses continued to stagger and could not score. With two minutes left in a deadlocked game, Los Angeles quarterback Bill Munson fumbled. Lionel Aldridge recovered the loose ball for the Packers. In the final minute, Jim Taylor apparently crossed the goal line, but the officials ruled him down inches shy of the end zone. With 37 seconds left, Chandler kicked a seven-yard field goal, giving Green Bay a 6-3 win. For the first time since battling the Bears in a rainstorm in 1938, the Packers played in a game where neither team scored a touchdown.

After the second quarter's midpoint, Los Angeles never entered Packer territory. Each defense had five quarterback sacks. Once again, the Packers won because of turnovers—turning the ball over only once while recovering three Ram fumbles and intercepting Munson once. Munson threw for only 69 yards, and Starr completed four passes for 73 yards. In the *Los Angeles Times,* Mal Florence wrote that the Packers were no longer the Green Bay teams of the early 1960s but were "imitators—like substituting a medium-priced Scotch for an expensive brand name." After the game, a combative Lombardi explained why he replaced Starr with Bratkowski. "I thought it would give us a lift. We weren't doing anything with the other boy." Asked whether Starr would start against Minnesota next week, the head coach answered, "How the hell do I know? You live from day to day in this business." And always in control, Lombardi challenged a Los Angeles reporter whose question he did not like: "Are you a comedian? I don't like comedians. This isn't a funny game."

Time would not enhance Lombardi's tolerance for comics. Against the Rams, Steve Wright, a second-year offensive tackle, injured his foot and played poorly. When the players met on Tuesday morning for their team meeting with Lombardi, Wright joked with teammates about the game's low score: "Six-three, can you believe it? Batter up." But Wright failed to see that his head coach, still incensed over his team's offensive play, had just entered the room. Turning red with anger, Lombardi kicked a trash can so hard that he hurt his foot. For several minutes, Lombardi roared, often staring at Wright: "How in the hell can you be laughing and joking and happy playing the way you're playing? How can you be celebrating? How can you be pleased with your performance?"

* * * * *

In its last four games, Green Bay, despite outstanding defensive play, had scored just 36 points. But after nine weeks, the Packers defense was allowing only 13.3 points per game, three times had denied opponents a touchdown, and had 32 turnovers. Though often struggling, the Green Bay offense had turned the ball over only 14 times. Turnovers explained Green Bay's 7-2 record.

Strong in all three defensive units, Green Bay prized quickness and the ability to penetrate with its defensive linemen. Fourth-year tackle Ron Kostelnik at 260 pounds provided size and strength. The line's longtime anchors were defensive tackle Henry Jordan and defensive end Willie Davis. Jordan lost his hair early and looked a decade older than his 30 years. He and his wife Olive, a sprightly brunette who watched over the wives of younger players, were favorites in the close-knit Packers fraternity. Like Max McGee, Jordan was known for his humor and wit, though his wisecracks always made people laugh and McGee's occasionally made people wince. Liked for his unpretentious ways and respected for his stalwart play, Jordan had been a star heavyweight wrestler at Virginia. His listed weight was 250 pounds, but he often weighed less and relied on speed and experience rather than bulk. Through film study and instinct, Jordan at the line of scrimmage was a master at recognizing the tip-offs of offensive linemen, at how the amount of weight a guard placed on his left hand or how he extended his right foot signaled a run or a pass. From 1960 through 1964, Jordan each year was named first-team All-Pro.

For his fumble recovery and two sacks against Los Angeles, Lionel Aldridge was named the NFL's Defensive Player of the Week. A fourth-round draft pick in 1963, Aldridge started as a rookie for Green Bay. His childhood years were grim. He was born in 1941 in hardscrabble Avoyelles Parish in Central Louisiana. He never knew his father, his mother left the family to find work in Detroit and never returned, and he was raised by grandparents until his grandfather died. Lionel was then sent to Pittsburgh, California, outside San Francisco, to live with his uncle and aunt. He shined in several sports in high school and played football at Utah State. Articulate with a deep voice, he pursued broadcasting in the offseason, and the team's other Black players, trying to conceal their race, enlisted Aldridge to call the owners of houses and apartments they wanted to rent. But Lionel was sensitive and angered quickly. His relationship with Willie Davis, the team's popular defensive captain, was tense. Davis believed Aldridge was jealous over the media applause the veteran lineman received. It was later learned that Aldridge battled schizophrenia. A Black man, Aldridge was secretly engaged to Vicky Wankier, who was White and moved after her college graduation to Milwaukee to be near Lionel. For both, the relationship caused strain. For having a relationship with a White woman, Aldridge feared being blackballed in the league like Cookie Gilchrist years earlier. Vicky became estranged from her family in Utah and experienced disapproval from the wives of some Packer players, both White and Black.

* * * * *

In Week Nine, though Unitas was questionable, Baltimore opened as a three-point favorite over Minnesota, a hot team that had won five of its last six games. In the conference race, the Vikings were only two games behind Baltimore and a game behind Green Bay. For a Minneapolis columnist, the Baltimore showdown was Minnesota's "most important game since the Vikings joined the league in 1961." Minnesota was leading the league in rushing offense. But against the Colts, the Vikings would be missing halfback Tommy Mason, who had injured his knee a week earlier against Los Angeles, and were facing the league's top rushing defense.

On Thursday, Unitas was limited in practice, but Raymond Berry raved to reporters about how quickly third-year quarterback Gary Cuozzo, his roommate, was mastering the nuances of Baltimore's offense. On the night before the game, Shula visited Cuozzo, confirming that he would be starting at quarterback. In 1963, the Colts signed Cuozzo, who started at Virginia for three years, as an undrafted free agent. The son of a New Jersey dentist with a brother close to finishing dental school, Cuozzo at Virginia was a Phi Beta Kappa pre-med major. Though recognizing his talent and passing skills, NFL teams believed Cuozzo would be attending medical school after graduation and removed his name from their draft boards. With a decision to make at the end of his first training camp, Cuozzo approached Shula, asking whether he would make the team. Told that he would, Cuozzo called the admissions office at Yale Medical School to advise that he would not be enrolling in September as a first-year medical student. To those like the Colts team surgeon, Dr. E. J. McDonnell, who questioned his judgment, Cuozzo explained that he liked playing football. In 1964, he began during the offseason his studies at the University of Tennessee's dental school.

The game was played before a sellout Metropolitan Stadium crowd on a dreary mid-November day when the temperatures hovered at freezing and the Minnesota cheerleaders wore yellow raincoats. Minnesota controlled the football in the first quarter but could not score. In the second quarter, Fran Tarkenton, finishing an 11-play drive, fired a six-yard touchdown pass to Hal Bedsole, open in the right corner of the end zone. Minnesota led 7-0. The Colts managed a field goal.

With less than two minutes left in the half, Minnesota was still ahead 7-3 but had to punt. Catching the kick at the Baltimore 10, Alvin Haymond burst straight ahead, running past Vikings for 20 yards, and then cut left to the sideline. He was tackled at the Vikings' 34-yard line for a 56-yard return. The Colts were pushed back to the Minnesota 43. Nineteen seconds were left. On third and 19, Cuozzo threw a long touchdown pass to Jimmy Orr, who beat defensive halfback Earsell Mackbee by several yards. In the first half, Minnesota dominated statistically—16 first downs to three, 39 plays to 15, and 104 yards rushing to 20. But at halftime, the Colts led 10-7, and their defensive coaches made adjustments to stop Minnesota's running game.

In the second half, Baltimore's passing attack exploded. On the Colts' first series, Gary Cuozzo found Jimmy Orr in the end zone for a 22-yard pass and a 17-7 lead. Once again, Mackbee was the trailing defender. With the benches for both teams on the same side of the field, the Colts could hear the Vikings defensive backs coach pleading with head coach Norm Van Brocklin to switch to zone coverage from the man-to-man defense Van Brocklin favored. Van Brocklin refused his assistant's entreaties, saying he expected rookie Mackbee to compete like a man.

The Vikings fought back. Tarkenton scrambled for 36 yards and then tossed a 17-yard touchdown to Paul Flatley, cutting Baltimore's lead to 17-14. Still in the third quarter, Cuozzo threw downfield to Lenny Moore. Three steps ahead of linebacker Lonnie Warwick, Moore caught the pass at the Minnesota five and scored for a 29-yard touchdown. The Colts were ahead by two scores 24-14.

Watching Minnesota's game film, Baltimore coaches had seen that the Vikings' kickoff-return team retreated too quickly to block. On the following kickoff, the Colts surprised the Vikings with an onside kick and recovered the ball at the Minnesota 46. "Shula caught the Vikings as flatfooted as a wallflower at a Watusi dance," wrote the *Sun's* Cameron Snyder. With the Colts reaching the Vikings' six-yard line, Cuozzo ran to his left and threw across his body to Berry crossing the back of the end zone for another Baltimore touchdown. After three quarters, Baltimore led 31-14. In the final period, Cuozzo pitched his fifth touchdown pass of the game, a 14-yard strike to Willie Richardson who beat Earsell Mackbee. "That's it, Mackbee, you son of a bitch," Van Brocklin yelled, "set a record!" The final score was 41-21. The Colts were now 8-1.

As a quarterback, Van Brocklin, "the Dutchman," was feared for his remarkable arm and competitive drive. As a 38-year-old head coach, he was feared for his quick and violent temper and acid tongue. Asked after the game whether he considered pulling Mackbee, the Vikings coach answered, "No, I wanted to leave him in and let him take a good beating. Besides, everybody we put in at that position is worse than the guy who played it before him." Van Brocklin's postgame censure of his team was just as searing: "The Vikings learned today what it means to be outplayed, outhit, and outscored by a team which wanted to win a little more badly. Baltimore did that, and that's why they're contending for the Western Division championship, and we're just where we are." "People," he added, "don't know how to pay the price of greatness."

On Monday, the day after the loss, Van Brocklin summoned three newspaper reporters who covered the Vikings to his office and announced he was quitting as Minnesota's head coach. He had not told anyone with the team's management. Vikings general manager Jim Finks and owner Max Winter made urgent calls, trying to convince the mercurial Van Brocklin to return. After a late-night meeting with Finks, the Dutchman reversed his resignation decision. He apologized for the turmoil he had caused and began his preparations for Sunday's game against Green Bay.

* * * * *

The Colts' next opponent was the Philadelphia Eagles for a November 21 meeting at Memorial. Entering their 33rd year, the Eagles had three NFL championships but only 13 winning seasons and had endured three consecutive losing seasons. In his second season in Philadelphia, Joe Kuharich was the Eagles' head coach. He had earlier coached Notre Dame for four years and in South Bend never had a winning season. With their capable offense, the Eagles could be a dangerous team. With a 3-6 record, they were not a good one. On offense, Philadelphia had a veteran quarterback, Norm Snead, and three outstanding players—halfback Timmy Brown, tight end Pete Ratzlaff, and tackle Bob Brown. For the year, Tim Brown ranked second in rushing yards. He commuted weekly to New York for acting classes. Ratzlaff, a 210-pound tight end from North Dakota, had played in Pro Bowl games. At age 34, he was having his best season. The second player picked in the 1964 NFL draft, offensive tackle Bob Brown at 280 pounds was 35 pounds bigger than most offensive linemen and a mauler. As a rookie, he was named second-team All-Pro. In his second year, the talented Brown was even more dominant.

Against the Eagles, Johnny Unitas was expected to play. The Colts were favored by 15 points. On a gray day at Memorial Stadium, Lenny Moore had one of his greatest games but was overshadowed by Jimmy Orr on one play. On the opening series, Moore, leaping between two defenders, caught Unitas's downfield pass at the Philadelphia 23 and ran into the end zone for a touchdown. Jerry Logan returned a Norm Snead interception 36 yards for another score, and Baltimore took an early 14-0 lead. But the Eagles continued to fight. Snead threw a 15-yard touchdown pass to Pete Ratzlaff, and Ollie Matson scored on a three-yard scamper around left end. At halftime, the game was tied 17-17.

In the third quarter, after a short Baltimore punt, the Eagles took the lead 24-20 on a seven-yard touchdown pass to Ray Poage. Behind their offensive stars, the Colts would come back. Early in the fourth quarter, with the ball at the Eagles' one, Lenny Moore vaulted over a wall of Eagles into the end zone, and Baltimore led 27-24.

Reaching for a pass at the goal line early in the game, Jimmy Orr injured his shoulder. He quickly showered, dressed in his street clothes, and left the stadium for examination and X-rays at nearby Union Memorial Hospital. Entering the hospital's emergency room, Orr could hear the game's radio broadcast and was rushed into a waiting room for an evaluation ahead of waiting patients. When the X-ray studies were read as negative for a fracture, an assistant trainer raced Orr back to Memorial Stadium only a half mile away. With seven minutes left, Orr dressed in uniform emerged from the Orioles dugout, running towards the Colts bench. Told by trainers that Orr had returned and could play, Don Shula simply looked at Orr and pointed to the field with Baltimore's offensive unit. Baltimore fans watched the popular receiver running towards and then onto the field. They responded with a low rumble that grew into a deafening roar. Not knowing what was happening, guard Dan Sullivan standing on the field was momentarily frightened by the wild applause that became progressively louder.

On the second play after his return, the wily flanker told Unitas, "I can get the corner"—the slightly sloped right corner of the end zone on the stadium's closed end that Baltimore fans named "Orrsville" because of the many touchdowns Orr had caught there. With Eagles defensive back Al Nelson reaching for his injured right shoulder, Orr in stride caught Unitas's pass for a 22-yard touchdown. He left the field with his right arm limp at his side and the home crowd's wild applause. Afterwards, asked why he did not throw to Orr on the first play after his return, Unitas joked, "I thought he might be out of breath after running from the hospital."

The Colts won 34-24, their eighth straight victory. Lenny Moore scored two touchdowns, rushed for 54 yards, and gained another 163 yards on seven receptions. He was named the league's Offensive Player of the Week. But the game belonged to Jimmy Orr, a South Carolina native who once caught passes for the Georgia Bulldogs. Orr was small for his sport and slow in a straight dash, but with quickness when running pass routes, he exploded in and out of his breaks and seemed always open. Orr combined consistent game production with a flair for big plays. With his cheerful nature, zest for good times and quality Scotch, and charmingly thick

Southern drawl, Orr was a favorite among his teammates, whose wives adored Jimmy but were thankful they were not married to him.

The *Baltimore Evening Sun* led its game coverage with the headline "Orr's Dramatics Nail Down Colt Victory." "I saw it and I'm still not sure I believe it," wrote *Baltimore Sun* columnist Bob Maisel. In his *News American* column titled "Orr Deserves Year's Top Drama Award," John Steadman ventured that even Hollywood screenwriters, crafting a "class B" melodrama, would have dismissed Orr's return and touchdown catch as "too preposterous to believe." And guard Alex Sandusky exclaimed, "That was the most sensational thing I ever saw! I think it beats Ruth pointing to the bleachers and hitting a home run."

* * * * *

In Week 10, the Packers traveled to Minneapolis to play a 5-4 Vikings team that began the season with championship hopes and whose head coach, Norm Van Brocklin, had just abruptly quit and then changed his mind. Because of Green Bay's troubles on offense and an expectation that Viking players would rally around Van Brocklin, Minnesota at home surprisingly opened the week as a two-point favorite. Groping for improvement on offense, Lombardi ordered that the Packers' practices in the week before the game be physical. For the November 21 game, temperatures in the low 30s with the possibility of snow were predicted.

For the first three quarters, the game was close. In the first quarter, the Packers' defense, in a five-play goal-line stand, stopped Tarkenton on fourth down and inches. At 4:39 in the opening period, Minnesota kicked a field goal for an early 3-0 lead. But on fourth and one at the Minnesota 46, Starr ran for 38 yards and then threw a 15-yard touchdown pass to Carroll Dale to give the Packers a 7-3 advantage. In the second period, the teams traded field goals. At the half, Green Bay led 10-6.

At 8:35 in the third quarter, Tarkenton completed a 27-yard touchdown to Paul Flatley, and Minnesota regained the lead 13-10. But in the fourth period, helped by Minnesota turnovers, the Packer offense awakened from its month-long slumber. On the quarter's second play, Starr threw deep to Boyd Dowler, who stretching out caught the pass between two Viking defenders at the Minnesota five-yard line and scored to put Green Bay ahead 17-13. The Vikings then fumbled three times leading to three Packer touchdowns—one was a 20-yard return by defensive halfback Doug Hart who recovered Bill Brown's second fumble. The Packers won 38-13, pushing their record to 8-2.

Though Green Bay had three turnovers, Minnesota had six with four lost fumbles and two interceptions. Against the Vikings, the Packers scored more points than they had in their last four games. With his ankle injury healed, Jimmy Taylor was finally able to change direction when running and rushed for 111 yards on 25 carries. And with Forrest Gregg returning to right tackle, Starr had time to throw and passed for three touchdowns. After the game, Lombardi singled out his two veteran stars. "The big difference was having Starr and Taylor going good today. Today we had it again." Bart Starr expressed gratitude and showed humility: "I'm real grateful to Coach Lombardi for sticking with me—I stunk out the joint the last couple of weeks."

In the locker room, a jubilant Lombardi sought deeper meaning in the win. "Gentlemen, you go ahead and celebrate this one," the Packers head coach told his players. "What you're witnessing here is why winning is the only thing. It is the only thing that will make you feel like this, make you experience what you're feeling right now. It is the only thing that creates this kind of environment, this atmosphere. Nothing else will ever come close to making you feel the way you do right now other than winning. Now I want you to remember this feeling as we finish out this season."

* * * * *

For Thanksgiving Day, the 9-1 Colts traveled to Detroit to play the Lions. The contest would be the first regular-season NFL game televised in color. Six weeks earlier, the season had looked so promising for the Lions after they won their first three games. But losing their last two games to San Francisco and Chicago, the Lions were now a 5-5 team, four games behind Baltimore in the Western Conference. With its punishing defense loaded with Pro Bowl players, Detroit could be formidable and was always physical. But the Lions were an inconsistent and at times undisciplined team. In frustration, head coach Harry Gilmer switched his quarterbacks—Milt Plum, an eight-year veteran, and George Izo, a career backup. Since 1934, the Lions had played football at home on Thanksgiving nearly every year, usually to a national radio or television audience. Before sellout crowds, they often played their best football. The Colts were favored by 10 points, but they physically were a beat-up team. Tony Lorick, Jimmy Orr, Ted Davis, Ordell Braase, and Alex Sandusky were all listed as questionable against the Lions. In the offensive line, George Preas and Jim Parker were nursing injuries. Lenny Moore was sick with a high fever.

Like a cheap racehorse, Baltimore started the game fast but then faded. After completing his first five passes, Unitas threw to Alex Hawkins, who beat cornerback Bruce Maher for a five-yard touchdown catch. But Maher later intercepted Unitas, and Pat Studstill made a diving catch of Plum's 13-yard pass in the left corner of the end zone, tying the game 7-7. On Baltimore's next series, Dick LeBeau picked off Unitas. On fourth down and inches, Amos Marsh, a bruising running back at 220 pounds, found the end zone, giving Detroit a 14-7 lead. Late in the second quarter, Marsh ran 62 yards nearly untouched for his second touchdown, giving Detroit a 21-10 lead.

In the third period, Detroit added a field goal. As the quarter ended, the Lions led 24-10. But on the fourth quarter's third play, Unitas threw long to John Mackey, who caught the ball between two Lions at the Detroit 13 and scored for a 52-yard touchdown, slicing the Lions' lead to 24-17.

With two minutes left in the game, Mackey scored again, catching a 15-yard touchdown. The game was tied 24-24. After kicking off, Baltimore held, forcing the Lions to punt. With 1:02 remaining, at their own 19, the Colts had a chance to win. But in three plays, they lost 13 yards and had to punt from their six-yard line. Detroit had all three of its timeouts. On third down, Unitas was sacked. After a quarterback sack, the clock stopped until receivers downfield huddled or the punt team entered the field on fourth down. When Baltimore's punting unit entered the field, the Lions failed to call a timeout. Defensive tackle Alex Karras tried to call a timeout, frantically shaping his hands in a "T" gesture. The officials correctly ignored his attempt. On the field, only Detroit's defensive captain, Joe Schmidt, could call a timeout, and he failed to do so. The Lions lost 17 seconds.

Tom Gilburg's punt was short, and punt returner Pat Studstill made a fair catch at the Baltimore 42. The stadium clock showed 24 seconds. But on a fair catch in the last two minutes, the clock did not stop. Detroit's head coach, Harry Gilmer, did not know the rule. As seconds disappeared from the scoreboard, Detroit fans screamed. Again, the Lions lost valuable seconds. And on a fair catch, Detroit had the right to request a free kick—a field-goal attempt at the spot of the ball without any rush, much like a kickoff. Gilmer failed to send out placekicker Wayne Walker for a 42-yard free kick. Instead, he called a pass play. Plum's sideline pass fell incomplete. Only 11 seconds were left. Detroit still had timeouts and time for Plum to throw another pass for a closer kick. But Gilmer ordered Walker onto the field to attempt a long field goal from midfield. Walker topped the ball. Baltimore escaped with a 24-24 tie.

Battling fatigue and injuries, the Colts played their worst game of the year. Unitas completed only 14 of 34 passes. The Lions used two defensive backs to cover Jimmy Orr and assigned Dick LeBeau to follow Raymond Berry. The two receivers caught only three passes for 41 yards. Often stunting or crossing over when rushing the quarterback, Detroit's defensive linemen punished Unitas throughout the game, sacking him four times in the second half. Reporters asked Detroit's bad-boy defensive tackle Alex Karras whether on one play he had actually pulled up when hitting Unitas. Known for his old-school ways and disdain for quarterbacks,

Karras surprised many by admitting that he had, noting how much he respected Unitas who never complained. "I'd hate to think in this league that any player would take a cheap shot at him," he said. "I know I wouldn't."

Amos Marsh, competing against Baltimore's injured starters and replacement players, ran for 146 yards against statistically the league's best rushing defense. After the game, defensive coordinator Charlie Winner applauded how middle linebacker Dennis Gaubatz played with a badly sprained ankle. After linebackers Ted Davis and Jackie Burkett left the game with injuries, the Colts had no one else left on the bench who could play linebacker. "The guy played the last five minutes on sheer guts," said Winner.

* * * * *

Against Detroit, Unitas turned to tight end John Mackey, who gave the Colts 102 receiving yards and two scores. Raymond Berry and Jimmy Orr were craftsmen at receiver. John Mackey at tight end was a powerful, 225-pound athlete who could run. Orr joked that the Colts were the only NFL team where the tight end was faster than the starting wide receiver and flanker. The son of a Baptist minister, Mackey won praise and awards in football, basketball, and track and field at Long Island's Hempstead High School. At Syracuse, where he roomed with Ernie Davis, Mackey played fullback and defensive end before he was moved to tight end. In college, he caught only 27 passes. But seeing special athleticism and potential, the Colts in 1963 drafted Mackey in the second round, the 19th player picked.

The Colts' offensive ends coaches, Jim Mutscheller and later Dick Bielski, tutored Mackey on running routes and catching the football, and veterans Johnny Unitas and Raymond Berry through example inspired him to join their passing drills after regular practices ended. As a rookie in 1963, Mackey started every game and was voted to the Pro Bowl. He averaged nearly 21 yards per catch and caught seven touchdowns, often in highlight plays where in the open field he knocked aside and bulldozed defensive backs and linebackers.

In 1964, Mackey in an exhibition game ran full speed into the goalpost. After the collision, he walked into the defensive team's huddle. Two days later, he finally remembered his wife Sylvia's name. That year, he also battled a thigh injury, and his production suffered. Healthy in 1965, John Mackey was the most dynamic tight end who had ever played and, even more than Chicago's Mike Ditka, was changing what people thought a tight end could do.

* * * * *

On Thanksgiving evening, the Packers celebrated the holiday at the Elks Club in Green Bay. It would be the high point of their week. On Friday, they flew to Los Angeles to play again the Rams, a team with talent but a 1-9 record. The week before, Los Angeles lost to the 49ers 30-27 with San Francisco kicking the winning field goal in the game's final seconds. Rams quarterback Bill Munson injured his knee against the 49ers. Roman Gabriel would play quarterback for the Rams. At six-foot-four and 225 pounds, Gabriel looked like a linebacker. Last year in Milwaukee, with Gabriel as their quarterback, the Rams upset the Packers 27-17.

On the last Sunday in November at the Los Angeles Coliseum, the day was sunny and clear. Fans in the crowd of 39,733 could see in the distance the Hollywood Mountains. On the first play from scrimmage, Rams halfback Willie Brown fumbled at the Los Angeles 16, and Green Bay recovered. On first down, Green Bay gained nine yards and on the next two downs nothing. The Packers settled for a 14-yard field goal and an early 3-0 lead. The Rams began a 17-play drive that lasted 10 minutes. Fullback Ben Wilson knocked over Packer defenders on a four-yard touchdown run, and the Rams took a 7-3 lead. In the second quarter, Los Angeles added two field goals and led 13-3 at halftime.

Both offenses sputtered in the third quarter. The Packers could not run. The Rams' celebrated defensive line dominated Green Bay's offensive line, repeatedly knocking down passes. Early in the fourth quarter, Lombardi, for the second time in three weeks, benched a healthy Bart Starr for backup

Zeke Bratkowski. With 9:50 left in the game, Los Angeles kicked a 43-yard field goal for a 16-3 lead. Forty seconds later, Deacon Jones sacked Bratkowski in the end zone for a safety, and the Rams led 18-3. With seven minutes remaining, Elijah Pitts caught a short pass and ran 70 yards for an 80-yard touchdown, and Green Bay cut the lead to 18-10. But the Rams controlled the ball and kicked another field goal. They won their second game of the year 21-10.

The Los Angeles victory was no fluke. While the Rams had 102 rushing yards, the Packers running the football managed on 16 carries only 22 yards. In the *Los Angeles Times,* Mal Florence asked who were the visitors in their green and gold disguises pretending to be the Green Bay Packers. The Rams, he wrote, "exposed the imposters for what they are, a mediocre 8-3 team." After the game, Lombardi acknowledged that in Week 11, his team had fallen further behind Baltimore in the conference standings. "We need help now," he admitted.

* * * * *

In November's final days, coaches in Green Bay and Baltimore had to prepare for their next game and future seasons. With both the NFL and AFL eager to sign future players, the NFL held the first two rounds of its 1966 draft on Saturday, November 27. The complete draft lasted 20 rounds and took 30 hours. Picking first, the expansion Atlanta Falcons selected Texas middle linebacker Tommy Nobis. The Packers picked 20 players. In the first round, they selected Illinois running back Jim Grabowski and Minnesota offensive tackle Gale Gillingham. A year earlier, Green Bay had drafted as a future pick Texas Tech running back Donny Anderson. Baltimore drafted 22 players. Its first two selections were offensive linemen: Kentucky's Sam Ball and Missouri's Butch Allison.

* * * * *

In losing to Los Angeles, the Packers hit their lowest point in the season's first 11 weeks. Against the Rams, they played badly. Entering December, they were not peaking but struggling. And now they would need help to overtake Baltimore in the conference race. On the flight home to Green Bay after the game, Lionel Aldridge, after several beers, was heard singing. Though an excellent teacher who knew his trade, Vince Lombardi was foremost a master psychologist who knew his players and his team. Lombardi's demand for perfection began the moment Packer players entered St. Norbert's halls for training camp and never waned. To motivate his players, Lombardi could inspire, threaten, hug, and demean. Fearing that another season was slipping away, Lombardi decided that the moment was desperate and that dramatic action was needed.

At the team's Tuesday morning meeting on November's last day, Lombardi in a rage ordered his assistant coaches to leave the room. His body was shaking. "You guys don't care if you win or lose," he screamed with his piercing voice. "I'm the only one who cares. I'm the only one who puts his blood and guts and heart into the game. You've got the concentration of three-year-olds. You're nothing! I'm the only one that gives a damn if we win or lose."

Forrest Gregg, the team's All-Pro offensive lineman known for his intensity, suddenly stood. Anger reddened his face. He moved forward as though he wanted to physically confront his coach. Teammates held him back. "God damn it, coach," Gregg shouted. "Excuse me for the profanity, excuse the language, coach--it makes me sick to hear you say something like that. We put our ass on the line for you every Sunday. We live and die the same way you do, and it hurts." Bob Skoronski, the team's offensive captain respected for his intelligence and judgment, was also standing. "That's right. Damn it, don't you tell us that we don't care about winning. That makes me sick. It makes me want to puke. We care about it every bit as much as you do. It's our knees and our bodies out there that we're throwing around."

Taken aback, Lombardi asked, "Now that's the kind of attitude I want to see. Who else feels that way?" Willie Davis, personally picked by Lombardi to be the team's defensive captain, was leaning too far back in his chair. When the chair started to fall over, Davis jumped upward. Embarrassed and uncertain what to do, Davis yelled, "Yeah, me too. I feel that way!" Quickly, the room was filled with Packer players shouting that they wanted to win.

But regardless of how badly the Packers wanted to win, they trailed Baltimore by more than a game in the Western Conference with only three games left. In its standings, the NFL did not consider ties and ranked teams by their winning percentage based on wins and losses. Green Bay would play the Colts in Baltimore in Week 13. If the Colts won that game, they would win the conference. And even if Green Bay beat Baltimore and won its last three games, the Colts would need to lose a second time in December, though Baltimore had to play Chicago on December 5. The season's final month was about to begin.

Western Conference – November 30, 1965							
	W	L	T	PCT	PF	PA	PD
Baltimore	9	1	1	.900	342	212	130
Green Bay	8	3	0	.727	226	154	72
Chicago	7	4	0	.636	318	231	87
San Francisco	6	5	0	.545	360	303	57
Detroit	5	5	1	.500	201	221	-20
Minnesota	5	6	0	.455	311	355	-44
Los Angeles	2	9	0	.182	183	298	-115

9

December: Three Weeks Left

Unlike the Western Conference, the race in the Eastern Conference was over. After beating Pittsburgh, Cleveland with a 9-2 record had again won its conference—no other team in the East had a winning record—and could begin to rest players nursing injuries. Asked about the race in the West, Ray Scott, the CBS broadcaster for Green Bay games, said, "Right now, I think the Bears are the best team in the Western Division. I still think the Packers can win this thing." Calling Cleveland's 1964 Championship win "one of the great upsets in football," Scott predicted, "Whichever team wins the Western Division will whip the Browns."

Baltimore's next opponent was the team Ray Scott hailed as the league's best, the Chicago Bears. Even though the Week 12 game would be played in Baltimore, the Colts were surprisingly four-point favorites. The Bears had won seven of their last eight games, often by three or four touchdowns. And they were healthy. The Colts were not. At linebacker, Gaubatz and Ted Davis had injured ankles, and Don Shinnick with his broken arm would need another week before he could play. Defensive end Ordell Braase was doubtful with a strained groin muscle.

On a chilly, wintry gray afternoon in Memorial Stadium, Baltimore played the first of three December games. Hoping for a Colts win and a Packers loss, the *News American's* game-day headline read "Colts Can Clinch Title Today." The

Colts lost the game. Some feared they lost the conference. There were 12 fumbles, with Baltimore losing four of its five fumbles and Chicago three of seven. The Colts turned the ball over six times. There were 23 penalties, 16 against the Bears for 142 yards. Typical of a Chicago game, there were three fights. After a Baltimore kickoff return, Alex Hawkins and the Bears' Charlie Bivens traded punches and were ejected. In the first quarter, Gale Sayers, running wide to his right, side-stepped a Colt defender in the backfield, turned the corner, and ran 61 yards past everyone else. It was the game's only touchdown.

Under the game plan devised by Chicago's defensive coordinator George Allen, the Bears constantly changed the defense they were playing. Chicago's linebackers physically challenged the Baltimore receivers at the line of scrimmage and often dropped back into coverage to disrupt the short passing routes that the Colts favored. In the game's first 25 minutes, Unitas completed only three passes for 24 yards. With 4:42 to play in the first half, disaster for Baltimore struck. After Unitas threw a pass downfield, defensive end Stan Jones hit Unitas from behind at the ankles, and tackle Earl Leggett slammed into the quarterback's knees, bending him backward before he collapsed to the ground. Unitas lay on the field clutching his right knee. He struggled to stand. That night, Unitas had surgery at Union Memorial Hospital for a torn knee ligament. His season was over.

Gary Cuozzo, one of the league's top backup quarterbacks, replaced Unitas. He had modest success, completing 12 of 30 passes for 172 yards, but with two interceptions. In the fourth quarter, Cuozzo threw a 48-yard touchdown pass to Jimmy Orr, but a Baltimore lineman was penalized for tripping, negating the score.

Shorthanded because of injuries and challenged by Colt turnovers, Baltimore's defense battled courageously. After the Sayers touchdown, Chicago added only two field goals. But the Chicago defense was even more dominant. For the day, the Colts rushed for only 59 yards. The halftime score was 10-0, but in the second half, the game was never really in doubt. Chicago won 13-0. In his postgame comments, Shula criticized his offensive unit: "It was the worst game, I think, I ever saw our offense play." But facing Green Bay next week in a game that could decide the Western Conference, Shula added, "It just wasn't our day, and we'll have to forget about it." After the game, Chicago coach George Halas was gracious. "This has to rank as one of the great Bear victories because we defeated a truly great Baltimore team."

* * * * *

Entering December in a tight conference race, Green Bay for inspiration looked to history. In 1960, the Packers won the West by winning their last three games while the Colts, crippled in their November brawl with Chicago, lost their last four. The team statistics for Green Bay sketched its 1965 season after 11 weeks. The Packers were still championship contenders because of their defense—second in total team defense or yards given up, first in scoring defense, and first in defensive takeaways. But the numbers showed Green Bay's struggles on offense—12th in total offense or yards gained, and ninth in scoring offense. Beginning with its October 24 contest against Detroit, the Green Bay offense began struggling both on the ground and in the air. In Lombardi's early years in Green Bay, the offensive line was celebrated as a team strength on great teams. But seeing too often his quarterbacks battered and sacked and his running backs met behind the line of scrimmage, the Packers' head coach knew the league's better defensive fronts were physically beating his offensive line.

A former college guard, Lombardi was a hands-on coach who ran the Packers offense. For two years, with Jim Ringo's trade, Jerry Kramer's lengthy illness, and injuries to Thurston and others, he switched and reassigned offensive linemen searching for the right lineup. He moved right tackle Forrest Gregg to left guard, started Steve Wright at right tackle, and played Dan Grimm at right guard.

Green Bay's best and most versatile lineman was Forrest Gregg, the team's second-round draft pick in 1956. Born in tiny Birthright, Texas, Gregg was the third child in a family with 11 kids and, like his grandfather, was named after Confederate general Nathan Bedford Forrest. He played football at SMU with Raymond Berry. Weighing at most 245 pounds, Gregg did not physically overwhelm defensive linemen, but he combined quickness and a fiery temperament with superb technique—he had been especially effective against Baltimore's Gino Marchetti. Green Bay's 1956 scouting report on Gregg read: "Best all around tackle in our conference. Aggressive. Strong. Rugged. Big enough. I recommend." Since Lombardi's first year as Green Bay's head coach in 1959, Gregg was named first-team All-Pro four times. He was arguably Green Bay's most accomplished player.

For much of the 1965 season, Lombardi played Gregg at guard and Steve Wright, a second-year player, at right tackle. At six-foot-six and 260 pounds, Wright was one of the team's biggest players. In 1964, Green Bay picked him in the fifth round based solely on size and potential—he never started a game at Alabama. By nature, he was free-spirited. His father was a Purdue-educated engineer working at DuPont. Growing up in an upper-middle class home in Louisville, he lacked the desperate drive to succeed in football that many of his teammates from dramatically different backgrounds had. Wright hated his Alabama years and disliked his college coaches, including Bear Bryant. In Green Bay, he was impressed by the professionalism he saw. Veteran linemen like Skoronski and Thurston willingly offered instruction, and Lombardi mixed occasional encouragement with loud rebukes. Though often drawing Lombardi's wrath for lack of focus, Wright truly admired Lombardi, finding him the most driven man he had ever met but one who was innately fair. In Green Bay's first game against Los Angeles, Wright's foot was stepped on, cartilage was damaged, and a calcium deposit formed that limited his mobility. Playing again against Rams' defensive end Deacon Jones two weeks later, he was badly outmatched.

Seeing enough after the Rams embarrassed the Packers in Los Angeles in their Week 11 game, Lombardi moved Gregg back to right tackle. With Bob Skoronski at left tackle, offensive tackle was once again a team strength. Skoronski was the offensive team's captain. Like Gregg, he consistently received high game grades from coaches. Lombardi, a master of player motivation, learned quickly that Skoronski, who was sensitive and conscientious, responded more favorably to reasoned instruction than to loud ridicule. The Skoronski family was an American success story. His father was a first-generation American who worked in a Connecticut rubber factory. Bob turned down a scholarship to Notre Dame so he could play football with his brother at Indiana. Two younger brothers attended Harvard, and his sister earned a doctorate.

It was a miracle that Jerry Kramer, for years the Packers right guard, could play football in 1965 and that at age 29 he was still alive. Raised in Idaho, Kramer was both big—six-foot-three and 245 pounds—and athletic. In high school, he set a state record for throwing the shot put, and he was a competent placekicker. He was an All-Pro guard who embraced football's physical contact and was known for his aggressive run-blocking, especially when leading Green Bay's power-sweep plays. Kramer matched up well against the bigger defensive tackles known for their power and strength but was challenged by quick defensive tackles like Detroit's Alex Karras.

As an NFL player, Kramer battled not only NFL defensive players but also his team's management in heated contract negotiations. His first contract in 1958 paid $7,750 with a $250 bonus. In 1963, Kramer began negotiations with Lombardi, the team's general manager, asking for $19,000, a 46 percent increase over his $13,000 salary in 1962. Lombardi offered $14,300, his customary 10 percent raise. The contract talks became bitter. Lombardi offered $15,000 and threatened to reduce the amount to $14,000 if his offer were not immediately accepted. Kramer refused to sign. Rumors circulated that the determined lineman might play out his option and sign with another team willing to give the Packers compensation. As punishment, the team's coaches assigned Kramer to cover kickoffs in an exhibition game. An All-Pro stalwart, Kramer had broken an ankle in 1961 playing on special teams. Seeing

Kramer incensed after the game, Lombardi relented and the next day agreed to pay $17,500.

But Jerry Kramer was always fearless and, when growing up, had been foolhardy. His list of injuries, accidents, and surgeries was long. At 14, in a high-school wood-making class, a lathe tore into his side. At 15, on a duck hunt, his shotgun accidentally discharged, the blast ripping his right arm. At one time, amputation seemed likely. Kramer had four surgeries to repair damaged tendons and nerves, and he was never again able to completely close his right hand. At 17, he was chasing a calf that stepped on an old wooden board, which broke with a large piece of wood slamming upward into Kramer's groin. Surgeons removed a splinter that was over seven inches long and nearly an inch thick that was lodged in a muscle near Kramer's spinal column. As a college freshman, he engaged in a prank to ring a college bell on top of a dormitory building and began climbing down a rope tied to a third-floor balcony railing when the railing broke. Clinging to a rain ledge, Kramer was pulled to safety through a window by friends inside the dorm. And in college, he was ejected from a car driven at 100 miles per hour that had lurched off the road and begun rolling over, and he walked away.

As a college player, Kramer learned he had cracked a cervical vertebra. Playing football, he had several concussions. In 1960, he detached the retina in his left eye; after surgery to save his vision, he was told not to play football again. In 1961, he shattered his right ankle, had surgery, and missed only eight games. But his greatest health scare occurred in 1964. Kramer began losing weight and battled severe pain and high fever. A large tumor was found on his liver. The growth proved not to be cancerous. But after several operations at the Mayo Clinic, surgeons finally found in his large intestine slivers of wood ranging from two to four inches in length, remnants from his accident 12 years earlier. Kramer underwent eight surgeries but would recover, regain weight and strength, and play football in 1965.

Green Bay's other veteran starters on the offensive line were left guard Fuzzy Thurston and center Ken Bowman. Born in Altoona, Wisconsin, Frederick Thurston was the youngest of eight and the only child in his family born in a hospital. A sister nicknamed him "Fuzzy" because of his hair. When he was four, his father at 33 died of a heart attack. The family was poor, and meat was rarely served at meals. Thurston attended Valparaiso on a basketball scholarship and did not play football until his junior year of college. At six-feet and 240 pounds, he was smaller than Jerry Kramer. With nimble feet and quickness, he was better at pass protection than run blocking. But a shoulder injury in 1964 affected his play. On a serious football team, Fuzzy, with his self-deprecating humor and infectious celebration of life, was a favorite among Packer players, who made Thurston's Menasha supper club, the "Left Guard," a frequent excursion. At center, second-year Ken Bowman battled left shoulder dislocations and wore a harness that limited his shoulder's mobility.

With the season on the line, Vince Lombardi decided that he would win or lose with his veteran linemen starting. After moving Gregg back to right tackle, he returned Jerry Kramer and Fuzzy Thurston full-time to their guard positions.

* * * * *

Minnesota was the first of what the *Green Bay Press-Gazette* called "three 'this is it' games." The Vikings entered the season expecting to compete in the Western Conference. But they lost each of their last three games by 20 points or more and had a losing 5-6 record. Winter in Wisconsin had arrived. During the week, Packer players wore sneakers to practice on frozen fields. At game time in Green Bay, the temperature was 40 degrees but would drop, the wind was blowing with gusts of 20 miles per hour, and the sky was ashen with the game ending under the glare of stadium lights.

For the Vikings, the opening minutes seemed ominous. On the game's third play, Minnesota's Tommy Mason fumbled, and Adderley recovered. One play later, Starr tossed a 27-yard touchdown to Dowler standing alone for a 7-0 lead. On the ensuing kickoff, Viking returner Lance Rentzel fumbled, and Packer Dan Grimm covered the ball. The Packers reached the Minnesota four-yard line. But on fourth down and one, Tom Moore fumbled Starr's handoff, and the Vikings held. On Green Bay's next offensive series, Zeke Bratkowski replaced Starr, who had jammed his fingers in pregame warmups. At the end of the first period, Minnesota had a long drive and scored on a one-yard run, tying the game 7-7.

The Vikings kicked three field goals in the second quarter to go ahead 16-7. With 19 seconds left in the half, Minnesota seemed in control. On fourth down with the ball at midfield, the Vikings had a howling wind at their backs. Fred Cox attempted a 59-yard field goal, but his effort fell short. Willie Wood returned the kick, racing down the sideline 71 yards to the Minnesota 21. With seconds remaining in the half, Elijah Pitts scored on a three-yard run, cutting Minnesota's lead to 16-14.

In the third quarter, the Vikings kicked another field goal, and Bratkowski threw a 27-yard touchdown pass to Bill Anderson. The Packers led 21-19. With 11:41 left in the game, Chandler attempted a 25-yard field goal. Tipped by a Minnesota player, the ball skimmed over the crossbar. Green Bay was ahead 24-19.

With two minutes to play, Chandler lined up for a 27-yard field goal that would seal the win for Green Bay. He missed. The Vikings had one last chance. With a minute left, Tarkenton, scrambling in the backfield, heaved a touchdown pass to Viking receiver Tom Hall in the end zone. But Hall was caught pushing off on Herb Adderley, and Minnesota was penalized for offensive pass interference. Three plays later, it was fourth down for the Vikings at the Green Bay 36. Darting away from rushing Packer defenders, Tarkenton threw downfield to Red Phillips at the end zone. The pass was low. Holding the ball, Phillips knocked over the corner flag marking the goal line. The back judge ruled the pass incomplete, saying Phillips had trapped the ball and was out of bounds. Protesting the call, Viking players crowded the officials on the field, drawing a penalty for unsportsmanlike conduct.

Against high winds, both quarterbacks struggled. Tarkenton completed 11 of 30 passes for 106 yards, and Bratkowski six of 19 for 90 yards with three interceptions. Despite his team's four turnovers, Lombardi was pleased with the win.

"We were overrunning everything in the first half. It was the highest I've seen my team in a long time—two or three years. They were almost too high." In the other locker room, Norm Van Brocklin defended his decision to attempt the long field goal at the end of the first half. "The wind was blowing like a hurricane," he said. Asked about the last-minute interference penalty on Hall and the ruling that Phillips had trapped the ball, the Minnesota head coach surprisingly demurred: "Nothing to say. I have to consider the Madison Avenue image. That's what the National Football League seems to be coming to these days."

* * * * *

The Packers and Colts braced for their most important game of the year—their December 13 confrontation in Baltimore. For Baltimore, with Unitas on crutches watching practices, encouraging news was that defensive end Ordell Braase and linebacker Don Shinnick, though with a partial cast, seemed likely to play. Unnoticed in most NFL cities, league officials on Monday, December 6, flipped a coin, with representatives from Green Bay and Baltimore participating by telephone, to determine the site of a playoff game if the two teams after 14 games were tied for the conference championship. Green Bay won the toss.

With its practice fields frozen and its season dependent on Sunday's game, Green Bay on Tuesday traveled east to a motel in Gaithersburg, Maryland, outside Washington, where Lombardi introduced for the week a rigid training-camp schedule with a 10:30 p.m. curfew. Early in the week, Paul Hornung called a players' meeting. "Look, we've got a second chance at the title," he told his teammates. "Let's not let this one get away." In the week's practices, onlookers noticed that Hornung was running with unusual quickness and looking like the player he had been before his 1963 suspension and later injuries.

Of the top players in his era, Paul Hornung, nicknamed "the Golden Boy," was perhaps the most colorful. Home was Louisville. At the age of one, he weighed 38 pounds. When he was four, his parents separated, and Paul and his mother lived with his maternal grandparents. As a youngster, he was always the best athlete. Playing quarterback at Louisville's Flaget High School, he was a football star, becoming the most heavily recruited high school player ever in Kentucky. Bear Bryant, then coaching at the University of Kentucky, was determined to sign Hornung and once visited his home with Kentucky's governor.

Hornung signed instead with Notre Dame, where as a T-formation quarterback he set records but lost games. As a junior, he made All-American teams. As a senior, though Notre Dame finished with a 2-8 record, he won the Heisman Trophy over Tennessee's Johnny Majors, Oklahoma's Tommy McDonald, Stanford's John Brodie, and Syracuse's Jim Brown, who because of race received fewer votes than Oklahoma linebacker Jerry Tubbs. Notre Dame boosters introduced Hornung to the lures of nearby Chicago, like the celebrated Chez Paree nightclub reportedly owned by the Chicago mob, where Hornung dated a club dancer. Handsome, with wavy blond hair and a sensual face, Hornung was approached by 20th Century Fox about a movie contract with acting lessons.

With the first pick in the 1957 draft, Green Bay selected Hornung. Packer Ron Kramer, a close friend, said Hornung could be at times "an asshole" but was always a lovable one. Regardless of how long his night before had lasted, he always practiced and played hard. And Hornung was a team leader, a star player with charisma who did not demand special privileges and who treated younger players with courtesy. Because of his talent and personality, he was Vince Lombardi's favorite player and almost a surrogate son. Inside the Packers organization, it was believed that Lombardi took vicarious delight in Hornung's nighttime exploits. Requiring a superior athlete at halfback, Lombardi thought Hornung, like Frank Gifford in New York, was perfect for the position—a powerful and patient runner who could catch, block, and even pass well. Though not always fond of the term, Lombardi considered Hornung a great "money player"—a player who welcomed the spotlight and big games. In his 1963 book

Run to Daylight!, authored with W. C. Heinz, Lombardi wrote that Hornung in the middle of the field was "only slightly better than an average ballplayer, but inside that 20-yard line he is one of the greatest I've ever seen. He smells that goal line." Confident in his abilities and secure in his relationship with his head coach, Hornung was unfazed by Lombardi's rants about his play on the practice field or in film sessions.

Based on statistics alone, Paul Hornung was not a great player. His fame rested in part on his winning personality, his versatility, and the teams on which he played—Notre Dame and Green Bay in its championship years. As both a placekicker and a halfback, he several times led the league in scoring. But Hornung had only three seasons, 1959 through 1961, when he won postseason honors. His best year was 1960, when he led the league in scoring with 176 points and ranked first in rushing touchdowns with 13 and seventh in rushing yards with 671. Though his teammate Jim Taylor had 400 more rushing yards, Hornung in 1960 fully deserved his first-team All-Pro honors and finished second in the United Press International's voting for Most Valuable Player.

In 1961, Hornung rushed for only 597 yards but again led the league in scoring. Both the Associated Press and the UPI improbably named him the league's Most Valuable Player. After receiving the MVP honor, Hornung unquestionably was the star player in the 1961 NFL Championship Game when Green Bay routed the Giants 37-0 and Hornung ran and caught passes for 136 yards and scored 19 points. But that year, fullback Jim Taylor had 700 more rushing yards, more receiving yards, and six more touchdowns than Hornung, and MVP runners-up Jim Brown and Sonny Jurgensen had stronger seasons.

In 1962, Hornung battled injuries and had only 219 rushing yards—fewer than quarterbacks Frank Ryan and John Brodie. Suspended for gambling, Hornung missed the 1963 season. Returning in 1964, he struggled badly as a kicker and ran for only 415 yards compared to Taylor's 1,169 yards. Based largely on dramatic moments in big games, Hornung's reputation as special inside the opponent's 20-yard line also could be self-fulfilling with more carries and opportunities to score when Green Bay had the ball near the opponent's goal line.

Off the field, Hornung enjoyed a playboy lifestyle. He drove a Cadillac and claimed to own 25 suits and countless sports jackets. He was his sport's most celebrated bachelor and received from women each night telephone calls with requests to meet and each day letters with photographs. Hornung kept for every year a black book listing desirable women and their telephone numbers—his 1963 book had names for 36 cities. He had the curious habit of introducing women he dated several times as "his fiancée," a practice that doubtless led with girlfriends to greater late-night adventure but eventual resentment.

* * * * *

In excitement and consequence, the Week 13 showdown in Baltimore felt like a championship game. For Baltimore, a win meant the conference title. For Green Bay, a win meant taking the conference lead with one game remaining, and a loss meant elimination in the conference race for the third straight year. Colts' owner Carroll Rosenbloom invited to the game as guests his longtime friend Joe Kennedy with his son, Senator Robert Kennedy, and the senator's large family. Sadly, the weather did not match the game's stakes. Lacking snow or even a hard rain that would have offered a dramatic stage for television viewers, the afternoon with temperatures in the mid-40s was gloomy. A thick brew of mist and fog engulfed Memorial Stadium. On the field, players could barely see the stadium's upper deck. During the game, coaches standing on the sideline struggled to see plays at either end of the field.

Throughout the week, the point spread repeatedly moved. At game time, with their home-field advantage, the Colts were slight favorites, though in some quarters the game was a "pick 'em." With Green Bay secluded for the week, questions swirled as to whether Starr would play and, if so, how effectively. But for Willie Davis, the question at quarterback was

Gary Cuozzo in a big game. "He's got to show me," said Davis. "He's never gone through anything like this before."

Bart Starr played. Early in the game, he threw an interception to Lenny Lyles, who returned the ball 28 yards to the Green Bay 11. But the Colts offense could do little, and Baltimore settled for a 14-yard field goal. The Packers offense, halting in so many games, began an 80-yard drive. Jim Taylor, breaking tackles on a 23-yard flare pass, bullied his way to the Baltimore two-yard line. Paul Hornung then scored running behind left tackle Bob Skoronski to give Green Bay a 7-3 lead. After an 18-yard Baltimore punt, Starr faked a handoff to Taylor and threw to Hornung alone at the Baltimore 35 for a 50-yard touchdown. At the end of the first quarter, Green Bay led 14-3.

In the second quarter, Michaels kicked a 45-yard field goal to narrow the Packers' lead to 14-6. On the ensuing kickoff, Elijah Pitts fumbled, and Lenny Lyles recovered. Lenny Moore scored on a three-yard run, narrowing Green Bay's lead to 14-13. But with a minute remaining in the half, Taylor fumbled at the Green Bay 21. Bobby Boyd scooped the ball up, returning it to the four-yard line. The game in hitting and momentum swings was meeting expectations.

The Packers defense entered the field, determined to hold the Colts to a field goal and end the half only two points behind. On first down, a Baltimore run gained two yards. There were 51 seconds left. On second down at the Green Bay two, quarterback Gary Cuozzo believed the Packers were playing in their goal-line 6-1 defense and would be blitzing. For his next play, he called 1-32 trap pass. But the Packers were in their 4-3 defense. Seeing tight end John Mackey release from the line of scrimmage and begin his pass route, linebacker Dave Robinson dropped back into coverage. A Packer tackle broke free and lunged towards Cuozzo. The Colt quarterback hurriedly threw to Jerry Hill in the end zone. The ball floated. Robinson stepped in front of Hill and jumped high. He intercepted Cuozzo's pass and ran 90 yards downfield in the fog. Lenny Moore caught Robinson at the Baltimore 10. The stadium clock showed 14 seconds. On the next play, Starr found

Boyd Dowler open in the back of the end zone for a touchdown. In the space of seconds, the game dramatically turned. Instead of leading at the half by six points with a touchdown or at least by two points with a field goal, Baltimore trailed 21-13.

The third quarter brought the Colts greater misfortune. Early in the period, Gary Cuozzo was hit by Lionel Aldridge and then violently slammed downward by Willie Davis. Cuozzo's left shoulder was separated, and the quarterback left the game. On short runs, Paul Hornung scored two touchdowns. After three quarters, the Packers were in control 35-10.

In the final period, Cuozzo, after receiving injections to numb his pain, returned to the field, showing courage. And the Colts would show resolve. Jerry Hill squeezed into the end zone from the one, and Cuozzo hit Berry on a five-yard touchdown pass. With 5:58 left, the score was 35-27. But Green Bay's offense was not finished. On a third and 10, Starr threw long to Hornung at the Baltimore 30. Gambling for an interception, Jerry Logan misplayed the ball. Hornung scored easily for a 65-yard touchdown.

The final score was 42-27. It was Paul Hornung's best game in four years. In the season's first 12 games, Hornung had managed only three touchdowns. Against Baltimore in Week 13, he ran and caught passes for five touchdowns and 176 yards. "He was my choice all week," said Lombardi when asked about one of his favorite players. "It was a pressure game, and he's always been good under pressure. A great pressure player." And Green Bay's head coach singled out veteran guard Fuzzy Thurston for outstanding play. "I've been in the league for nine years," noted Paul Hornung after the game, "but I've never seen a team so completely up as we were today." On Monday, Lombardi playfully told reporters, "This time we decided to go with all the veterans to prove you fellows wrong when you said we were getting old."

In contrast to the celebration in the Green Bay locker room, the mood in Baltimore's was bleak. Don Shula called the loss "the toughest one to swallow since I've been coaching here." Always blunt in defeat, Shula focused his ire on

Gary Cuozzo's late first-half interception: "We killed ourselves. We had the ball at the four, took it to the two on the first play, and you had to think we could ram it in from there." Asked about Cuozzo's decision to pass, the Colts head coach added, "He made a bad call. It was just a bad decision on the guy's part. There is no other way to say it." Acknowledging bad execution on the play, Cuozzo defended his call: "That pass is one of our goal-line plays. It's not just something I dreamed up." The interception in the final minute of the first half was a game-changing play, but with seconds left in the second quarter, the Colts defense surrendered an easy touchdown. And even after the score, 30 minutes of football remained with Green Bay ahead by only eight points. As in the 1964 Championship Game, the Baltimore defense also played poorly, allowing Green Bay to score 42 points. "That's the worst game I can remember our playing in a long time," admitted defensive coach Charlie Winner after the game.

* * * * *

With only one week left in the season, Green Bay at 10-3 moved ahead of the 9-3-1 Colts in the conference standings with a higher winning percentage. After Green Bay's win in Baltimore, the Packers organization began contacting by mail its season-ticket holders across Wisconsin about buying tickets for a possible conference playoff game and the NFL championship; the prices for playoff tickets were $6, $5.25, and $4, and for Championship Game tickets $12 and $10.

In Week 13, the Bears embarrassed San Francisco 61-20 and were only a game behind the Packers. In the conference race, Chicago's win was important, but that game would be remembered for Gale Sayers's performance. On a wet day running on a muddy field, Sayers scored six touchdowns, tying the NFL record for the most touchdowns in one game set by Ernie Nevers in 1929 and Dub Jones in 1951. Playing against a defense specifically designed to stop him, Sayers, on only nine runs and two pass receptions, scored five touchdowns—including an 80-yard screen pass and runs of 50 and 21 yards. Sayers ended his scoring on an 85-yard punt return when again his explosive speed and sudden cuts at full speed stunned the 49ers' coverage-team players. "He's out of sight," said San Francisco safety Elbert Kimbrough after the game. "He's the greatest runner I've ever seen, and that includes Jim Brown." In his fifth decade of professional football, Bears coach George Halas exclaimed, "This was the greatest performance I've ever seen by one man." San Francisco assistant coach Y. A. Tittle, who played pro football for 17 years, agreed: "It was the most brilliant exhibition I've ever seen."

* * * * *

In December's first two weeks, Baltimore lost two critical games and critically two quarterbacks. In the *Baltimore Evening Sun*, Jim Walker gave a dire assessment of the Colts' chances in the West after the Green Bay loss: "In two hours and 27 minutes, the Horses plunged from Western Conference favorites to almost hopelessly out of the race." Baltimore's Week 14 game would be played on Saturday afternoon, December 18, in Los Angeles against the Rams. With Roman Gabriel playing quarterback, Los Angeles had won its last three games, including last week's 42-7 win over Cleveland.

On Tuesday, Gary Cuozzo had shoulder surgery. Baltimore's lone quarterback was Tom Matte, a halfback who had played quarterback in a T-formation offense under Woody Hayes at Ohio State. Hayes called Shula, praising Matte, though warning that his weakness was taking the snap from center. Shula and Don McCafferty simplified the Baltimore offense, reducing the number of formations the team would use from the customary 12 to three. For each formation, there would be only eight plays—a draw, a screen pass, four other runs, and two other passes. As Shula stressed to his team that the defense would have to win the game, the Colts searched desperately for a second quarterback. They contacted Lamar McHan, a former Colt and Packer in retirement in Arkansas. McHan had no interest, saying that he still hated flying and that his wife was hosting a bridge game on Saturday.

At Baltimore's urging and with the expectation of future compensation by the Colts, Art Rooney's Steelers placed 37-year-old quarterback Ed Brown on waivers. Wanting to see

Baltimore lose, Chicago first placed a claim on Brown before later withdrawing it. The Colts eventually picked up Brown, but he would not report to his new team until the Thursday night before a Saturday afternoon game. Immediately after his arrival, Ed Brown received a tutorial on the Baltimore offense given in Shula's hotel suite by Baltimore's coaches. Because Pittsburgh's offensive system used different numbers for running backs and the holes where they should run, Shula eliminated numbers in play-calling and renamed with pickup-game simplicity the plays that might be run like sweep right or trap left. Ed Brown practiced with his new team once on Friday.

During the week, Tom Matte, who needed as much practice time as possible, battled a stomach virus. As he entered Jerry Logan's car to ride to the airport for the team's Los Angeles flight, Judy Matte handed her husband a bucket. When team owner Carroll Rosenbloom on Friday night treated the team to dinner in Los Angeles, Matte was too sick to go. On game day, the Rams were a touchdown favorite. Before the game, Woody Hayes sent his former Buckeye quarterback a telegram that read: "I know you can do the job. Good luck."

In their pregame warmups on Saturday at the Los Angeles Coliseum, the Colts were quiet and looked dispirited, and their two quarterbacks, Matte and Brown, were missing routine throws. Both offenses started slowly. With 12:23 left in the second quarter, the Colts scored first when Lou Michaels kicked a 50-yard field goal. After a long Alvin Haymond punt return, Lenny Moore ran 28 yards for a touchdown, and Baltimore led 10-0. But in the last minute of the first half, Roman Gabriel threw a 10-yard touchdown pass to Tommy McDonald, cutting Baltimore's lead to 10-7.

Early in the second half, Gabriel hit Jack Snow on a 60-yard touchdown pass, and the Rams led for the first time 14-10. In the final quarter, Los Angeles increased its lead to 17-10 on a 12-yard Bruce Gossett field goal. But with the Colts at their own 32, Ed Brown threw over the middle to John Mackey, who at full speed caught the ball at the 50, eluded safety Ed Meador, and scored. The game was now tied 17-17.

With time fading, the Colts regained possession. On a crucial third down and four, Jerry Hill willed his way through Ram defenders for a first down, and Matte then ran for 20 yards. Michaels kicked a 23-yard field goal, putting Baltimore ahead 20-17. But with 3:10 left in the game, Los Angeles had time to score and quickly moved downfield. With a minute still to play, the Rams had first down at the Baltimore nine. On second down at the seven-yard line, Gabriel under pressure ran to his right and threw into the Baltimore end zone. Bobby Boyd intercepted the pass to save the win.

On offense, Don Shula called most plays. Matte ran for 99 yards but had no pass completions on two attempts. Ed Brown completed three of five passes. The Colts ran 47 times for 214 yards. Challenged to be aggressive, the Baltimore defense, rushing linebackers and safeties, blitzed Roman Gabriel 25 times and forced two interceptions. The Colts held the Rams to 57 rushing yards. Baltimore and Los Angeles sportswriters gushed over the Colts' effort. For Bob Maisel in his *Baltimore Sun* column, the Colts in Los Angeles "played what might have been the most satisfying football game in their history." Mal Florence in the *Los Angeles Times* wrote, "The Baltimore Colts may not win the Western Conference of the National Football League this season, but they conduct themselves like champions." After the game, Don Shula offered his praise: "What an effort the boys gave. I guess I have never seen its equal and never expect to see it again." Events one week later would show Shula a better coach than prophet. For the Baltimore Colts, there was nothing else to do but hope that San Francisco on Sunday could upset Green Bay.

* * * * *

Playing the 49ers in San Francisco on Sunday, the Packers needed a win to claim the Western Conference. But the 49ers, now 7-6, had won four of their last five games and led the NFL in points scored with the league's best passing offense. Knowing the stakes in his team's Week 14 game, Lombardi, in a rare moment of public reflection, confessed to reporters, "It seems to me that I've had to coach harder this year than ever before. And I'm exhausted."

For their final game against the Packers, on a sunny day with the temperature in the 60s, the 49ers drew 45,710 fans, their second-biggest crowd of the year at Kezar Stadium. Exciting their fans, the 49ers scored first, kicking a 21-yard field goal early in the second quarter. The Packers quickly responded. Faking a handoff to Taylor and then to Tom Moore on an end run, Starr threw a 43-yard touchdown pass to Boyd Dowler, who two steps ahead of Jerry Mertens caught the ball at the goal line. The first half ended with Green Bay ahead 7-3.

The third quarter saw three interceptions, two by Green Bay's defense, but only one led to points. Turning to his right, Brodie threw to Bernie Casey running an out pattern, but Herb Adderley jumped in front of Casey for the interception and ran 13 yards down the sideline for a touchdown, holding the football high in his left hand as he stepped into the end zone. With 5:48 remaining in the third quarter, the Packers held a 14-3 lead. But late in the quarter, Brodie pitched a 32-yard touchdown pass to John David Crow, who broke away from Adderley. And Brodie later found Dave Parks for a 12-yard touchdown pass with Doug Hart falling in the end zone. With 10:38 left in the game, the 49ers led 17-14.

Finishing a long drive, Jim Taylor scored, running the power sweep to his left for five yards behind Thurston and Gregg. Green Bay regained the lead 21-17. The scoreboard showed 6:18 remaining. Willie Wood intercepted Brodie at midfield, and Chandler kicked a 31-yard field goal. Now ahead 24-17, the Packers were two minutes away from winning the conference.

On the ensuing kickoff, a face mask penalty was called against Green Bay, and San Francisco began its drive at its own 44. Against football's best pass defense, Brodie went to work—13 yards to Parks, seven yards to Gary Lewis, and back to Parks for nine more yards. Sitting in the press box, San Francisco coach Y. A. Tittle called a play the 49ers had practiced during the week, opposite right 66 Y pole. Lining up at tight end, Vern Burke ran upfield and then slanted to the left towards the goalposts. Brodie stepped forward in the pocket and threw to Burke, who made a diving 27-yard catch at the goal line for a touchdown. It was Burke's second catch of the year. With 1:07 to play, the game was tied 24-24. But Green Bay still had time to kick a field goal and win.

The Packers returned the kickoff to their 32. Starr completed a 10-yard pass to the Green Bay 42 for a first down. The Packers needed only another 20 or 25 yards for a Chandler field goal. They had 52 seconds. Starr then missed on three straight passes. With only seconds left and a tie seemingly ensured, the Packers punted. But returner Kermit Alexander weaved his way 38 yards through onrushing Packers to the Green Bay 46. The game clock showed seven seconds left. With San Francisco wanting a shorter field goal attempt, Brodie threw downfield. The pass sailed over the left sideline and was incomplete. The 49ers' field goal team prepared to run onto the field, but the officials ruled the game was over. The 49ers protested that the clock should have been stopped on an incomplete pass and that the scoreboard showed two seconds. The officials responded that regardless of the scoreboard clock, their timekeeper determined that time had run.

With the 24-24 draw, Green Bay and Baltimore were now tied in the Western Conference with 10-3-1 records. The 49ers outgained Green Bay, 392 yards to 299. San Francisco's Dave Parks led all receivers with nine receptions for 149 yards. But turnovers once more kept Green Bay in the game—handing the ball over only once, the Packers intercepted Brodie three times and recovered two fumbles.

* * * * *

After winning in Los Angeles, most Colt players returned to Baltimore, though some flew to Las Vegas where Alex Hawkins and Bobby Boyd used their Desert Inn suite as a gathering place to watch the Green Bay game. In Baltimore, the Colts arranged for the local CBS affiliate, WMAR, to show the game on closed circuit for players, coaches, and their families in the studio used for the station's popular "Romper Room" children's show. The changed leads during the game brought standing ovations and loud disapproval before wild celebration when Vern Burke's last-minute touchdown tied the game and an exuberant Don Shinnick kissed the screen. Though the 49ers did not win, their draw meant the Colts still had a chance to win the conference. They would play the Packers for a third time on Sunday, the day after Christmas, in a playoff game in Green Bay. After the San Francisco game, Don Shula called his players in Las Vegas and told them to get back to Baltimore as fast as they could.

Western Conference – 1965 Regular Season							
	W	L	T	PCT	PF	PA	PD
Baltimore	10	3	1	.769	389	284	105
Green Bay	10	3	1	.769	316	224	92
Chicago	9	5	0	.643	409	275	134
San Francisco	7	6	1	.538	421	402	19
Minnesota	7	7	0	.500	383	403	-20
Detroit	6	7	1	.462	257	295	-38
Los Angeles	4	10	0	.286	269	328	-59

10

The NFL Western Conference Playoff: The Toughest Game Ever

Baltimore needed to win only one game—whatever the long odds, whatever Green Bay's lopsided advantage at quarterback, whatever the Packers' edge at home—just one game. The NFL had a rule that only players eligible in the last two games of the regular season could play in a postseason game. Baltimore petitioned the league for an exception to be made for Ed Brown, who was eligible only in the final week. A rule exception needed the unanimous support of all teams. The league denied the request. The failure of the Colts organization to look for a backup quarterback after Unitas's injury in week 12 proved costly. On Sunday, Baltimore's most important player would be a backup halfback playing quarterback, Tom Matte. If Matte were injured, the Colts' quarterback would be defensive halfback Bobby Boyd, who played quarterback at Oklahoma.

In the Baltimore locker room, Tom Matte was a favorite, known for his dedication to team, hard work, and high-pitched voice for which he was often teased. Matte's father, a Canadian who was part Iroquois, had played professional hockey and worked as a union millwright building skyscrapers. Growing up in Cleveland, Matte competed in several sports and became an Eagle Scout. In ninth grade, he played football against his father's wishes and shattered his knee, but he recovered to play football and club ice hockey at Ohio State where his fraternity brother was golfer Jack Nicklaus. As a Buckeye quarterback coached by Woody Hayes, he predictably ran three times more often than he passed, and as a senior, he received some votes for the Heisman Trophy. In 1961, Baltimore drafted Matte in the first round, looking for a versatile, big halfback like Paul Hornung. His best year was 1963 when Lenny Moore, battling injuries, missed games, and Matte ran and caught passes for 1,007 yards. But in his five seasons in the NFL, Matte had thrown only 29 passes.

As the Colts and Packers began their playoff-game preparations, the Associated Press announced its All-Pro teams and season honors. Jim Brown won Most Valuable Player; George Halas Coach of the Year; and Gale Sayers, who led the league in scoring, Rookie of the Year. Both Green Bay and Baltimore had four players who were named first-team All-Pro—for Green Bay, Forrest Gregg, Willie Davis, Herb Adderley, and Willie Wood; and for Baltimore, Johnny Unitas, Jimmy Orr, Jim Parker, and Bobby Boyd, who led the league in interceptions with nine. Making the AP's expansive second-team All-Pro listing were Packers Ray Nitschke and Don Chandler as a punter, and Colts Raymond Berry, Bob Vogel, Ordell Braase, and Steve Stonebreaker.

Predictably, the defenses in Detroit, Chicago, and Green Bay, all acknowledged to be among the league's best, each had four or more players named to the different All-Pro teams. Though statistically the Baltimore defense was as good as any other defense in the league, except possibly Green Bay's, the Colts' defensive unit had few players singled out for post-season honors. But in its November 29 issue, *Sports Illustrated* featured on its cover Dennis Gaubatz with the banner "Baltimore's Bulldog Defense." Tex Maule's cover story was titled "Heroes Without Any Headlines." Maule wrote that on Baltimore's defense, there were few headliners, just "a group of highly capable players with only vaguely familiar names." But he hailed the Colts' defense as good as the Chicago Bears defense in their 1963 championship season and perhaps the league's "most complicated."

* * * * *

On Tuesday, Don Shula faced his underdog team. "Gentlemen, Wilson will be starting in place of Berry," Shula announced. "Hawkins will be starting in place of Orr, and Tom Matte will be our quarterback against the Packers." "If they can't take a joke," he continued, adding a four-letter expletive and a third-person plural pronoun. The Baltimore players howled with approval. For a game plan, Shula out of necessity stressed simplicity and looked to the 1930s. Of course, the Colts' offense could not turn the ball over. For Baltimore to win, the defense would have to play its best game of the season—it could not give up big plays, it could not allow many points, and it had to get turnovers. Playing Green Bay only two weeks earlier, the Colts defense ceded 42 points. N. P. Clark wrote in the *News American* on Christmas Eve that for the undermanned Colts to win, Sunday's game for Baltimore's defenders would have to be a religious crusade.

On Saturday morning, Christmas Day, the Colts flew to Green Bay, staying at the Northland hotel. The *Green Bay Press-Gazette* reported on Baltimore's arrival with an inauspicious headline: "Colts Arrive With Minimum of Fanfare." But after arriving in Green Bay, the Colts received a telegram sent by Westinghouse employees in Baltimore with eight pages of signatures wishing their team good luck. Carroll Rosenbloom took his team for Christmas dinner to the Spot, Paul Hornung's favorite Green Bay restaurant. Confident in their ability and coaches, the Colts believed they could win. But seeing Baltimore's troubles at quarterback, the Packers expected to win. "If we can't win a must-game against a team as handicapped as the Colts," Willie Davis told reporters, "we don't deserve to win a championship."

* * * * *

At Lambeau Field, with 80 reporters covering the game, a third row in the press box was added. Showing the game in color, CBS paid the NFL $200,000 to broadcast the game but would earn over one million dollars in advertising revenue, charging $60,000 for one-minute commercials. The players were paid the amount of their regular-season weekly check. In the early morning hours before the game, field crews removed the tarpaulins covered with ice and the 40 tons of hay underneath that had been protecting the stadium's field for two weeks. At opening kickoff, the temperature was 33 degrees and would drop seven degrees during the game. Portable space heaters sat behind each bench. In the stands, few showcased team apparel. More fans wore the red coats and plaid shirts favored by hunters than Packers' green and gold.

Green Bay won the coin toss and elected to receive. On the first play from scrimmage, Bart Starr faked a handoff to Jim Taylor and threw to his left, completing an 11-yard pass to Bill Anderson. As the tight end turned forward, Lenny Lyles slammed into his midsection, knocking the football loose. Don Shinnick picked up the ball and began running down the right sideline. Several blockers escorted Shinnick to the end zone. Bart Starr ran in pursuit. At the goal line, Jim Welch hit Starr hard on his right side, knocking him sideways. Starr lay on the cold field. His ribs were badly bruised, and his back was hurting. Unable to raise his right arm above his shoulder, Starr would not return at quarterback but could hold on field goals and extra-point kicks. After three plays, Baltimore led 7-0. For the sixth time this season, Zeke Bratkowski replaced his friend Bart Starr as the Packers quarterback. Later in the first quarter, Paul Hornung and Lenny Moore exchanged fumbles, and Don Chandler barely missed a 47-yard field goal. After 15 minutes, Baltimore still led by seven points.

In the second quarter, Bratkowski, running to his right, found Hornung open and completed a 47-yard pass to the Baltimore 14. But Green Bay was penalized for having an ineligible receiver downfield, and the big play was nullified. Throughout the game, the Packers played a goal-line defense that crowded the line of scrimmage and dared Matte to pass. Baltimore's offense finally challenged. Standing behind the center, quarterback Tom Matte wore on his left wrist a plastic-covered wristband that listed plays printed by his wife, Judy, a fourth-grade teacher, and that Green Bay defenders repeatedly clawed at. At the Colts' 29, Matte, rolling to his left, ran for four yards, but Willie Davis, unable to stop his momentum, stumbled over the Baltimore quarterback lying on the ground and was called for a 15-yard personal foul. On third and six with the ball at the Green Bay 48, Matte, running backwards, shoved a pass forward to Lenny Moore, who ran for nine yards down the left sideline and a first down. Jerry Hill ran for 10 yards, Matte for five, and Hill for four more. On third and one, Lenny Moore gained five yards. The Colts would reach the Green Bay seven-yard line and kicked a short field goal. With 5:29 left in the first half, Baltimore led 10-0.

The Packers threatened. On a long pass to Bob Long, Jerry Logan was called for pass interference. The penalty was 47 yards. Green Bay had a first down at the Baltimore nine-yard line. On first down, Bratkowski hit tight end Anderson, who stepped out of bounds a half yard short of the goal line. Green Bay had three more downs to score. The Colts switched to a 5-1 defense. On second down, Jim Taylor tried to jump over the line. He was pushed back but gained a foot. The ball nearly touched the goal line. On third down, Horning ran to his left and was stopped for no gain. It was now fourth down. The Packers needed inches. Their offense stayed on the field. Taylor received the handoff and ran to his right. But Lou Michaels and Dennis Gaubatz rocked the Packer fullback who dropped the ball. The Colts held. On the sideline, Vince Lombardi, wearing a dark fedora and beige overcoat, yelled at his players leaving the field, demanding to know what "the hell" was going on. Shockingly, the Colts were ahead by 10 points at the half. During intermission, Lombardi challenged his team: "What are you doing here? You've come so close. How hard do you think it will be to get back here?"

When the second half began, the charcoal-gray sky became darker, and the stadium lights were turned on. Early in the third quarter, Baltimore, playing nearly flawless football, made a rare mistake. With the Colts punting on fourth down, center Buzz Nutter's snap to punter Tom Gilburg was high. Jumping and reaching upward, Gilburg caught the ball but then juggled it. Trying to run, Gilburg was tackled at the Baltimore 35. After a short Green Bay run, Bratkowski threw down the middle to Carroll Dale, who made a diving catch at the Baltimore one. On second down, running behind Jerry Kramer, Hornung scored to narrow Baltimore's lead to 10-7.

The game became a stalemate with Baltimore on offense trying to run against a stacked Packer defense but determined not to make a costly turnover, and the Colts on defense turning back repeated Green Bay thrusts. Near the end of the third quarter with the ball at midfield, Bratkowski drifted to his right. As he was about to be hit, Bratkowski floated a pass downfield that Bobby Boyd intercepted.

Early in the fourth period, Green Bay drove to the Baltimore 25. The Packers were in Chandler's field goal range. On second and 10, Bratkowski threw over the middle. Lou Michaels, retreating into pass coverage, timed his jump and deflected the pass, knocking the ball upward into the arms of safety Jerry Logan for another Colts interception.

After a rare Baltimore completion, a 16-yard sideline pass to Mackey, Baltimore punted for the sixth time. With Packer fans beginning to watch the clock, Green Bay started a new drive on its own 28. After a first down, with the ball at the Green Bay 42, Bratkowski dropped back to pass. Billy Ray Smith's arm hit the top of the quarterback's helmet. Bratkowski fell violently as though he had been shot for an eight-yard loss. Despite Smith's animated protests, the Colts were penalized 15 yards for a personal foul, and the Packers now had the ball at the Baltimore 43. Bratkowski hit Bill Anderson, playing concussed, for six yards over the middle. On third down and three at the Baltimore 36, Taylor ran for four yards and a first down. Bratkowski passed to Anderson for 12 more yards. The Colts defense finally stopped Green Bay, but only after the Packers reached the Baltimore 15. It was now fourth down. Huddling to ward off the icy weather, the Lambeau Field crowd stared at the scoreboard. Two minutes remained.

Vince Lombardi sent his placekicker, Don Chandler, onto the field to kick a 22-yard field goal that would tie the game. Bill Curry snapped the ball to holder Bart Starr, who quickly positioned the football, its laces facing forward. Chandler took two steps forward and kicked the ball. Baltimore players jumped upward to block the kick. The ball sailed over their outstretched arms. But it tumbled towards the right upright, a stub standing only 10 feet above the crossbar. In apparent disappointment, Chandler spun around, turning his back to the ball. Two Colts on the field, Billy Ray Smith and Don

Shinnick, waved their arms to the right and began celebrating. Field judge Jim Tunney stood 10 yards behind the goalpost and, from the kicker's vantage point, several yards to the left of the right upright. Fifty thousand in the stadium stood. Millions watched on television. Their eyes turned to Tunney. Three seconds seemed like a minute.

Jim Tunney raised his arms upward, signaling that the kick was good. The Colts' players and coaches railed at the officials. Television film footage, though not conclusive, seemed to show the ball passing wide of the right upright. But the game was now tied 10-10. The scoreboard read 1:58 left in the fourth quarter. After receiving the kickoff, the Colts, content to run, could not make a first down and had to punt. With the ball at their own 38 and 27 seconds remaining, the Packers lost four yards on a pass to Tom Moore. Bratkowski completed a 20-yard pass to Jim Taylor as the fourth quarter ended.

For only the second time in NFL history, teams would play a sudden-death overtime game. Like the 1958 NFL Championship that Baltimore won at Yankee Stadium, the first team to score would win, and the game would be played until a team scored. Playing at home because of a coin flip in the league office three weeks earlier, Green Bay again won the coin toss and wanted the ball. Tom Moore returned the opening kickoff to the Green Bay 22, where he was knocked backward by Lou Michaels. On first down, Taylor gained two yards off right tackle. Bratkowski missed Dale over the middle. On third and eight, Bratkowski's pass to Bill Anderson over the middle was knocked down by Jerry Logan. Chandler punted, and Alvin Haymond returned the punt nine yards to the Baltimore 41. On first down, Matte, trying to run around left end, was tackled by linebacker Lee Roy Caffey for a three-yard loss. Matte then took to the air, but his two passes fell incomplete. On fourth and 12, Gilburg kicked a 38-yard punt to Willie Wood, who lost three yards on the return when tackled by Alvin Haymond.

With the ball at the Green Bay 21, Bratkowski passed to Taylor for nine yards. On second and one, the Packers, wanting to pass again, lost eight yards when Billy Ray Smith sacked Bratkowski. On third down, Bratkowski misfired on his pass to Tom Moore, and Green Bay had to punt.

After a 38-yard punt, Baltimore had the ball at its own 41. Tom Matte took charge—nine yards up the middle to the 50, five yards and a first down on a quarterback draw to the Green Bay 45, and eight yards off right tackle to the Packers 37. On second and two, the Colts were now in field goal range. They were on the verge of winning. Like Chandler, Lou Michaels was one of the league's best placekickers, making during the regular season all 48 of his extra-point tries and 17 of 28 field-goal attempts. Without the Colts gaining another inch, Lou Michaels could win the game on a 44-yard field goal. And one more first down, another six or eight yards after a new set of downs, and Michaels would have an easy field goal to win the game and the conference.

On the field, defensive captain Willie Davis, who had been lining up on the outside shoulder of Baltimore's right tackle, decided to move inside and pushed Nitschke further outside to his left. On second and two, Lenny Moore running wide lost a yard. On third and three, Matte again called a quarterback draw and lost two yards. With the ball at the 40 on the right hash mark, Michaels trotted onto the field to attempt a 47-yard field goal. Knowing Michaels's range, Bart Starr, standing on the sideline, feared that Green Bay was going to lose. But Buzz Nutter's snap to holder Bobby Boyd was low. Reaching forward, Boyd caught and positioned the ball, but Michaels hesitated before he kicked. The ball sailed short of the goalposts and wide to the right.

With the ball at their 20, the Packers began their third offensive series in overtime. On the field for nearly five quarters, Baltimore's defensive players battled exhaustion. Replacing an injured Paul Hornung, Elijah Pitts gained four yards around right end. On second down, under pressure, Bratkowski passed to Bill Anderson over the middle for 18 yards to the Green Bay 43. On the next play, Pitts, showing a burst, ran for six yards over left tackle, and then Taylor fought for five yards and a first down at the Baltimore 47. Running on first down, Taylor picked up three more yards. On second and seven, Bratkowski found Carroll Dale standing at the right sideline for 18 yards to the Colts 26.

The Packers were now in field goal range. Lombardi considered sending in Chandler for a 34-yard field goal but decided to move the ball closer. Taylor was stopped for no gain, but then Pitts rushed for four yards and Taylor for four more. On fourth down with the ball at the Baltimore 18, Don Chandler entered the field. On the 29th play in overtime, Chandler kicked a 25-yard field goal for a 13-10 Green Bay victory, and the Packers won the Western Conference with a chance to capture next week the NFL championship. Lasting 73 minutes and 39 seconds, it was the longest game ever played in the NFL.

* * * * *

After the game, the Colts were still incensed over Jim Tunney's ruling that Chandler's field goal at the end of the fourth quarter was good. Lou Michaels challenged Chandler to publicly say his field goal was good. "It missed by three feet," Michaels told reporters, "and you can print that." In the Green Bay locker room, Chandler's comments about the kick were guarded. The Green Bay placekicker noted simply that an official near the upright had called the kick good. But the official, Jim Tunney, was not standing at or even directly behind the upright. Given the television end-zone footage of the field goal attempt and the reaction of Chandler and Colts players on the field as the ball whirled towards the right upright, the probability seems high that Chandler's kick was wide right. Predictably, in their coverage after the game, Baltimore's newspapers highlighted and denounced Tunney's field goal call. The *Green Bay Press-Gazette* downplayed the controversy, only two days later running an Associated Press article that the Colts felt cheated by the ruling, and the *Milwaukee Journal* largely ignored the uproar.

With a halfback playing quarterback, Baltimore needed not just nearly perfect play but good fortune to win. For much of the game, Baltimore received the breaks and close calls, but not in the critical last minutes of the fourth quarter. After the game, Don Shula complained that Billy Ray Smith had been penalized for hitting Bratkowski too hard. Though inadvertent and in that era not always called, Smith's blow to the quarterback's helmet under the rules was a personal foul. Statistically, Green Bay dominated—23 first downs to Baltimore's nine, and 362 yards to 175. But turnovers, Green Bay's strength throughout the year, gave the Colts a chance. The Packers turned the ball over four times, and the Colts only once. For Tex Maule in *Sports Illustrated*, the game simply showed "that all the courage in the world cannot compensate for the lack of a passing attack."

Among the Green Bay players, there was a sense of relief as much as joy. Though the game was cleanly played, the victorious Packers attested to the fierce hitting and answered locker room questions with superlatives. Forrest Gregg believed the game was the most physical he had ever played. Henry Jordan called it his "toughest" game ever. Herb Adderley said it was "the roughest game I've ever been in." But aside from its physical demands, the game emotionally was exhausting. For the players, especially late in the fourth quarter and in overtime when one major mistake—a missed tackle in the open field, a fumble, a poorly thrown ball—could lose the game, it was the back nine on Sunday at the Masters near the top of a crowded leaderboard. "I can't remember any game like this for nervousness and tension for the entire game," Henry Jordan told reporters. "Every time we went out there, we said, we can't have a letdown."

After the game, Vince Lombardi repeatedly praised the Colts and expressed pride in how his Packers team played. "I thought our team was superb under adverse circumstances." A day later, Lombardi said that though the 1965 Packers might not be his best team, "it has great character, which I think is more important." He later added, "Our game Sunday was football as it should be played. It was as fine a hitting game as I've ever seen. I don't remember one like it."

With the Colts players, there was some pride but largely pain. The Baltimore defense scored seven points, held the Packers to 10 points for 73 minutes, and stole the ball from

Green Bay four times. Given the moment and the opponent, it was the finest game a Colts defense in franchise history had ever played. But understandably, Bobby Boyd had little to say. “We lost. That's all that matters. I think I'd rather get beat 503 to 0 than this way.” Wendell Harris was also distraught. “This is one we'll never forget—never. Maybe we shouldn't have gotten this far in the shape we were in—but we did, and we lost. There's no way to measure how much it hurts.” Though he had been angry over his team's championship loss in Cleveland a year earlier, Carroll Rosenbloom was moved by what he had watched. “I've never been more proud of any team I've ever had,” Rosenbloom said. “We didn't deserve to lose. There was no justice out there today.”

Tom Matte playing quarterback ran 17 times for 57 yards, completed five passes for 40 yards, and did not turn the ball over. After the game, he threw his wristband listing plays on the locker room floor in disgust. Recognizing the artifact's importance, John Steadman, the *News American* sports editor and columnist, retrieved it. “Tom, you have every reason to be proud,” Don Shula told Matte as the Colts began leaving their locker room. Raymond Berry extended his hand to his teammate, saying simply, “I'm proud of you, Thomas.” Arriving Sunday night at Baltimore's Friendship Airport, the Colts were greeted by 700 fans who chanted “C-O-L-T-S.” They singled out Tom Matte with applause and hoisted him on their shoulders. It took Matte, surrounded by appreciative fans, 25 minutes to cross the airport terminal.

Even in defeat, the Colts' magnificent effort inspired Baltimore's newspaper scribes. “They just ran out of ‘miracles’,” John Steadman wrote in the *News American*, “but no, not out of fortitude, tenacity or the belief that they would, somehow, someway, find a way to improvise victory.” And in Monday's *Baltimore Evening Sun*, columnist Bill Tanton captured the story of the 1965 Baltimore Colts when he wrote: “They gave it everything they had.”

11

Two Final Games

Having just survived nearly five quarters of football, the Packers had one more game to play: the NFL Championship at home against the Cleveland Browns, the Eastern Conference champions. The Browns had not played in two weeks or been tested in a month. Though competing in a weaker conference, Cleveland finished the season 11-3, the league's best record. Underrated because of their conference and their defense, the Browns were two-point underdogs. But two Cleveland players, Jim Brown and offensive tackle Dick Schafrath, had been named first-team All-Pro, and four Browns—guard Gene Hickerson, center John Morrow, linebacker Jim Houston, and defensive end Bill Glass—second-team All-Pro. The Browns were also largely healthy, though Schafrath pulled a muscle in Friday's practice before the game and his playing would be a game-time decision.

For the Packers, fatigue, emotional and physical, was a concern. With an NFL Championship Game on Sunday, Lombardi gave his players an extra day of rest. On Wednesday, the Packers' practice was lackluster. Though still hurting, Starr was throwing at practice. Because of injury, Hornung and Dowler did not play in Sunday's overtime. Jim Taylor, hampered much of the year by foot and Achilles tendon injuries, now had a pulled groin muscle.

* * * * *

Preparing to stage its championship game, the NFL announced a new television contract with CBS—a two-year deal paying $37.6 million for the regular season with the network having a third-year option and the two sides finishing negotiations for postseason and Pro Bowl games. The teams in the two leagues continued to battle over signing recently drafted college seniors. The Packers announced the signing of Donny Anderson, the Texas Tech running back. Reports were that Anderson's contract was worth $600,000 and that the AFL's Houston Oilers had offered even more.

* * * *

On Friday, December 31, Cleveland arrived in Green Bay. The Browns elected to stay at the Holiday Inn in Appleton, 30 miles outside Green Bay, rather than the Northland, Green Bay's hotel of choice for visiting teams. Cleveland's concern was the New Year's Eve parties the Northland would be hosting. Regarding the weather, it was Green Bay in January. Immediately after the Packers' playoff win, Jim Brown was prophetic: "Chances of first-rate field conditions this time of year in Green Bay certainly aren't good. Sweeps may become too dangerous. It may be well for us to work on some more straight-ahead stuff." On Saturday, the first day of the new year, the temperature peaked at 25 degrees. Like a week earlier before the conference playoff game, the Lambeau Field crew workers in early morning hours on game day began removing the tarpaulins and 40 tons of hay protecting the field. But as the tarps and hay were removed, four inches of snow began falling. Shortly before the game began, rain and light snow began pelting Green Bay with temperatures at or slightly above 30 degrees. On the morning of the game, both Jim Taylor and Paul Hornung saw the falling snow and felt confident, thinking the Browns on offense in the wintry conditions would now be as slow as the Packers.

The snow and rain turned the field into mud and coated the highways leading into Green Bay with ice and slush. The Cleveland team buses leaving Appleton were supposed to reach Lambeau Field in 40 minutes. The trip instead took 80 minutes. The Browns arrived at the stadium 70 minutes before the start of the Championship Game, leaving time only for hurried warmups. Road conditions were so bad that the

Packers' radio announcers, Ted Moore and Blaine Walsh, missed the game's early plays, and a Green Bay television sportscaster, Les Sturmer, began their radio broadcast.

Near the end of the game, the field had turned to mush, and black swatches covered the uniforms of the linemen and running backs. Ironically, in the 1964 Championship Game, Cleveland's weather with strong winds off Lake Erie favored the Browns. The weather in Green Bay a year later created field conditions that hurt Cleveland, making difficult Jim Brown's cutbacks and end runs.

For their Championship Game, the NFL and CBS had the Wisconsin winter as a striking backdrop with television cameras showing falling snow, and players and bundled-up fans creating white puffs in the frigid air when they exhaled. The Packers scored first on a 47-yard touchdown pass to Carroll Dale that Starr underthrew, causing cornerback Walter Beach to lose his footing. The Browns answered with a 17-yard touchdown pass to Gary Collins, a big receiver whose length and size challenged Herb Adderley. Because of a bad center snap, Lou Groza missed the extra-point attempt, but he later kicked a field goal to give Cleveland a 9-7 first-quarter lead. In the second quarter, Green Bay kicked two field goals, and Cleveland added one. The Packers led at the half 13-12.

With straight-ahead runs, Green Bay controlled the second half. Paul Hornung in the third quarter scored on a 13-yard run. In the fourth quarter, Chandler kicked his third field goal of the game. Green Bay won its ninth NFL championship 23-12. The score did not reflect the Packers' dominance. The Packers led in first downs 21 to 8. On the ground, Green Bay outdistanced Cleveland 204 yards to 64. In the last two quarters, Cleveland ran just 16 plays and gained only 26 yards.

Jim Brown, tracked by Ray Nitschke throughout the game, had 12 carries for 50 yards. Paul Hornung, again saving his best efforts for the biggest games, had 105 yards rushing and a touchdown. But Jim Taylor, always wanting to outshine Jim Brown whenever the two played against each other, was the Packers' workhorse—96 tough yards on 27 carries. He was named the game's Most Valuable Player. After the game,

Lombardi sought out Taylor, whose uniform was darkened by mud. "Let me shake your hand again, Jimmy," he told his weary fullback. "You did a great job, a great job. And I know you were hurt."

For the game's older spectators, a championship decided on a sloppy field with player jerseys caked with mud was redolent of league games played decades earlier. For Cleveland's owner, Art Modell, the field was a reason for the loss. "The field conditions hurt us more than them," Modell glumly observed. Some Cleveland players suggested the team's hotel selection and chaotic morning trip to the stadium contributed to their poor play. But Browns quarterback Frank Ryan was more charitable, calling Green Bay's defense the best he had played against in years.

For Vince Lombardi, this was his third NFL championship in five years, but this season seemed different because his 1961 and 1962 Championship teams had won so easily. After the game, Lombardi blended elation with insight. "This is the best win I've ever had. It came so hard, all year long. Everything was hard this season. The playoff. Everything. I never worked so hard in my life for anything." And he repeated what he said months earlier before the season had begun and a week earlier after Green Bay's playoff win: "This team has more character than any other team I've ever had."

* * * * *

One week later in Miami, the Baltimore Colts played the Dallas Cowboys in the Playoff Bowl, featuring the teams that finished second in their conference. Because of Baltimore's quarterback concerns, the Cowboys, led by Don Meredith, were favored by four points. For the Colts, the week in South Florida was largely time in the sun after a two-hour practice each morning. "I'm going to put a lot of pressure on you guys," Shula playfully told his team during the week. "I'm going to let Matte throw the ball, and I don't know what will happen." Shula did allow Matte to throw, and the Colts embarrassed Dallas 35-3. Leading 14-0 at the half, Baltimore took total command in the third quarter, scoring two touchdowns.

The game's numbers showed how complete Baltimore's win was. The Colts had 22 first downs to Dallas's 13 and 199 rushing yards to 106. Jerry Hill had a big day—90 yards running with two touchdowns and a 52-yard reception. But Tom Matte was voted the game's Most Valuable Player, completing seven of 17 passes for 165 yards and throwing two touchdowns to Jimmy Orr. For winning the game, each Colts player received $1,200, and in defeat, each Cowboy $500. For the Colts, the lopsided victory lessened, if only by a tad, the sting of their playoff loss in Green Bay. Retiring offensive linemen Alex Sandusky and George Preas ended their careers with a win. On the morning after the game, linebacker Steve Stonebreaker talked of next season: "Just five months, 16 days, and 21 hours until training camp."

EPILOGUE

In 1965, the New York Giants' four placekickers missed 21 of their 25 field-goal attempts. On May 17, 1966, at the NFL owners' meeting in Washington, the Giants announced the signing of free-agent kicker Pete Gogolak, whose contract with the AFL's Buffalo Bills had just ended. It was a three-year agreement paying $32,000 per year. NFL Commissioner Pete Rozelle approved the contract. Until the Gogolak signing, the NFL and AFL competed to sign newly drafted players, with the amounts of recent contracts alarming teams, but refrained from pursuing veteran players in the other league. Many NFL owners were appalled by the signing. Given recent developments in the AFL, they feared with reason what might come.

Six weeks earlier on April 7, AFL Commissioner Joe Foss resigned under pressure. Merger talks between the leagues had stalled. A day after Foss's departure, the AFL owners selected as their new commissioner football's most combative and errant team executive—Al Davis, the Oakland Raiders head coach and general manager. In late April, the AFL's owners gathered again. The headline for the *New York Times* article on the owners' meeting read, "Davis, New Commissioner, Opposes Merger with N.F.L." More telling were the article's subheads—"'War' Declared on A.F.L.'s 'Rival'" and "Davis Expounds Hard Line Here and Says He Has Dictatorial Powers." The Gogolak signing three weeks later meant an escalation in hostilities between the leagues and a change in the rules of engagement, developments that Al Davis welcomed. The new AFL Commissioner began plotting his league's response—stealing the NFL's starting quarterbacks. AFL teams quickly offered huge contracts to the Rams' Roman Gabriel and the 49ers' John Brodie.

And at the NFL owners' May meeting, the league reacted to the controversy over Don Chandler's field goal in the recent playoff game, raising the height of the uprights above the crossbar and ordering that goalposts be painted yellow. The old rule was that uprights had to be at least 10 feet high. The new rule was that uprights had to be 20 feet above the crossbar.

In June 1966, the two pro football leagues finally agreed to merge. Ironically, the AFL owners spearheading merger talks had concealed their negotiations from their new commissioner, Al Davis, whose election convinced NFL owners that the time to merge had come. The battles to hide just-drafted college players and sign them to exponentially higher contracts were over, and the battles to steal veteran star players from each other were quelled. The merger agreement called for an NFL-AFL Championship Game beginning with the 1966 season, NFL Commissioner Pete Rozelle to run both leagues, a common draft after the 1966 season, complete merger of the two leagues in 1970, expansion to 26 teams by 1968 with plans to later add two more teams, and compensation payments to the New York Giants and the San Francisco 49ers for sharing their markets with respectively the New York Jets and the Oakland Raiders.

For their merger, the leagues needed Congress to pass an antitrust exemption. Hostile in 1961 to the antitrust legislation that allowed the NFL to negotiate television contracts for all teams, New York Congressman Emanuel Celler, the autocratic and crusty chairman of the House Judiciary Committee, opposed any antitrust exemption permitting the merger. He refused to even allow his committee to vote on an antitrust bill. Fortunately for New Orleans seeking a franchise and the NFL seeking the exemption, Louisiana had at the time in Washington two congressional giants—Congressman Hale Boggs and Senator Russell Long. Boggs, whose daughter Cokie Roberts would later become a prominent radio and television reporter, was the House Majority Whip and later a

House Majority Leader who perished in 1972 when his Cessna plane disappeared in Alaska. Russell Long, Huey's son, was the Senate Majority Whip and the masterly chairman of the powerful Senate Finance Committee. Receiving criticism at home for supporting in 1965 the Voting Rights Act, Boggs secured Rozelle's assurance that, on congressional passage of the antitrust exemption, New Orleans would be awarded an NFL franchise. Bypassing Celler, Boggs and Long attached the antitrust exemption to a tax bill certain to pass. On October 21, 1966, Congress passed the tax legislation, and the NFL had its exemption. Ten days later, on November 1, the NFL awarded a franchise to New Orleans. It was All Saints' Day in a heavily Catholic city, and the new team was named the Saints. On May 24, 1967, the AFL awarded a franchise to Cincinnati, and its owner would be Paul Brown.

* * * *

Politically, socially, and culturally, the 1960s were a decade of dramatic change for the nation. World War II had devastated or fundamentally weakened every major combatant country but the United States, which during the war achieved a level of national unity and purpose greater than at any other time in the country's history. The United States emerged from a global war triumphant, largely confident, prosperous, and far less scarred in loss of life and destruction of homeland than its allies and adversaries. After the war, the challenges posed by the Soviet Union and global Communism led to political consensus and cultural conformity. But by 1965, with the killing of a popular president still remembered, the country was in transition—a fuller reckoning with race and racial justice had begun, sexual mores were changing, popular culture was being transformed, and American involvement in the quagmire that was Vietnam was deepening with opposition to that war growing.

Driven by television and the rivalry between and eventual merger of the established NFL and the insurgent AFL, professional football in the 1960s underwent change in how and where the game was played, how many watched it, and who played in it. The 1965 NFL season was a transitional year in pro football between past and future. And that year offered an exciting race for the NFL's Western Conference with Baltimore trying to avenge its 1964 championship loss, Green Bay trying to win another title, and Chicago trying to overcome a disastrous September with two historically exceptional first-year players. The conference was not decided until after Christmas when Green Bay and Baltimore, tied after 14 games, battled in a playoff game in the Wisconsin winter for nearly 74 minutes that was decided for only the second time in league history in sudden-death overtime.

When Green Bay and Baltimore competed in 1965, their assemblage of talent playing on the field and coaching from the sidelines was staggering. Though a handful had already seen their best years, the Packers and Colts together had 16 future Pro Football Hall of Fame players. Green Bay had 11—Jim Taylor (1976), Bart Starr (1977), Forrest Gregg (1977), Ray Nitschke (1978), Herb Adderley (1980), Willie Davis (1981), Paul Hornung (1986), Willie Wood (1989), Henry Jordan (1995), Dave Robinson (2013), and Jerry Kramer (2018). Baltimore had five, all on offense—Jim Parker (1973), Raymond Berry (1973), Lenny Moore (1975), John Unitas (1979), and John Mackey (1992). (The other 12 NFL teams fielded in 1965 40 more players who would later be inducted into the Hall of Fame. They included 1965 first-team All-Pro players Jim Brown, Gale Sayers, Dick Butkus, Deacon Jones, Bob Lilly, Bob Brown, Alex Karras, Mick Tinglehoff, and Paul Krause.) In 1994, a committee of media and league representatives selected for the NFL's 75th Anniversary All-Time Team Unitas, Berry, Gregg, Parker, and Nitschke. And the two teams had other players worthy at least of Hall of Fame consideration. For the NFL's 1960s All-Decade Team, Hall of Fame voters picked Green Bay receiver Boyd Dowler and Baltimore cornerback Bobby Boyd.

Vince Lombardi and Don Shula, the teams' head coaches, not only later entered the Pro Football Hall of Fame but became two of the greatest coaches in pro football history. After his 1965 championship, Lombardi would win the next two NFL championships and the first two Super Bowl games—the

Ice Bowl in 1967, won on Bart Starr's quarterback sneak with 13 seconds left, has been permanently etched on any ledger of memorable NFL games. After the Packers' 1967 Super Bowl win, Lombardi stepped down as Green Bay's head coach. He was physically and emotionally spent, and he surely knew that the Packers as a team were growing older and had peaked in talent. A year later, he became head coach and general manager of the Washington Redskins. In Lombardi's first year in Washington, the Redskins showed marked improvement, and Washington quarterback Sonny Jurgensen talked with genuine excitement about playing for Vince Lombardi. But in the summer of 1970, Lombardi was diagnosed with colon cancer, which was described as virulent. On September 3, 1970, he died in a Washington hospital. He was 57 years old. Having waited so long to be a head coach, Lombardi died 11 years after he coached his first game in Green Bay.

With his success in football and known embrace of traditional values, Lombardi transcended sports and became a cultural icon. *The New York Times* ran Lombardi's obituary on its front page. His funeral Mass took place at St. Patrick's Cathedral, a soaring Gothic-style landmark in Midtown New York that was in so many ways a distant world from Sheepshead Bay in Brooklyn where Lombardi grew up. Cardinal Terence Cooke celebrated the Mass and gave the eulogy. With 11 blocks of Fifth Avenue closed, a thousand onlookers stood behind barricades outside the cathedral, watching as 3,000 mourners came to honor Lombardi. It was the biggest funeral at St. Patrick's since Robert Kennedy's service two years earlier. On the same day, President Nixon attended a memorial Mass for Lombardi at St. Matthew's Cathedral in Washington, celebrated by Washington's Cardinal Patrick O'Boyle. Earlier in Green Bay, 2,000 honored Lombardi at an ecumenical memorial service.

The NFL quickly renamed its Super Bowl trophy the Vince Lombardi Trophy. A year after his death, Lombardi was inducted into the Pro Football Hall of Fame, and President Nixon attended the ceremony in Canton. Vince Lombardi was a complex man who embraced simple verities. Tom Landry, the Dallas coach, once said the reason that the Packers bonded so tightly together was the fear and anger Lombardi instilled. It was an overly simplistic assessment of Lombardi that his former Green Bay players rejected. Vince Lombardi was more than a coach obsessed with winning and known for loud player rebukes. To his players, he was the best teacher they ever had—an exacting but fair disciplinarian who worked harder than anyone else and who made them the best they could be. In later years at their reunions, former Packers, tough men who played the toughest of team sports, shared their Lombardi memories with tearful eyes.

In 1965, Don Shula was still at the beginning of his coaching career. He coached Baltimore for four more seasons. For Shula, Super Bowl III, played in January 1969, eclipsed the 1964 Championship Game loss to Cleveland as the nadir of his coaching career. Playing the New York Jets, the Colts were favored by 19 points. But Jets quarterback Joe Namath three days before the game guaranteed a Jets win and, in a barroom encounter, even taunted Colts defensive end Lou Michaels with predictions of a Jets upset. New York's head coach was Weeb Ewbank, whom Baltimore owner Carroll Rosenbloom had fired six years earlier so he could hire Shula. In the game, the Jets embarrassed the Colts 16-7. It was the first time an AFL team won the Super Bowl. The loss irreparably ruptured Shula's relationship with Rosenbloom.

After a disappointing season in 1969, Shula left Baltimore to become head coach and general manager of the Miami Dolphins. Shula coached the Dolphins for 26 years. Always a superior coach, Shula, with age and experience, became an even better coach. With the balanced offense and strong defense he always wanted, Shula's early Miami teams played in three Super Bowls and won twice, and his 1972 Dolphins team went undefeated. Later, with Dan Marino as his quarterback, Shula embraced an explosive passing offense, maximizing the talent and skills of his roster, and the Dolphins played in two more Super Bowls. The day after his 66th birthday in January 1996, after 33 years as an NFL head coach, Shula stepped down as Miami's coach. One year later, he entered the Pro Football Hall of Fame. In May 2020, he died at 90 years old. To this day, with 347 wins, Don Shula has won more games as a head coach than anyone else in NFL history.

* * * * *

Carroll Rosenbloom was the first NFL owner in the television age to seriously campaign for a new stadium, but his efforts to replace Memorial Stadium in Baltimore were thwarted. Though born and raised in Baltimore and owning the Colts, he did not live in the city and emotionally no longer seemed attached to it. Always restless and ambitious, Rosenbloom somehow arranged in 1972 a swap of NFL franchises with an impulsive Bob Irsay, whose background was running an air conditioning and heating company. On the day that Irsay bought the Los Angeles Rams from the estate of Dan Reeves for $19 million, he traded his Los Angeles franchise to Rosenbloom for the Colts franchise and $4 million. For Rosenbloom, the result was a team in Los Angeles, an escape from Baltimore, and a savings of $4.4 million in capital gains taxes by exchanging the Colts franchise rather than selling it. Dallas general manager Tex Schramm called the franchise trade "one of the most ridiculous transactions in the history of professional sports."

In Los Angeles, Carroll Rosenbloom remained competitive in demanding that his team win and forceful with local authorities in seeking a new stadium. In the 1970s inside the league, Rosenbloom, though always outspoken, joined Al Davis as a maverick owner. After Los Angeles signed a Detroit receiver whose contract had expired, Pete Rozelle infuriated the Rams' new owner by awarding the Lions in compensation Rams fullback Cullen Bryant. Represented by Rosenbloom's personal attorneys, Bryant filed an antitrust suit against the NFL to block the commissioner's decision. Few doubted that Rosenbloom had instigated and was funding the lawsuit. At a November 1975 owners' meeting, Rosenbloom viciously attacked Rozelle in an hour-long tirade, declaring at the end, "I will never attend another meeting as long as that man is in the chair." Walking out of the conference room, he paused near Rozelle. "I'll get even," he threatened. "If I can't get you in here, I'll get you out there." Six months later, the Internal Revenue Service began a criminal investigation of Rozelle. Those inside the league remembered that Rosenbloom had boasted that with his political and legal connections, he could get anyone investigated by the IRS.

On April 2, 1979, Rosenbloom at age 72 drowned when swimming alone in the early afternoon in the Atlantic near a rented villa at Golden Beach, Florida. The waters where the drowning occurred had treacherous undercurrents. A coroner's investigation found no evidence of foul play and ruled the death accidental. Some believed that Rosenbloom had suffered a minor heart attack. But a family member questioned whether he would have entered the ocean alone. A PBS documentary later speculated that Rosenbloom, with his gambling history and organized-crime associations, had been murdered but offered no hard evidence.

After Rosenbloom's death, his 1972 exchange of franchises dramatically affected the two cities whose teams had been traded and the business of professional football. In 1966, Rosenbloom finally married Georgia Wyler, with whom he had a second family in South Florida for years during his first marriage. On her husband's death, Georgia inherited a 70 percent interest in the Rams franchise. One year after Rosenbloom died, Georgia Rosenbloom remarried and took the last name of her sixth husband, Dominic Frontiere. In 1980, she executed Rosenbloom's agreement for the Rams to leave the Los Angeles Coliseum and move to nearby Anaheim.

Denied permission by the league to move his Raiders from Oakland to Los Angeles, Al Davis filed an antitrust suit against the NFL and in 1982 won. With Davis's court victory, the nation's antitrust laws, passed ostensibly to serve the public by encouraging competition among competing businesses, perversely licensed wealthy NFL owners to treat their franchises as another asset owned to maximize their wealth. Any notion that a pro football franchise belonged to the city to which it had been awarded and owed some public service obligation to its host city was dead, and league consent for franchise relocation became a farce.

On March 29, 1984, Bob Irsay, at odds with Maryland officials over a new stadium, abandoned Baltimore for Indianapolis, borrowing a fleet of Mayflower moving vans to transport in early morning hours the team's equipment and other personal property to Indiana. In 1988, Bill Bidwill moved the St. Louis Cardinals to Phoenix. In 1995, Georgia Frontiere moved the Rams to St. Louis, and Bud Adams signaled that he would be moving the Oilers from Houston, the nation's fourth largest city, to Tennessee. In 1996, unable to secure public funding for a new stadium in Cleveland, Art Modell moved his team to Baltimore, which ironically built a new football stadium, but he would at least leave behind in Cleveland the Browns' name and identity. In later years, the Rams returned to Los Angeles; the Chargers fled San Diego; and the Raiders, after leaving Oakland for Los Angeles, left Los Angeles for Oakland, and then left Oakland for the second time for Las Vegas, the nation's gaming capital built in its early years by mob money. Since 1982, NFL teams have abandoned seven different cities and relocated 10 different times.

* * * * *

After their playing days, Green Bay and Baltimore players led lives typical of former NFL players of their era. In a time when many professional schools welcomed part-time students, Willie Davis earned his master's degree in business administration from the University of Chicago and became successful in business. Gary Cuozzo became an orthodontist and returned to his native New Jersey to open his practice. Ken Bowman finished law school at the University of Wisconsin and practiced law in Wisconsin before later becoming an Arizona magistrate judge. Predictably, many worked in sports broadcasting and did well in those business ventures favored by former NFL players like restaurants and car dealerships. In 1982, Gino Marchetti sold his restaurant chain to Marriott for over $48 million. Some stayed in football to coach or scout. Bart Starr, Forrest Gregg, and Raymond

Berry became NFL head coaches; though none overall experienced great success, Gregg with Cincinnati and Berry with New England led their teams to a Super Bowl. Boyd Dowler and Zeke Bratkowski worked as NFL assistants for years and became offensive coordinators. Dick Szymanski became the Colts' personnel director and general manager.

Some players sought to help others less fortunate. Convinced by Raymond Berry to join the Fellowship of Christian Athletes, Bob Vogel on missions traveled to Central America and visited prisons. He and his wife Andrea for decades gave a home, at times for months, to 48 foster children and eventually adopted one. Don Shinnick after football continued his prison ministry work. Bart and Cherry Starr long supported a Wisconsin organization for helping troubled teens, Rawhide Youth Services, and started the Starr Children's Fund to fight pediatric cancer at Children's of Alabama hospital.

But professional achievement and acclaim offer no protection against life's tragedies and mortality. Several players passed far too early—Henry Jordan at 42 was felled by a heart attack while jogging, Ron Kostelnik at 53 and Ray Nitschke at 61 suffered heart attacks while driving, Lee Roy Caffey at 52 succumbed to colon cancer, and Steve Stonebreaker at 56 took his own life. Lionel Aldridge battled schizophrenia and for a time was homeless; an advocate later in life for those homeless and mentally ill, he died at 56 from congestive heart disease and other complications of severe obesity. Bart Starr and Gary Cuozzo lost adult sons to drugs but found strength in their strong religious faith and purpose in speaking to audiences of young people over what their families had experienced. And for too many players, their later years revealed the ugly side of professional football, ending an insouciant ignorance and a feigned innocence over the long-term effects of violent collisions and especially of repeated head trauma.

In 2002, the most intrepid of football players, Johnny Unitas, died of a heart attack at 69 years old. Learning of Unitas's death, Raymond Berry noted his teammate's "utter disregard for his own safety." For Unitas, the years after football were challenging. Running a restaurant, he later filed a Chapter 11 bankruptcy action seeking reorganization after bad business decisions. Because of football injuries, Unitas in his later years could not hold a fork with his right hand and scrawled autographs with the pen wedged between his thumb and little finger. In addition to heart bypass surgery, he had two knee replacement operations and unsuccessful surgery on his right arm.

The day after Unitas died, the *Baltimore Sun's* September 12, 2002 edition covered his passing and career with nearly nine pages of coverage, including much of its front page. Headlines for articles in the front news section read "Toughest Colt lifted up a city" and "Hero for a working-class town." The *Sun* offered a moving lead editorial that highlighted his impact and captured his essence: "He didn't invent the forward pass, and he didn't invent the NFL, but neither was the same after he had done with them. Johnny Unitas, in the blue and white of Baltimore, did invent the quarterback-as-star. An ordinary guy among men, he came to pro football knowing what real life was about. That doesn't happen anymore."

Unitas's obituary in the *New York Times* quoted Ernie Accorsi, the New York Giants general manager who had worked with the Colts in the late 1960s. "What made him the greatest quarterback of all time wasn't his arm or his size," Accorsi said of Unitas. "It was what was inside his stomach. I've always said the purest definition of leadership was watching Johnny Unitas get off the team bus." NFL Films' Steve Sabol, always conscious of image and drama, said, "He was really Gary Cooper in *High Noon*." It was "like being in the huddle with God," recalled John Mackey. A Unitas biographer, Mike Towle, highlighted the passage from John Facenda, the voice of NFL Films, that after Unitas played, other quarterbacks were compared to him, but when John Unitas played, he was compared to no one else. His Baltimore coach, Don Shula, who later coached Bob Griese and Dan Marino in Miami, called Unitas the first of the game's great modern quarterbacks. In his assessment of Unitas, Hall of Fame quarterback Len Dawson was even more glowing: "It's hard to say who's the best because so many things change as eras change. But he was the best." In its September 23, 2002 issue, *Sports Illustrated* celebrated Unitas's career with several long pieces. Fittingly, Frank Deford's lead article was titled "The Best There Ever Was." Through football, Johnny Unitas perhaps escaped a life of manual labor in Pittsburgh, achieved sports greatness, and became venerated in Baltimore, his adopted city. As Vince Lombardi and his mentor Red Blaik might have said, Unitas was willing to pay the price. But the price that he and others paid to play professional football was high.

A year before the Colts legend died, *Sports Illustrated,* for an article titled "The Wrecking Yard," featured on its cover Unitas, who looked grave, his nose scarred and his right hand resting on a football. Exploring the effects of serious injury on pro football players decades later, the article suggested that at gatherings of retired NFL players, orthopedic surgeons should hand out business cards. On the Colts, Ordell Braase had three hip replacements and a knee replacement done, and Dennis Gaubatz had two hip and two knee replacement surgeries. But the article indicated that overall those who played pro football in the 1950s and early 1960s seemed to have fewer and less serious health problems after football than those who began playing in and after the 1970s when weight training was embraced and the players were bigger and stronger. With its focus on orthopedic injuries, the 2001 article discussed head trauma in passing.

Concussions were common in the era when John Unitas and Paul Hornung played, and concussed players were expected to return to the field after minutes on the sideline. Not until much later would the danger of repeated head trauma be more fully understood, and the diagnosis of chronic traumatic encephalopathy (CTE) associated with recurrent head injury be recognized. With age comes cognitive decline. Dementia and serious neurological disorders like Alzheimer's are not uncommon among the elderly. Without imaging testing of brain tissue after death, skeptics can at least question whether head trauma from football caused a particular player's later dementia. But it seems clear that repeated head trauma afflicted a high number of Packers and Colts who played in the 1960s. John Mackey died in 2011 from complications of CTE, which was confirmed by testing. His wife Sylvia, a flight attendant, feared a decade earlier that her husband had serious neurological damage when on September 11 he watched on television the World Trade Center towers collapse and hours later could not remember what had happened. Paul Hornung, who died in 2020 from complications of severe dementia, sued years earlier helmet manufacturer Riddell. There were other Packer and Colt players who died from complications of Alzheimer's, Parkinson's, or other degenerative brain disease that had impaired their lives for years--Bill Pellington in 1994; Don Shinnick in 2004; George Preas in 2007; Jim Welch in 2017; Bob Skoronski in 2018; Roy Hilton, Forrest Gregg, and Ordell Braase in 2019; Mike Curtis, Doug Hart, and Willie Wood in 2020; Neal Petties in 2023; and Wendell Harris in 2024. And regardless of the listed cause of death, still others like Fuzzy Thurston in 2014 and Bobby Boyd and Alex Hawkins in 2017 died after long battles with Alzheimer's and dementia.

* * * * *

This story, a narrative of the NFL in 1965 told through the Western Conference race between Green Bay and Baltimore, is not one of how the National Football League has changed over the past half century with its many television platforms, staggering team profits, unprecedented franchise values, and once unimaginable player contracts—they came later. Rather, it is the story of professional football in an earlier time when, though the future could be glimpsed, the past still lived. In 1965, the Packers were not dominant like the Green Bay championship teams of 1961 and 1962, and the Colts were not as strong as their championship teams in 1958 and 1959. And in 1965, even with the eight teams in the AFL drawing away talent, the NFL with 14 teams was more competitive than in earlier years because of the many talented Black players in the league.

Ultimately, Green Bay won its 1965 playoff classic because at quarterback it had a capable backup like Zeke Bratkowski, and Baltimore, after losing Unitas and Cuozzo in December, did not, despite Tom Matte's valor. And even if officials in the playoff game had ruled Don Chandler's last-minute field goal in regulation wide and Baltimore had won, the Colts still faced their quarterback dilemma in a Championship Game, and their opponents, the Cleveland Browns, would have been favored. But during the 1965 season, Lombardi repeatedly described his Packers as a team of character. They were. And so were the Baltimore Colts. The overtime playoff game that decided the Western Conference that year was the climax of an epic 15-week struggle by two teams whose players, in repeatedly overcoming adversity, epitomized ancient virtues like fortitude and pride without hubris. The 1965 Western Conference playoff in drama and grit remains special, a classic that those who watched six decades ago still remember and that ennobled those on both teams who competed. It was, as Vince Lombardi said, football as it should be played.

ACKNOWLEDGMENTS

Many provided much-needed help with the writing of this book. It is my delight to publicly acknowledge and thank them for their contributions.

On January 22, 2021, the *New York Times* ran a story titled "Every Two Months, One of My Teammates Dies." Nicely written by Ben Shpigel, the article reported that in the prior 27 months, nine starters on Green Bay's 1965 championship team had passed. For the purposes of my book, mortality reduced substantially the number of players from whom I could seek an interview. The infirmities of old age decreased further the number capable of giving an interview that was meaningful. To those players still living, I tried to ascertain their last address and sent letters explaining what I was doing and asking for an interview. In some instances, the address I had was incorrect. An additional challenge was that I had no experience in sports journalism that I could cite and, at the outset, no friends in the league and media who could contact former players and others and help in scheduling visits. In at least two instances, my interview requests were expressly declined. But seven former players did respond to my written requests and later telephone entreaties and granted interviews. The player interviews varied greatly in duration, and some players had better memories than others. But I remain forever grateful and moved that Gary Cuozzo, Carroll Dale, Boyd Dowler, Dennis Gaubatz, Dave Robinson, Bob Vogel, and Steve Wright agreed to visit with me regarding their pro football experience. The Green Bay Packers organization helped in arranging my interview with Robinson. Family members of players proved supportive, and I thank Sylvia

Mackey, Judy Matte, and John Unitas Jr. for their anecdotes, insight, and research suggestions.

Wanting to speak with fans who attended the 1964 NFL Championship Game and 1965 games in which the Packers or Colts played, I placed classified ads in the *Baltimore Sun, Cleveland Plain Dealer*, and *Green Bay Press-Gazette*. A surprisingly high number of fans in the Baltimore and Cleveland areas responded, many of whom exhibited remarkable memories with colorful game anecdotes and offered valuable research suggestions. Their passion for the teams they cheered for 60 years ago remains unmistakable and inspirational. Bruce Amsel, Frank Orteca, Joseph Valore, Richard Wirth, Norm Brady, Michael Nakal, Alan Resnick, and Jerry Gillett were especially helpful. Bob Campbell in Rosedale, Maryland; Roger Cohen in Rye, New York; and Jeff Sepesi in Eden Prairie, Minnesota (a Browns fan who attended the 1964 NFL Championship) read a selected chapter and offered constructive comments. John Ziemann, who was a member of the Baltimore Colts Band, was an amazing resource and corrected the often-repeated story that it was Colts' Band members who played taps at the Cleveland Browns hotel on the morning of the 1964 Championship Game. And Tom Pigeon in Green Bay, who still works as a Lambeau Field guide and whose knowledge of Packers history is encyclopedic, shared with me his memories of Green Bay football before and during the Lombardi years and read my manuscript. His comments were invaluable.

Our nation's librarians are an underappreciated treasure, especially at this time. In my research efforts, I was helped by librarians in Mandeville, Covington, and Lafayette, Louisiana; at the Hornbake Library's special-collections room at the University of Maryland; and at countless other libraries across the country that provided me with books and newspaper microfilm that I requested. And Baltimore's Babe Ruth Museum provided me with access to its Johnny Unitas collection and other Colts-related materials in its archives; Michael Gibbons at the museum was particularly helpful.

Several former work colleagues provided technical help: Cheryl Alleman and Jane Raggio with typing and formatting and especially Paul Durand, whose mastery of all things computer-related is matched by only his generosity in helping those who need most his expertise. Anne Constable read early drafts and offered endless encouragement. Others who read an early draft and offered valuable suggestions were David Ballas, a long-time New Orleans high school football coach and my cousin Karen's husband who sadly has just passed, and Bob Myers. Loyola University Professor C. W. Cannon and fellow participants in a New Orleans Writers Workshop course read and critiqued chapters, as did Gayle and Mike Weber and Doug Truxillo. My daughter, Brittany Petre, proofread a final draft, a task as difficult as it is essential. And finally, thanks to Michael Braun at Orange Hat Publishing/Ten16 Press for his patience, editing skills, and belief that my manuscript was worthy of being published; and to Dana Breunig for her design creativity. Of course, I am totally responsible for any errors in this work. But to everyone who agreed to read a chapter, called me in response to a newspaper ad, shared his or her memories, and at any time provided help or simply encouragement, thank you.

In writing this book, I wanted to properly honor those who played professional football in 1965. I hope in some measure I succeeded.

NOTES

Chapter 1

5 Colts Fan Sign: interview, Frank Orteca
8 Collier on Warfield: *Baltimore Sun,* December 23, 1964, 17
8 Best Rookie Receiver: *Baltimore Sun,* December 24, 1964, 15
8 Modzelewski Talks to Browns: *Sports Illustrated,* January 4, 1965, 11
8 Pellington Cut by Brown: Mark Ribowsky, *Shula: The Coach of the NFL's Greatest Generation (*New York: Liveright Publishing Corporation, 2019*)*, 41
8 Reputation for Vicious Play: Alex Hawkins, *My Story (And I'm Sticking to It)* (Chapel Hill: Algonquin Books, 1990), 77
8 "Hangman": Upton Bell with Ron Borges, *Present at the Creation: My Life in the NFL and the Rise of America's Game* (Lincoln: University of Nebraska Press, 2017), 300
9 Doak Walker Incident: *New York Times,* May 1, 2019, A-24
9 "I Touched You Once": David Lombardi, "NFL 100: At 34, Gino Marchetti's Larger-than-Life Legacy Remains an Inspiration to Many," *The Athletic,* August 10, 2021
9 Western Conference Dominance: "How the West Has Won," *Sports Illustrated,* November 23, 1964, 35
10 Game Preview: *Sports Illustrated,* December 21, 1964, 24 and 25
11 Brown's Innovations: Richard C. Crepeau, *NFL Football: A History of America's New National Pastime* (Urbana, Chicago and Springfield: University of Illinois Press, 2014), 39 and 40
11 Single-Bar Facemask: Andrew O'Toole, *Paul Brown: The Rise and Fall and Rise Again of Football's Most Innovative Coach* (Cincinnati: Clerisy Press, 2008), 2008
11 "You Choke": Mark Bowden, *The Best Game Ever: Giants vs. Colts, 1958, and the Birth of the Modern NFL* (New York: Atlantic Monthly Press, 2008), 56
12 Image Erased: Bell, *Creation,* 323
12 Marshall's Telephone Call: O'Toole, *Paul Brown,* 234
13 Brown Watching from Car: Terry Pluto, *When All the World Was Browns Town: Cleveland's Browns and the Championship Season of '64* (New York: Simon & Schuster, 1997) 56
13 Players to Confront Brown: Jim Brown with Steve Delsohn, *Out of Bounds* (New York: Kensington Publishing, 1989), 103
13 "Taken My Team": O'Toole, *Paul Brown,* 251
14 Collier's Film Study: Michael MacCambridge, *America's Game: The Epic Story of How Pro Football Captured a Nation* (New York: Random House, 2004), 35 and 36
15 Exchanging Game Film: *Sports Illustrated,* January 11, 1965, 24
15 Cleveland's Defensive Strategy: *Sports Illustrated,* January 4, 1965, 10
16 Colts Deny Complacency: *Baltimore Sun,* December 24, 1964, 13 and 15

16 Rosenbloom's Comment to Modell: Pluto, *Browns Town*, 121
16 Heaton Prediction: *Cleveland Plain Dealer*, December 27, 1964, 2C
16 Colts Overconfident: *Cleveland Plain Dealer*, December 26, 1964, 27
16 Movie Theater Encounter: Jack Gilden, *Collision of Wills: Johnny Unitas, Don Shula, and the Rise of the Modern NFL* (Lincoln: University of Nebraska Press, 2019), 112
16 Jim Brown Hearing Taps: "Top 10 Moments: Browns Win 1964 Championship Game 27-0 against Baltimore Colts," Cleveland.com video, John Wooten interview; interview, John Ziemann (Colts Marching Band not stay at same hotel as Browns)
16 Orr Seeing Wind: Hawkins, *My Story*, 139
17 Band Instruments Confiscated: interview, John Ziemann
18 Colts' Missed Assignments: *Sports Illustrated*, January 4, 1965, 12
20 Postgame Comments by Parrish and Skorich: *Sports Illustrated*, January 4, 1965, 10
20 Gordon White's Article: *New York Times*, December 28, 1964, 42
20 Shula's Postgame Comments: *Baltimore Sun*, December 28, 1964, 26
20 "Shula Disgusted" Headline: *Cleveland Plain Dealer*, December 28, 1964, 33
21 Hawkins on Shula Blaming Offense: Gilden, *Collision*, 77
21 Colts' Flight Back: Ribowsky, *Shula*, 78

Chapter 2

22 Laughing Five Blocks Away: David Maraniss, *When Pride Still Mattered: A Life of Vince Lombardi* (New York: Simon & Schuster, 1999), 160 and 161
22 "Mr. High-Low": Maraniss, *Pride Mattered*, 161
22 Wept at Ordination: Robert W. Wells, *Vince Lombardi: His Life And Times* (Madison: Wisconsin House, 1971), 89
24 Failed Pregnancies: Maraniss, *Pride Mattered*, 75 and 87
24 Marie's Hospitalization: Maraniss, *Pride Mattered*, 362
25 Lombardi Family: Maraniss, *Pride Mattered*, 16 and 17
25 Vince's Schooling: Maraniss, *Pride Mattered*, 26
25 St. Francis Prep: Wells, *Vince Lombardi*, 28
26 "Never a More Aggressive Man": Maraniss, *Pride Mattered*, 51
26 Pregame Talk: Maraniss, *Pride Mattered*, 70
28 Colonel Reeder: Maraniss, *Pride Mattered*, 141
29 West Point Cheating Scandal: Maraniss, *Pride Mattered*, 131
30 Swiacki's Help: Vince Lombardi with W. C. Heinz, *Run to Daylight!: Vince Lombardi's Diary of One Week with the Green Bay Packers* (Englewood Cliffs, NJ: Prentice-Hall, 1963), 130
31 Fordham Job: Maraniss, *Pride Mattered*, 162 and 163
31 Eagles' Offer: Maraniss, *Pride Mattered*, 182

32 Green Bay Economy: Cliff Christl, *The Greatest Story in Sports: The Green Bay Packers 1919-2019* (Green Bay: Green Bay Packers, 2021), 128; Betsy Foley, *Green Bay: Gateway to the Great Waterway* (Woodland Hills, CA: Windsor Publications, 1983), 104
34 Select Committee Acts: Christl, *Greatest Story,* 328
35 Reasons to Take the Job: Maraniss, *Pride Mattered,* 200
35 Freezing Weather: *Green Bay Press-Gazette,* January 27, 1959, 1
35 "A Free Hand": *Green Bay Press-Gazette,* January 29, 1959, 21
36 Vainisi's Folders: Gilden, *Collision,* 83
36 Jackie Vainisi's Response: Maraniss, *Pride Mattered,* 253
37 Lombardi at Oneida Club: *Green Bay Press-Gazette,* July 20, 1965, 9
37 Lombardi's Prediction: *Milwaukee Sentinel,* July 13, 1965, part 3, 2

Chapter 3

38 Rosenbloom's Background: *Sports Illustrated,* December 13, 1965, 86-90
39 Havana Casino and Chesler: Crepeau, *NFL Football,* 75; Gilden, *Collision,* 43
39 Rosenbloom in New York: *Sports Illustrated,* December 13, 1965, 90
39 Rosenbloom's Appearance: Gilden, *Collision,* 41
39 *SI's* Profile: *Sports Illustrated,* December 13, 1965, 86-90
40 Second Family: Gilden, *Collision,* 43
40 Matching Winner's Share: Hawkins, *My Story,* 83
40 Illegal Payments: Bell, *Creation,* 139
40 Unitas Not Trust: Gilden, *Collision,* 44
41 Money Out Window: Ted Patterson, *Football in Baltimore: History and Memorabilia* (Baltimore: Johns Hopkins University Press, 2000), 86
41 Watner Sells Team: Bell, *Creation,* 29
42 "Just Announced It": MacCambridge, *America's Game,* 79
42 Baltimore's Power Structure: Frank DeFilippo, "When Powerbrokers Ruled Baltimore," *Maryland Matters,* June 17, 2019
42 Bethlehem Steel employment: Bell, *Creation,* 70
43 "Big Green Bay": John F. Steadman, *Football's Miracle Men: The Baltimore Colts' Story* (Cleveland: Pennington Press, 1959), 22
43 Colts Band and Corrals: *Baltimore Colts 1965 Press-Radio-TV Guide,* 10 and 14
43 Baltimore's Attendance: Steadman, *Miracle Men,* 29
43 "Willie the Rooster": Steadman, *Miracle Men,* 25
44 "Welcome Home": Patterson, *Football in Baltimore,* 150
44 Raising the Team Banner: interview, Norm Brady
44 Shula and Unitas at Immaculate Heart of Mary: interview, Norm Brady
46 Promising a Winner: Arthur J. Donovan, Jr. with Bob Drury, *Fatso: Football When Men Were Really Men* (New York: William Morrow and Company, 1987), 134
46 Paul Brown Calling Marshall: Steadman, *Miracle Men,* 139
46, "The Professor": *1957 Baltimore Colts Press-Radio-TV Guide,* 10

47 Changed Color of Helmets: Bell, *Creation,* 55
47 Worse Than World War II: "Toughest Colt lifted up a city," *Baltimore Sun,* December 12, 2002 online story,
48 Moore Walks Out: Hawkins, *My Story,* 114
48 Marchetti Promoting Shula: Jeff Davis, *Rozelle: Czar of the NFL* (New York: McGraw-Hill, 2008), 206
48 Shula Interview: Don Shula with Lou Sahadi, *The Winning Edge* (New York: E. P. Dutton & Company, 1973), 85 and 86
49 Shula's Scholarship: Ribowsky, *Shula,* 15
50 Shula's Final Exhibition Game: Shula, *Winning Edge,* 51 and 52
50 Teaching Browns' System: Shula, *Winning Edge,* 59
50 "Future Coach": *1957 Baltimore Colts Press-Radio-TV Guide,* 39
51 Collier Advised Shula to Accept: Carlo DeVito, *Don Shula: A Biography of the Winningest Coach in NFL History* (New York: Sports Publishing, 2018), 46
52 "Holler Guy": *1963 Baltimore Colts Press-Radio-TV Guide,* 5
52 Unitas Waving Off Field-Goal Team: Ribowsky, *Shula,* 75; William Gildea, *When the Colts Belonged to Baltimore: A Father and a Son, a Team and a Time* (Baltimore: Johns Hopkins University Press, 1994), 142 and 143
52 "Tell the Coach To Go to Hell": *Sports Illustrated,* September 23, 2002, 68
52 Shula Willing to Replace Unitas: *Baltimore Sun,* October 28, 1963, 23
53 Winner's Background: Gilden, *Collision,* 179 and 180; Bowden, *Best Game,* 60
55 "Nightmarish Slaughter": *Baltimore Colts 1965 Press Guide,"* 16 and 17

Chapter 4

56 Bert Bell's Death: Bell, *Creation,* 3; Robert S. Lyons, *On Any Given Sunday: A Life of Bert Bell* (Philadelphia: Temple University Press, 2010), 306 and 307; *New York Times,* October 12, 1959, 1
56 Bell's Health: MacCambridge, *America's Game,* 101
56 Buying the Eagles: Bell, *Creation,* 13; Lyons, *Given Sunday,* 313
57 Bell's Background: MacCambridge, *America's Game,* 41 and 42
57 To Penn or Hell: *New York Times,* October 12, 1959, 23
58 Telephone Expenses: *New York Times,* October 12, 1959, 23
58 Drawing Up Schedule: Bowden, *Best Game,* 11
58 "Like a Chain": Lyons, *Given Sunday,* 57
59 Berwanger Not Signed: *Berkeley Daily Gazette,* December 11, 1940, 23
59 Listing Injured Players: McCambridge, *America's Game,* 49
59 Bell Tearful: McCambridge, *America's Game,* 112
61 "You'll Grow into It": MacCambridge, *America's Game,* 149
61 Greater Formality: MacCambridge, *America's Game,* 150
61 Right Person, Right Place: Crepeau, *NFL Football,* ix; MacCambridge, *America's Game,* 151
61 "Gift From Providence": *Sports Illustrated,* January 6, 1964, 21

62 Rozelle's Youth: Davis, *Rozelle,* 25-27
62 Impressed Newell: Davis, *Rozelle,* 1 and 2
62 Ken Macker: Davis, *Rozelle,* 59 and 60
63 Rams in Turmoil: Davis, *Rozelle,* 72
63 Marketing the Rams: Davis, *Rozelle,* 73
64 Salary Increase: *New York Times,* May 24, 1962, 43
64 NFL and TV in 1960: MacCambridge, *America's Game,* 171
65 Network Bids: MacCambridge, *America's Game,* 190 and 191
65 Modell's Conversation: MacCambridge, *America's Game,* 191
66 AFL's TV Contract: MacCambridge, *America's Game,* 200 and 201; *New York Times,* January 30, 1964, 59
66 Sabol's Bid: Crepeau, *NFL Football,* 77; Davis, *Rozelle,* 147
67 Meeting at 21 Club: online article by David Lidsky, *CNN Money,* September 1, 2002
67 Showing at Toot's Shors: MacCambridge, *America's Game,* 182 and 183
67 NFL Buying Blair: Davis, *Rozelle,* 156; MacCambridge, *America's Game,* 183
67 Laguerre's Background: Michael MacCambridge, *The Franchise: A History of Sports Illustrated Magazine* (New York: Hyperion 1997), 78, 81-84, and 88
68 Becoming Managing Editor: MacCambridge, *Franchise, 102*
68 Restructuring the Magazine: MacCambridge, *Franchise,* 104
68 Push for "Fast Color": MacCambridge, *Franchise,* 109
69 Memo to Luce: MacCambridge, *Franchise,* 124
69 NFL Never Treated So Well: MacCambridge, *America's Game,* 159
69 Harris Survey: MacCambridge, *America's Game,* 212
69 Coffee with Hornung: Paul Hornung as told to Al Silverman, *Football and the Single Man* (Garden City, N.Y.: Doubleday & Company, 1965), 21 and 22
70 Halas Quoted: *Chicago Tribune,* January 4, 1965, part 3, 1
70 Casares Story: Davis, *Rozelle,* 166
70 Summoned to New York: Paul Hornung, *Single Man,* 23
70 Lie Detector and Confession: MacCambridge, *America's Game,* 176 and 177
70 Karras's Involvement: Bob Carroll, *When the Grass Was Green: Unitas, Brown, Lombardi, Sayers, Butkus, Namath, and All the Rest; The Best Ten Years of Pro Football* (New York: Simon & Schuster, 1993), 108
70 Scope of Investigation: *Sports Illustrated,* April 29, 1963, 22
70 NFL Announces Penalties: *New York Times,* April 18, 1963, 1 and 41
71 Coming of Age: *Sports Illustrated,* January 6, 1964, 21
71 Calling Salinger: Crepeau, *NFL Football, 76;* MacCambridge, *America's Game,* 185 and 186
72 Jane Rozelle: Davis, *Rozelle,* 64, 254, and 257
72 Werblin on Stars and Namath: *Sports Illustrated,* July 19, 1965, 66 and 68
73 Merger Rumors: *Sports Illustrated,* May 31, 1965, 24 and 25

Chapter 5

75 Lombardi Still Upset: Jim Taylor with Kristine Setting Clark, *The Fire Within* (Chicago: Triumph Books, 2010), 106

75 Grass Drill Reps: Bill Curry, *Ten Men You Meet in the Huddle: Lessons from a Football Life* (New York: ESPN Books, 2008), 87; Steve Wright with William Gildea and Kenneth Turan, *I'd Rather Be Wright* (Englewood Cliffs, NJ: Prentice-Hall, 1974), 47

75 Hanner's Collapse: Bart Starr with Murray Olderman, *Starr: My Life in Football* (New York: William Morrow and Company, 1987), 48

76 Taylor's Scouting Report: Green Bay Packers Hall of Fame, exhibit

76 Best Conditioned Athlete: George Plimpton, *One More July: A Football Dialogue with Bill Curry* (New York: Harper & Row, 1977), 11

77 Most Punishing Runner: Vince Bagli and Norman L. Macht, *Sundays at 2:00 with the Baltimore Colts* (Centreville, MD: Tidewater Publications, 1995) 9 and 86

77 "Got To Sting 'Em": Starr, *Starr*, 77

77 One of the Meanest: *Baltimore Afro-American*, October 6, 1964, 14

77 "Ain't Played Against Him": *Sports Illustrated*, November 29, 1965, 32

77 Biting Modzelewski: Starr, *Starr*, 78

77 Taunting Huff: Christl, *Greatest Story*, 418; Ray Nitschke as told to Robert Wells, *Mean on Sunday: The Autobiography of Ray Nitschke* (Garden City, NJ: Doubleday & Company, 1972), 99

77 Huff's Compliment: Nitschke, *Mean*, 101

78 Smoking Cigars: Wright, *Rather Be Wright*, 69

78 Mother's Death: Nitschke, *Mean*, 7

79 Meanest Kid: Nitschke, *Mean*, 15

79 "Vicious" Player: Nitschke, *Mean*, 28

79 Power Sweep Introduced First: Christl, *Greatest Story*, 359

79 Roots in Sutherland's Single-Wing: George L. Flynn ed., *Vince Lombardi on Football* (New York: Van Nostrand Reinhold, 1973), 17

80 Madden at Seminar: Lombardi, *Daylight*, 12 and 13

80 "Complex Simplicity": *Green Bay Press-Gazette*, August 18, 1965, 23

80 Just Fast Enough: Christl, *Greatest Story*, 361

82 Hitting Sport: Taylor, *Fire Within*, 26

82 "Passers a Bad Risk": *Life*, October 24, 1955, 133

83 Rap the Quarterback: *Time*, November 30, 1959, 61

83 Donovan's Two Greatest: Lou Sahadi, *Johnny Unitas: America's Quarterback* (Chicago: Triumph Books, 2004), 235

83 Conerly Seeing Unitas: MacCambridge, *America's Game*, 93

83 Olsen on Unitas Holding Ball: Sahadi, *Johnny Unitas*, xxiv

84 Most Savage Game Seen and Atkins Exchange: Hawkins, *My Story*, 98

84 Parker Sickened: Gilden, *Collision*, 86

84 Unitas Stuffed Nose: Raymond Berry with Wayne Stewart, *All the Moves I Had: A Football Life* (Guilford, Conn.: LP, 2016), 64

85 *Tribune* photograph: *Chicago Tribune*, November 14, 1960, part 4, 1

85 "Take Him Out": *Baltimore Evening Sun*, November 14, 1960, 31
85 Snyder's Tribute: *Baltimore Sun,* November 14, 1960, 15
85 "Unitas Beat Us": *Baltimore Evening Sun,* November 14, 1960, 31
85 "Is He Human": *Baltimore Evening Sun,* November 14, 1960, 31
86 Father's Affair: John C. Unitas Jr. with Edward Brown, *Johnny U and Me: The Man Behind the Golden Arm* (Chicago: Triumph Books, 2014), 27
87 Letters to Father: MacCambridge, *America's Game*, 90
87 Three Dollars Per Game: John Unitas Jr., *Johnny U,* 49
87 Like Throwing a Screwball: Sahadi, *Johnny Unitas*, 50.
88 "Best Camp": *Green Bay Press-Gazette,* August 11, 1965, 25
89 "Got To Say Satisfied": *Green Bay Press-Gazette, August 15, 1965, C-1*
89 "Packers in Mid-Season Form": *Green Bay Press-Gazette,* August 22, 1965, C-1
89 "Better Game Than Thought": *Green Bay Press-Gazette,* August 30, 1965, 13
90 Lombardi Opposed Name Change: Cliff Christl, "The drawn-out battle over the name Lambeau Field," Packers.com, June 1, 2017
90 Not Want To Share Spotlight: John Wiebusch, ed., *Lombardi (*Chicago: Follett Publishing Company, 1971*)*, 89
91 "Where Blood Is": *Baltimore Sun,* July 30, 1965, 18
92 Michaels Fighting: Hawkins, *My Story,* 129
92 Michaels Drinking: Hawkins, *My Story,* 135 and 147
92 Shula's Praise: *Baltimore Sun,* August 16, 1965, 17
92 "Not Need Monsters": *Baltimore Sun,* August 19, 1965, 31
94 Number of Black Players: MacCambridge, *America's Game,* 165
94 Experience in Miami: Lenny Moore with Jeffrey Jay Ellish, *All Things Being Equal: The Autobiography of Lenny Moore* (Champaign: Sports Publishing, 2006), 101
95 Wives of Black players in Green Bay: interview, Dave Robinson
95 Staying at Ft. Benning: Christl, *Greatest Story,* 390
95 Davis's Background: Willie Davis with Jim Martyka and Andrea Erickson Davis, *Closing the Gap: Lombardi, the Packers Dynasty, and the Pursuit of Excellence* (Chicago: Triumph Books, 2012), 1, 8, and 9; Jerry Kramer with Dick Schapp, *Distant Replay: The Green Bay Packers; The Stars of Football's Greatest Team Look Back* (New York: Putnam's Sons, 1985), 156 and 157
95 Lombardi Courting Davis: Davis, *Closing Gap*, 59-61
96 Offer to Curry: Curry, *Ten Men*, 161
96 Refused Service: interview, Sylvia Mackey
96 Pro Football Preview: *Sports Illustrated, September 13, 1965*, 41-73
97 Jim Brown Profile: *Time,* November 26, 1965, 86
97 Ayers Allegations and Jim Brown's Trial: *Baltimore Sun,* July 15, 1965, 29 and 30; *Akron Beacon Journal,* July 23, 1965, A-1
97 Brown's High School Basketball Record: Mike Freeman, *Jim Brown: The Fierce Life of an American Hero* (New York: Harper Collins, 2006), 74
97 Not Starting in Syracuse Basketball: Freeman, *Jim Brown,* 88

98 "Favorite Coach": Freeman, *Jim Brown,* 115
98 Brown's Leadership on Team: O'Toole, *Paul Brown,* 223
98 NFL Called "Glamour Sport": *Sports Illustrated,* September 13, 1965, 42

Chapter 6

99 Parker Quits Lions: *Detroit Free Press,* August 13, 1957, 1
100 Standing Ovation: *Pittsburgh Post-Gazette,* September 20, 1965, 28
100 Lombardi at Half: Davis, *Closing Gap,* 195
101 Post-Game Comments: *Green Bay Press-Gazette,* September 20, 1965, 13
101 Lombardi's Tuesday Comments on Pittsburgh Game: *Milwaukee Sentinel,* September 21, 1965, 22
101 Rosenbloom Wants New Stadium: *Baltimore Sun,* September 18, 1965, 13 and 17
102 *SI* Promotes Minnesota: *Sports Illustrated,* September 13, 1965, 42 and 46
102 "Turkish bath": *Baltimore Sun,* September 20, 1965, 17
102 Sandusky on Temperature: *Baltimore Evening Sun,* B-10
102 Hottest Game: *Baltimore Sun,* September 20, 1965, 23
103 "Preached Containment": *Baltimore Evening Sun*, September 20, 1965, B-10
103 Van Brocklin Critical of Tarkenton: *Baltimore Evening Sun,* September 20, 1965, B-11
103 "Eating His Lunch": *Baltimore Sun,* September 20, 1965, 17
104 Packers Defense To Be Challenged: *Green Bay Press-Gazette,* September 26, 1965, C-1.
104 Lombardi Seeking Excellence: Davis, *Closing Gap, x;* Starr, *Starr,* 45
105 Berry at Camp: Mike Curtis with Bill Gilbert, *Keep Off My Turf* (Philadelphia and New York: J. B. Lippincott Company, 1972), 24
105 Weak SI Joint: Berry, *All the Moves,* 12 and 13
105 Exercise Regimen: Berry, *All the Moves,* 34 and 35
105 Types of Passes: Bowden, *Best Game,* 81
106 Running Routes: Berry, *All the Moves,* 66 and 67
106 Lenny Moore's Background: Michael Olesker, *The Colts' Baltimore: A City and its Love Affair in the 1950s* (Baltimore: Johns Hopkins University Press, 1972), 133
106 Best All-Around Athlete: Berry, *All the Moves,* 99
106 Moore So Gifted: Bagli and Macht, *Sundays at 2:00,* 46
107 Using Injuries To Avoid Practice: Bagli and Macht, *Sundays at 2:00,* 97
107 Doubts about Moore: Gilden, *Collision,* 55 and 56; Moore, *All Things Being Equal,* 110 and 122
107 Meeting with Rosenbloom: Moore, *All Things Being Equal,* 126
107 "Showdown" Game: *Baltimore Evening Sun,* September 25, 1965, 9
107 "Must" Win: *Green Bay Press-Gazette,* September 26, 1965, C-1
108 Baltimore Writers Attending: *Milwaukee Sentinel,* September 23, 1965, part 2, 2

108 Adderley To Follow Orr: *Baltimore Evening Sun,* September 27, 1965, B7
109 McGee Suggesting Play: *Milwaukee Sentinel,* September 27, 1965, part 2, 2
109 Better Team Lost: *Baltimore News American,* September 27, 1965, 1-A
109 Shula After Game: *Baltimore Sun,* September 27, 1965, C-1
109 "Blew It": *Sports Illustrated,* October 4, 1965, 78
110 Lombardi After Game: *Baltimore Evening Sun,* September 27, 1965, B-7 (Baltimore defense); *Baltimore Sun,* September 27, 1965, C-2 (superb defenses); *Green Bay Press-Gazette,* September 27, 1965, 13 (lost a couple), and September 28, 1965, 13 (game tension)
110 Knocks Out Player: Herb Adderley and Dave Robinson with Robert Boyles, *Lombardi's Left Side* (Overland Parks, KS: Ascend Books, 2012), 148
111 Wants To Play Defense: Lombardi, *Daylight,* 68
111 "Do Best You Can": Kramer, *Distant Replay,* 165
111 Robinson's Background: interview, Dave Robinson; Herb Adderley and Dave Robinson with Robert Boyles, *Lombardi's Left Side* (Overland Parks, KS: Ascend Books, 2012), 47, 55, and 63; Kramer, *Distant Replay,* 156 and 157
112 First Gator Bowl: Adderley and Robinson, *Left Side,* 73; Steve Doerschuk, "HOF '13: Dave Robinson toasts his beloved wife, career," CantonRep.com, July 31, 2013
112 Paterno Scouting for Packers: Adderley and Robinson, *Left Side,* 76
113 First Contract: Adderley and Robinson, *Left Side,* 78 and 79

Chapter 7

115 Halas's Background: Jeff Davis, *Papa Bear: The Life and Legacy of George Halas* (New York: McGraw-Hill, 2005), 32, 33, 44, and 49; MacCambridge, *America's Game,* 7
117 German Translation: Davis, *Papa Bear,* 156 and 157
117 Importance of Green Bay Game: Davis, *Papa Bear,* 118
118 1960 Was Toughest Game: *Green Bay Press-Gazette,* October 2, 1965, P-1
118 Offsides Charge: *Green Bay Press-Gazette,* October 4, 1965, 15
119 Lombardi Irate: Gary D'Amato and Cliff Christl, *Mudbaths and Bloodbaths: The Inside Story of the Bears-Packers Rivalry* (Madison: Prairie Oak Press, 1997), 203
119 "Dark Scowl": *Green Bay Press-Gazette,* October 4, 1965, 15
119 Fans Too Quiet: *Green Bay Press-Gazette,* October 5, 1965, 20
119 Halas Comments After Game: *Chicago Tribune,* October 4, 1965, 2-1
119 McGee on Sayers: *Green Bay Press-Gazette,* October 4, 1965, 15
120 "Beautiful Passer": *Sports Illustrated,* September 13, 1965, 61
120 If Hold to 20 Points: *San Francisco Examiner,* October 7, 1965, 54
121 Shula "Disappointed": *Baltimore Sun,* October 4, 1965, C-6
121 Unitas Problems Shaving: *Baltimore Evening Sun,* October 4, 1965, B-8
121 "Try To Kill Quarterback": *Baltimore Sun,* October 4, 1965, C-9

122 Pushed in Practices: *Green Bay Press-Gazette*, October 6, 1965, 33
122 McGee on Chandler's Run: *Green Bay Press-Gazette,* October 13, 1965, 43
122 "Would Have Kept Running": *Milwaukee Sentinel,* October 12, 1965, part 2, 3
123 Lombardi Content: *Green Bay Press-Gazette,* October 11, 1965, 11
123 "We Had Determination": *Green Bay Press-Gazette,* October 12, 1965, 17
123 Christiansen on Starr: *San Francisco Examiner,* October 11, 1965, 61
124 First Game Ball: *Baltimore Sun,* October 11, 1965, C-1
124 Timing with Receivers: *Baltimore Sun,* October 11, 1965, C-1
124 "Skullduggery and Unitas": *Baltimore Evening Sun,* October 11, 1965, B-7
124 Nearly Perfect First Half: *Baltimore Sun,* October 11, 1965, C-9
124 "Playing In Frenzy": *Green Bay Press-Gazette,* November 23, 1962, 13
125 Karras Hated Packers: Taylor, *Fire Within,* 107
125 Karras Taunting Lombardi: Maraniss, *Pride Mattered,* 371
126 "You're All Packers": *Green Bay Press-Gazette,* October 18, 1965, 13
126 Hill's Assault: *Sports Illustrated,* November 11, 1963, 19 and 20
127 "Finest Half Hour": *Green Bay Press-Gazette,* October 18, 1965, 13
127 "Packers Have Pride": *Green Bay Press-Gazette,* October 18, 1965, 13
127 "Starr A Great Game": *Green Bay Press-Gazette,* October 18, 1965, 13
127 "Best Half I've Had": *Milwaukee Sentinel,* October 18, 1965, part 2, 6
127 Starr's Background: Starr, *Starr,* 13–17
127 Lacked Brother's Courage: Curry, *Ten Men,* 121
128 College Hazing: "NFL legend Bart Starr was victim of 'brutal' Alabama hazing," AI.com website, February 29, 2016
128 Dee Tipping Off Green Bay: Starr, *Starr,* 29
128 "So Prissy": Christl, *Greatest Story,* 348
128 McHan Leaving the Field: Christl, *Greatest Story,* 379
128 McHan Accosting Lombardi: Christl, *Greatest Story,* 380; Starr, *Starr,* 62
129 Lombardi Going with Starr: Starr, *Starr,* 63
129 Trying To Trade for Meredith: Christl, *Greatest Story,* 434
129 Bill George Incident: Christl, *Greatest Story,* 395; Jerry Kramer, *Jerry Kramer's Farewell to Football* (New York and Cleveland: World Publishing Company, 1969), 138 and 139
129 "I Was Wrong": Starr, *Starr,* 73
132 Redskins Game a Social Event: *Sports Illustrated,* October 4, 1965, 52
132 "Not Look Good": *Baltimore Sun,* C-1, October 25, 1965
133 Daley's Game Article: *Green Bay Press-Gazette*, October 25, 1965, 13
134 Lombardi Postgame After Dallas: *Green Bay Press-Gazette,* October 25, 1965, 13
134 "As Good a Defensive Game": *Green Bay Press-Gazette*, October 25, 1965, 13
134 McGee at Tulane: Hornung, *Single Man,* 212
135 Dowler's Background: interview, Boyd Dowler
135 Dowler Underrated: Christl, *Greatest Story,* 378
135 Rosenbloom Hiring Architects: *Baltimore Sun,* October 19, 1965, C-1

136 "Pretty Girl": *Baltimore Evening Sun*, October 25, 1965, B-10
137 Preas and Sandusky Complimentary: *Baltimore Sun*, October 25, 1965, C-1
137 Fans Intimidate Officials: *Baltimore Sun*, October 26, 1965, C-1
137 "Should Have Won": *Baltimore Sun*, October 29, 1965, C-1
138 Mackey on 49ers' Hitting: *Baltimore Sun*, November 1, 1965, C-1
138 Shula and Rosenbloom Relieved: *San Francisco Examiner*, November 1, 1965, 56
138 Packers "Incredibly Lucky": *Milwaukee Sentinel*, October 26, 1965, part 2, 2
138 "How Good": *Green Bay Press-Gazette*, October 28, 1965, 19
139 Halas on Chicago Closing Practices: *Green Bay Press-Gazette*, October 25, 1965, 14
139 Misjudging Sayers: *Milwaukee Journal*, November 1, 1965, part 2, 11
140 "Hoping I Could Sting Him": *Chicago Tribune*, November 1, 1965, part 3, 2
140 Packers Too Cautious: *Green Bay Press-Gazette*, November 1, 1965, 13
140 Lombardi Says Better Than 1963 Bears: *Milwaukee Journal*, November 1, 1965, part 2, 11
140 Ditka Says Better Than 1963: *Milwaukee Journal*, November 1, 1965, part 2, 11
140 Who Will Win West: *Green Bay Press-Gazette*, November 3, 1965, 47

Chapter 8

142 Sayers and Butkus Best since 1940: *Baltimore Sun*, October 21, 1965, C-4
142 Butkus's Background: Dan Pompei, "Bear for All Seasons," *Chicago Tribune* website, December 15, 2012,
142 Not Let Butkus Scrimmage: Davis, *Papa Bear*, 419
143 Otto Graham on Butkus: *Sports Illustrated*, August 16, 1965, 47 and 48
143 Butkus at College All-Star Game: *Sports Illustrated*, August 16, 1965, 47
143 "Wrong About That Guy": Curry, *Ten Men*, 182
143 Butkus Looking for Hate: Carroll, *When the Grass Was Green*, 151
145 "Vice Versa" Headline: *Chicago Tribune*, November 7, 1965, 2-2
145 "Sand in Eyes": *Baltimore Sun*, November 8, 1965, C-2
146 "No Longer Than First Kiss": *Chicago Tribune*, November 8, 1965, 3-6
146 Berry Surprised by Call: *Baltimore Evening Sun*, November 8 1965, B-10
146 Jim Walker's Lead: *Baltimore Evening Sun*, November 8, 1965, B-10
146 Halas Complaining about Officials: *Baltimore Evening Sun*, November 8, 1965, B-10
146 Most Bruising Game: *Baltimore Evening Sun*, November 8, 1965, B-10
146 Lombardi Contract Extension: *Milwaukee Sentinel*, November 5, 1965, part 2, 3
147 Detroit Game Headline: *Green Bay Press-Gazette*, November 8, 1965, 13
148 Starr's Ankle Twisted: *Milwaukee Sentinel*, November 9, 1965, part 2, 4
148 Best Game Since 1953: *Green Bay Press-Gazette*, November 8, 1965, 13

148 Better Than Thanksgiving Game: *Green Bay Press-Gazette,* November 8, 1965, 13; *Detroit Free Press,* November 8, 1965, 1-D
148 The Lions Remembered: *Green Bay Press-Gazette,* November 8, 1965, 13
148 "Offensive Line Overpowered": *Green Bay Press-Gazette,* November 8, 1965, 13
148 Team "Too Tense": *Green Bay Press-Gazette*, November 9, 1965, 17
149 "Imitators": *Los Angeles Times,* November 15, 1965, III-8
149 Replacing Starr: *Green Bay Press-Gazette,* November 15, 1965, 13; *Milwaukee Sentinel,* November 15, 1965, part 2, 2
150 "Are You a Comedian": *Green Bay Press-Gazette,* November 15, 1965, 13
150 Wright Injury: interview, Steve Wright
150 Wright Joking: Davis, *Closing Gap,* 200 and 201
151 Aldridge's Background: Howie Magner, "The Long Walk Home," *Milwaukee* magazine website, December 30, 2014
151 Tension between Aldridge and Davis: Davis, *Closing Gap,* 166
151 Shunned by Wives: Magner, "Long Walk," *Milwaukee* magazine website
152 "Most Important Game": *Baltimore Sun,* November 15, 1965, C-6
152 Cuozzo Mastering Offense: *Baltimore Evening Sun,* November 11, 1965, D-8
152 Cuozzo Passing on Medical School: interview, Gary Cuozzo
153 "Wallflower at Watusi Dance": *Baltimore Sun,* November 15, 1965, C-6
154 Van Brocklin Getting on Mackbee: Hawkins, *My Story,* 153 and 154
154 Van Brocklin's Comments after Game: *Baltimore Evening Sun,* November 15, 1965, B-9; *Minneapolis Star,* November 15, 1965, 32; *Baltimore Sun,* November 15, 1965, C-6
155 Tim Brown's Acting Interest: *Baltimore Sun,* November 20, 1965, B-1 and B-5
156 Orr at the Hospital: *Baltimore Sun*, November 22, 1965, C-1 and C-7; *Baltimore Evening Sun*, November 22, 1965, C-8
156 Why Unitas Threw on Second Play: *Baltimore Evening Sun,* November 22, 1965, C-8
157 Maisel Column: *Baltimore Sun,* November 22, 1965, C-1
157 Steadman's Comment: *Baltimore News American,* November 22, 1965, 1A
157 "Most Sensational Thing": *Baltimore Evening Sun,* November 22, 1965, C-9
158 "The Big Difference": *Milwaukee Sentinel,* November 22, 1965, part 2, 2
158 Starr Thankful: *Green Bay Press-Gazette,* November 22, 1965, 17
158 "Celebrate This One": Davis, *Closing Gap,* 201 and 202
158 Game in Color: DeVito, *Don Shula,* 68
160 Not Know Time Would Run: *Baltimore Evening Sun,* November 26, 1965, B-14
161 No Cheap Shot on Unitas: *Sports Illustrated,* December 6, 1965, 27
161 "Played on Sheer Guts": *Baltimore Evening Sun,* November 26, 1965, B-14

161 Help Running Patterns: John Mackey with Thom Loverro, *Blazing Trails: Coming of Age in Football's Golden Era* (Chicago: Triumph Books, 2003), 15 and 77

162 Goalpost Collision: Mackey, *Blazing Trails*, 96 and 97; interview, Sylvia Mackey

163 Pretending to be Packers: *Los Angeles Times,* November 29, 1965, III-1

163 "Need Help Now": *Milwaukee Sentinel,* November 29, 1965, part 2, 2

164 Singing on Flight: Plimpton, *One More July,* 24

164 Lombardi Tirade: Forrest Gregg and Andrew O'Toole, *Winning in the Trenches* (Cincinnati: Clerisy Press, 2009), 105 and 106; Plimpton, *One More,* 24

164 Davis Jumping Up: Davis, *Closing Gap,* 203

Chapter 9

167 Scott's Prediction: *Green Bay Press-Gazette,* December 4, 1965, P-1

167 "Can Clinch Conference": *Baltimore News American,* December 5, 1965, 1D

169 Shula's Comments After Game: *Baltimore Evening Sun,* December 6, 1965, B-14; *Baltimore Sun,* December 6, 1965, C-4

169 Halas Gracious: *Chicago Tribune,* December 6, 1965, 3-1

170 Gregg's Background: Gregg and O'Toole, *Winning in Trenches*, 17

170 Gregg's Scouting Report: Green Bay Packers Hall of Fame, exhibit

170 Wright's Background: Wright, *Rather Be Wright,* 5-7; interview, Steve Wright

170 Admiration for Lombardi: interview, Steve Wright

170 Injury Against Rams: Wright, *Rather Be Wright,* 58 and 59; interview, Steve Wright

171 Skoronski's High Grades: Richard Ryman, "Bob Skoronski, Packers Hall of Fame tackle, dead at 84," *Green Bay Press-Gazette* website, October 31, 2018; "HISTORY/HOF/ Bob Skoronski," packers.com website, May 2, 2019

171 Skoronski Family: Kramer, *Distant Replay,* 131; Starr, *Starr,* 102 and 103

171 Contract Negotiations: Jerry Kramer and Dick Schapp, *Instant Replay* (New York: New American Library, 1968), 14-16

172 Kramer's Injury and Accident History: Kramer, *Distant Replay,* 15 and 16; Kramer, *Farewell,* 47-51, 60, and 61; Lombardi, *Daylight,* 56 and 57

172 Kramer's Surgeries: Kramer and Schapp, *Instant Replay,* 57; Len Wagner, "The Amazing Jerry Kramer," *Green Bay Packers 1965 Yearbook,* 7-9 and 40

173 Thurston's Background: Fuzzy and Sue Thurston with Bill Wenzel, *What a Wonderful World: The Fuzzy Thurston Story* (Fuzzy Thurston and Bill Wenzel, 2006), 28-32

173 Wearing Shoulder Harness: Starr, *Starr,* 109 and 110

173 "This Is It" Games: *Green Bay Press-Gazette,* December 5, 1965, D-1

175 Team Too High: *Green Bay Press-Gazette,* December 6, 1965, 15

175 "Like a Hurricane": *Green Bay Press-Gazette,* December 6, 1965, 20

175 "Madison Avenue Image": *Milwaukee Sentinel,* December 6, 1965, part 2, 6
176 Hornung's Background: Hornung, *Single Man,* 59-61
176 Hornung's Recruitment: Maraniss, *Pride Mattered, 280*
176 Movie Contract: Hornung, *Single Man,* 130
176 Ron Kramer's Assessment: Maraniss, *Pride Mattered,* 282
176 Taking Vicarious Delight: Maraniss, *Pride Mattered,* 279; Wiebusch, *Lombardi*, 163
177 Near the Goal Line: Cliff Christl, "Lombardi on Hornung: The best all-around back ever," packers.com website, October 18, 2018; *Green Bay Press-Gazette,* December 13, 1965, 17
177 "Greatest I've Ever Seen": Lombardi, *Daylight,* 33
178 Hornung's Social Life: Hornung, *Single Man,* 234-236, 238, and 239
179 "He's Got to Show Me": *Green Bay Press-Gazette,* December 11, 1965, 9
180 "My Choice All Week": *Green Bay Press-Gazette,* December 13, 1965, 17
180 "Going With All Veterans": *Milwaukee Sentinel,* December 14, 1965, part 2, 2
180 Shula After Game: *Baltimore Sun,* December 13, 1965, C-8
181 "Not Something I Dreamed Up": *Baltimore Evening Sun,* December 18, 1965, B-9
181 "Worst Defensive Game": *Baltimore Evening Sun,* December 13, 1965, B-9
182 Sayers Applauded: *Green Bay Press-Gazette,* December 13, 1965, 18
182 Walker's Assessment: *Baltimore Evening Sun,* December 13, 1965, B-9
182 Formations and Plays Reduced: Shula, *Winning Edge,* 91
182 Contacted McHan: Hawkins, *My Story,* 157
183 Brown's Tutorial: Shula, *Winning Edge,* 92; *Baltimore Sun,* December 19, 1965, A-1
183 Matte's ride to airport: interview, Judy Matte
183 Woody Hayes Telegram: *Green Bay Press-Gazette,* December 23, 1965, 14
183 Looked Flat Before Game: Shula, *Winning Edge,* 93
184 "Most Satisfying Game": *Baltimore Sun,* December 19, 1965, A-1
184 "Like Champions": *Los Angeles Times,* December 19, 1965, D-1
184 "What An Effort": *Baltimore Sun,* December 19, 1965, A-1
184 "Coaching Harder": *Milwaukee Sentinel,* December 18, 1965, part 2, 1
186 Colts in Las Vegas: Hawkins, *My Story,* 157
186 Game on Closed Circuit: *Baltimore Evening Sun,* December 20, 1965, C-9

Chapter 10

189 Matte's Background: interview, Judy Matte; Gilden, *Collision*, 169 and 170
190 Baltimore's Defense: *Sports Illustrated,* November 29, 1965, 30 and 31
191 Shula Telling Colts Game Plan: Hawkins, *My Story,* 159
191 "Crusade": *Baltimore News American,* December 24, 1964, 7C
191 Colts' Arrival: *Green Bay Press-Gazette, December* 26, 1965, D-1

191 Colts Believed They Could Win: interview, Bob Vogel
191 "If Can't Beat the Colts": *Green Bay Press-Gazette,* December 22, 1965, 13
191 CBS Broadcast: *Green Bay Press-Gazette,* December 22, 1965, 13
193 Lombardi Screaming at Players: interview, Tom Pigeon
193 "Come So Close": Davis, *Closing Gap,* 209
196 Starr Fearing a Loss: *Sports Illustrated,* January 3, 1966, 12
197 "Missed by Three Feet": *Green Bay Press-Gazette,* December 28, 1965, 14
198 "All the Courage": *Sports Illustrated,* January 3, 1966, 10
198 Most Physical Game: Gregg, *Winning in Trenches,* 109
198 "The Toughest": *Green Bay Press-Gazette,* December 27, 1965, 13
198 "Roughest Game": *Baltimore Evening Sun,* December 27, 1965, B-9
198 Jordan on Great Tension: *Green Bay Press-Gazette,* December 29, 1965, 13
198 Team "Superb": *Green Bay Press-Gazette,* December 27, 1965, 13
198 "Great Character": *Green Bay Press-Gazette,* December 28, 1965, 13
198 Lombardi on Game Later: *Green Bay Press-Gazette,* December 28, 1965, 13
199 "Rather Get Beat 503 to 0": *Baltimore Sun,* December 27, 1965, C-1
199 Harris on Game: *Baltimore Evening Sun,* December 28, 1965, B-10
199 Rosenbloom Proud: *Green Bay Press-Gazette,* December 27, 1965, 14
199 Shula and Berry Comforting Matte: *Baltimore Evening Sun,* December 27, 1965, B-10
199 Arrival in Baltimore: *Green Bay Press-Gazette,* December 27, 1965, 14
199 Ran Out of Miracles: *Baltimore News American,* December 27, 1965, 3B
199 Tanton Column: *Baltimore Evening Sun,* December 27, 1952, B-10

Chapter 11

201 Brown on Field Conditions: *Green Bay Press-Gazette,* December 27, 1965, 14
201 Morning of Championship Game: Christl, *Greatest Story,* 454
201 Horning and Taylor Seeing Snow: *Milwaukee Journal,* January 3, 1966, 11
201 Browns' Buses Delayed and Announcers Late: Christl, *Greatest Story,* 454
203 Congratulating Taylor: *Green Bay Press-Gazette,* January 3, 1966, 16
203 Modell on Field Conditions: *Green Bay Press-Gazette,* January 3, 1966, 14
203 Best Defense: *Green Bay Press-Gazette,* January 3, 1966, 13
203 "So Hard This Year": *Sports Illustrated,* January 10, 1966, 18
203 "More Character": *Green Bay Press-Gazette,* January 3, 1966, 13
203 "Let Matte Throw": Mike Klingaman and Edward Lee, "Tom Matte, former Baltimore Colt who starred in NFL playing as running back and emergency quarterback, dies," *Baltimore Sun* website, November 3, 2021
204 Next Season: *Baltimore Sun,* January 11, 1966, C-3

Epilogue

205 Al Davis Elected: *New York Times*, April 29, 1966, 53
209 Lombardi Obituary: *New York Times*, September 4, 1970, 1
209 Lombardi Funeral: *New York Times*, September 8, 1970, 41
210 Namath Taunting Michaels: Mike Klingaman, "Not One to Leave it Short," *Baltimore Sun* website, October 21, 2009
211 Franchise Trade: MacCambridge, *America's Game*, 296
211 "Ridiculous Transaction": MacCambridge, *America's Game*, 297
211 Rosenbloom Threatens Rozelle: David Harris, "New Troubles in the NFL," *New York Times Magazine*, September 7, 1986, Sect. 6, 31
214 Vogel Caring for Foster Children: interview, Bob Vogel
214 "Utter Disregard for Safety": *New York Times*, September 12, 2002, Sect. C, 11
215 Editorial and Headlines: *Baltimore Sun*, September 12, 2002, AI, A13, and A22
215 Accorsi on Unitas: *New York Times*, September 12, 2002, Sect. C, 11
215 Like Gary Cooper: *Sports Illustrated*, September 23, 2002, 21
215 "In Huddle with God": *New York Times*, December 26, 1971, Sect. S, 3; Mackey, *Blazing Trails*, 59
215 "Compared to No One Else": Mike Towle, *Johnny Unitas: Mister Quarterback* (Nashville: Cumberland House Publishing, 2003), 156
215 "First of Great Modern Quarterbacks": *Baltimore Sun*, September 12, 2002, 10D
215 Dawson on Unitas: *Baltimore Sun*, September 12, 2002, 10D
216 Article on Injuries: William Nack, "The Wrecking Yard," *Sports Illustrated*, May 7, 2001
217 Mackey with CTE: Ron Cassie, "Head in the Game," *Baltimore* magazine website

SOURCES

Books

Adderley, Herb, and Robinson, Dave, with Robert Boyles. *Lombardi's Left Side,* Overland Parks, KS: Ascend Books, 2012

Bagli, Vince, and Macht, Norman L. *Sundays at 2:00 with the Baltimore Colts,* Centreville, Md.: Tidewater Publishers, 1995

Barone, Michael, and Ujifusa, Grant. *The Almanac of American Politics 1994,* Washington D.C.: National Journal, 1994

Bell, Upton, with Ron Borges. *Present at the Creation: My Life in the NFL and the Rise of America's Game,* Lincoln: University of Nebraska Press, 2017

Bengston, Phil, and Hunt, Todd. *Packer Dynasty,* Garden City, N.Y.: Doubleday & Company, 1969

Berry, Raymond, with Wayne Stewart. *All the Moves I Had: A Football Life,* Guilford, Conn.: LP, *2016*

Blaik, Earl H., with Tim Cohane. *You Have to Pay the Price,* New York: Holt, Rinehart and Winston, 1960

Bowden, Mark. *The Best Game Ever: Giants vs. Colts, 1958, and the Birth of the Modern NFL,* New York: Atlantic Monthly Press, 2008

Brown, Jimmy, with Myron Cope. *Off My Chest,* Garden City, N.Y.: Doubleday & Company, 1964

_____, with Steve Delsohn. *Out of Bounds,* New York: Kensington Publishing, 1989

Carroll, Bob. *When the Grass Was Green: Unitas, Brown, Lombardi, Sayers, Butkus, Namath and All the Rest; The Best Ten Years of Pro Football,* New York: Simon & Schuster, 1993

Christl, Cliff. *The Greatest Story in Sports: Green Bay Packers 1919-2019 (Vols. 1 and 2),* Green Bay: Green Bay Packers, 2021

Crepeau, Richard C. *NFL Football: A History of America's New National Pastime,* Urbana, Chicago and Springfield: University of Illinois Press, 2014

Curry, Bill. *Ten Men You Meet in the Huddle: Lessons from a Football Life,* New York: ESPN Books, 2008

Curtis, Mike, with Bill Gilbert. *Keep Off My Turf,* Philadelphia and New York: J. B. Lippincott Company, 1972

D'Amato, Gary, and Christl, Cliff. *Mudbaths and Bloodbaths: The Inside Story of the Bears-Packers Rivalry,* Madison: Prairie Oak Press, 1997

Davis, Jeff. *Papa Bear: The Life and Legacy of George Halas,* New York: McGraw-Hill, 2005

_____. *Rozelle: Czar of the NFL,* New York: McGraw-Hill, 2008

Davis, Willie, with Jim Martyka and Andrea Erickson Davis. *Closing the Gap: Lombardi, the Packers Dynasty, and the Pursuit of Excellence,* Chicago: Triumph Books, 2012

DeVito, Carlo. *Don Shula: A Biography of the Winningest Coach in NFL History,* New York: Sports Publishing, 2018

Donovan, Arthur J., Jr., with Bob Drury. *Fatso: Football When Men Were Men,* New York: William Morrow and Company, 1987

Eckhouse, Morris. *Day by Day in Cleveland Browns History,* New York: Leisure Press, 1984

Flynn, George L., editor. *Vince Lombardi on Football,* New York: Van Nostrand Reinhold, 1973

Foley, Betsy. *Green Bay: Gateway to the Great Waterway,* Woodland Hills, CA: Windsor Publications, 1983.

Freeman, Mike. *Jim Brown: The Fierce Life of an American Hero,* New York: HarperCollins, 2006

Gildea, William. *When the Colts Belonged to Baltimore: A Father and a Son, a Team and a Town,* Boston: Houghton Mifflin Harcourt Publishing Company, 1994

Gilden, Jack. *Collision of Wills: Johnny Unitas, Don Shula, and the Rise of the Modern NFL,* Lincoln: University of Nebraska Press, 2018

Gregg, Forrest, and O'Toole, Andrew. *Winning in the Trenches: A Lifetime in Football,* Cincinnati: Clerisy Press, 2009

Gunther, John. *Inside U.S.A.,* New York: Harper & Brothers, 1947

Hawkins. Alex. *My Story (And I'm Sticking to It),* Chapel Hill: Algonquin Books, 1990

Hornung, Paul, as told to Al Silverman. *Football and the Single Man,* Garden City, N.Y.: Doubleday & Company, 1965

Horrigan, Joe. *NFL Century: The One-Hundred-Year Rise of America's Greatest Sports League,* New York: Crown Publishing Group, 2019

Kirwan, Pat, with David Seigerman. *Take Your Eye Off the Ball: How To Watch Football by Knowing Where to Look,* Chicago: Triumph Books, 2010

Kramer, Jerry, and Schapp, Dick. *Instant Replay: The Green Bay Diary of Jerry Kramer,* New York: New American Library, 1968

_____, *Jerry Kramer's Farewell to Football,* New York and Cleveland: World Publishing Company, 1969

_____, with Dick Schapp. *Distant Replay: The Green Bay Packers; The Stars of Football's Greatest Team Look Back,* New York: Putnam's Sons, 1985

Lombardi, Vince, with W. C. Heinz. *Run to Daylight!: Vince Lombardi's Diary of One Week with the Green Bay Packers,* Englewood Cliffs, NJ: Prentice-Hall, 1963

Lyons, Robert S. *On Any Given Sunday: A Life of Bert Bell,* Philadelphia: Temple University Press, 2010

MacCambridge, Michael. *The Franchise: A History of Sports Illustrated Magazine,* New York: Hyperion, 1997

_____. *America's Game: The Epic Story of How Pro Football Captured a Nation,* New York: Random House, 2004

Mackey, John, with Thom Loverro. *Blazing Trails: Coming of Age in Football's Golden Era,* Chicago: Triumph Books, 2003

Maraniss, David. *When Pride Still Mattered: A Life of Vince Lombardi,* New York: Simon & Schuster, 1999

Moore, Lenny, with Jeffrey Jay Ellish. *All Things Being Equal: The Autobiography of Lenny Moore,* Champaign: Sports Publishing, 2006

Neft, David, Cohen, Richard M., and Deutsch, Jordan A. *The Sports Encyclopedia: Pro Football,* New York: Simon and Schuster, 1982

Nitschke, Ray, as told to Robert Wells. *Mean on Sunday: The Autobiography of Ray Nitschke,* Garden City, N.Y.: Doubleday & Company, 1973

Olesker, Michael. *The Colts' Baltimore: A City and its Love Affair in the 1950s,* Baltimore: Johns Hopkins University Press, 2008

____. *Front Stoops in the Fifties: Baltimore's Legends Come of Age,* Baltimore: Johns Hopkins University Press, 2013

O'Toole, Andrew. *Paul Brown: The Rise and Fall and Rise Again of Football's Most Innovative Coach,* Cincinnati: Clerisy Press, 2008

Patterson, Ted. *Football in Baltimore: History and Memorabilia,* Baltimore: Johns Hopkins University Press, 2000

Peirce, Neal, and Hagstrom, Jerry. *The Book of America: Inside 50 States Today,* New York: W. W. Norton & Company, 1983

Plimpton, George. *One More July: A Football Dialogue with Bill Curry,* New York: Harper & Row, 1977

Pluto, Terry. *When All the World Was Browns Town: Cleveland's Browns and the Championship Season of '64,* New York: Simon & Schuster, 1997

Poiley, Joel. *Last Man Standing: How Tom Matte's Memorable 1965 Season Highlighted a Remarkable NFL Career,* Lanham, Md.: Rowman & Littlefield Publishing Group, 2024

Ribowsky, Mark. *Shula: The Coach of the NFL's Greatest Generation,* New York: Liveright Publishing Corporation, 2019

Sahadi, Lou. *Johnny Unitas: America's Quarterback*, Chicago: Triumph Books, 2004

Shula, Don, with Lou Sahadi. *The Winning Edge,* New York: E.P. Dutton & Company, 1973

Smith, D.P., III. *The Golden Arm Gentleman,* Charleston, S.C.: Palmetto Publishing, 2022

Starr, Bart, with Murray Olderman. *Starr: My Life in Football,* New York: William Morrow and Company, 1987

Steadman, John F. *Football's Miracle Men: The Baltimore Colts' Story,* Cleveland: Pennington Press, 1959

____. *The Greatest Football Game Ever Played: When the Baltimore Colts and the New York Giants Faced Sudden Death,* Press Box Publishers, 1988

Taylor, Jim, with Kristine Setting Clark. *The Fire Within,* Chicago: Triumph Books, 2010

Thompson, Chuck, with Gordon Beard. *Ain't the Beer Cold!,* South Bend: Diamond Communications, 1996

Thurston, Fuzzy and Sue, with Bill Wenzel. *What a Wonderful World: The Fuzzy Thurston Story,* published by Fuzzy Thurston and Bill Wenzel, 2006

Towle, Mike. *Johnny Unitas: Mister Quarterback,* Nashville: Cumberland House Publishing, 2003

Unitas, John C., Jr., with Edward Brown. *Johnny U and Me: The Man Behind the Golden Arm,* Chicago: Triumph Books, 2014

Wells, Robert W. *Vince Lombardi: His Life and Times,* Madison: Wisconsin House, 1971

Wiebusch, John, editor. *Lombardi,* Chicago: Follett Publishing Company, 1971

____, and Silverman, Brian, editors. *A Game of Passion: The NFL Literary Companion,* Atlanta: Turner Publishing, 1994

Wright, Steve, with William Gildea and Kenneth Turan. *I'd Rather Be Wright,* Englewood Cliffs, NJ: Prentice-Hall, 1974

Zimmerman, Paul. *The New Thinking Man's Guide to Pro Football,* New York: Simon and Schuster, 1984

Newspapers (including websites)

AI.com website
Akron Beacon Journal
Baltimore Afro-American
Baltimore Evening Sun
Baltimore News American
Baltimore Sun
Berkeley Daily Gazette
Canton Repository
Chicago Tribune
Cleveland Plain Dealer
Fort Worth Star-Telegram
Green Bay Press-Gazette
Los Angeles Times
Milwaukee Journal
Milwaukee Sentinel
Minneapolis Star
New York Times
Philadelphia Inquirer
Pittsburgh Post-Gazette
San Francisco Examiner

Magazines and Similar Sources (including websites)

The Athletic
Baltimore
CNN Money
Esquire
Fortune
Life
Maryland Matters
Milwaukee

Newsweek
Sports Illustrated
Time

Team and Team-Related Publications (including websites)

Baltimore Colts 1953, 1957-1966 Press-Radio-TV Guides
Green Bay Packers 1965 Yearbook, by Art Daley and Jack Yuenger
Packers 1965 Press Book
Packers.com

Player and Player Spouse Interviews

Gary Cuozzo
Carroll Dale
Boyd Dowler
Dennis Gaubatz
Sylvia Mackey
Judy Matte
Dave Robinson
Bob Vogel
Steve Wright

Selected Index

www.ingramcontent.com/pod-product-compliance
Lightning Source LLC
Chambersburg PA
CBHW010041090426
42734CB00019B/3240